WILLOW™

Buffy the Vampire Slayer

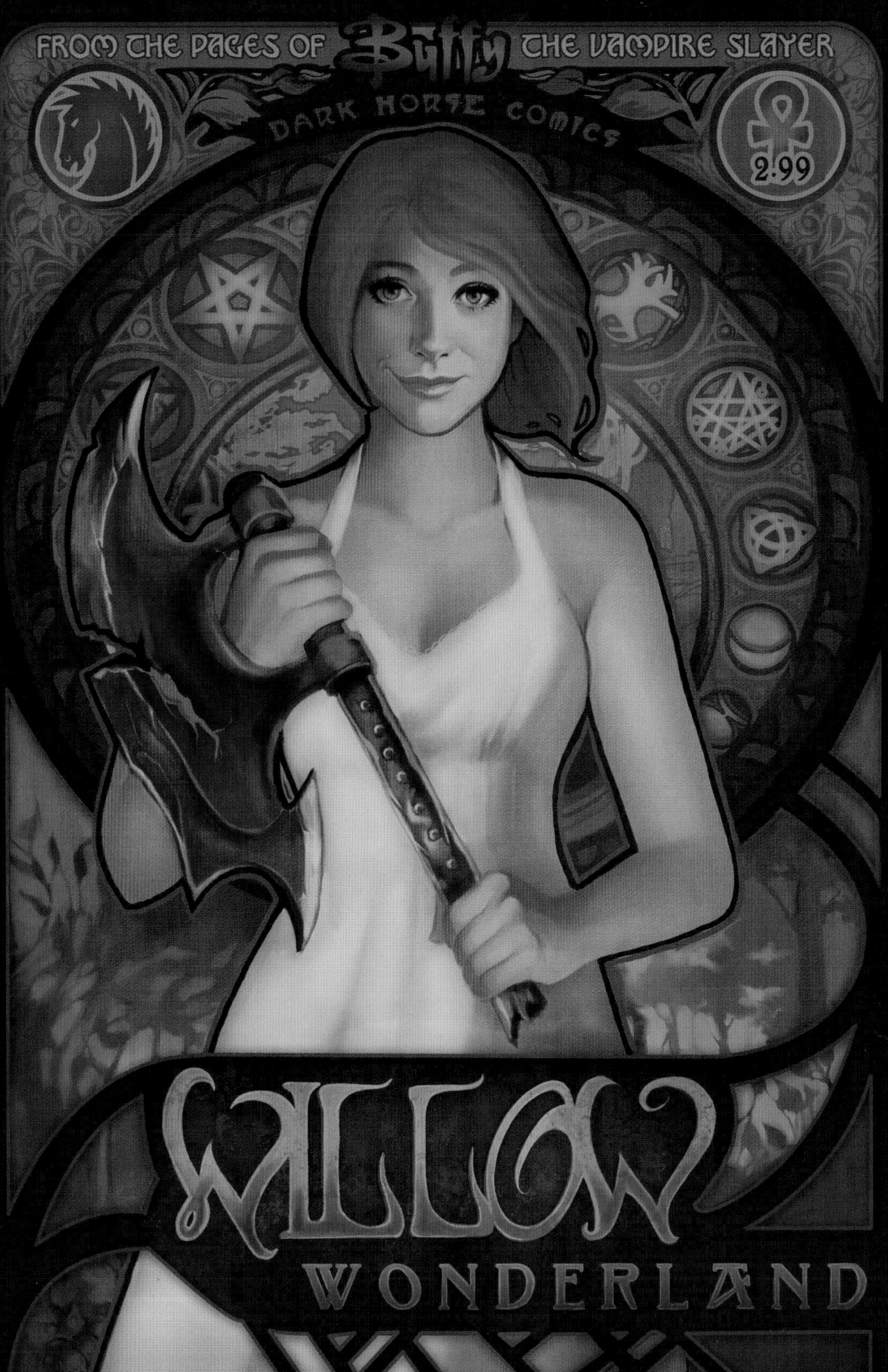
FROM THE PAGES OF Buffy THE VAMPIRE SLAYER
DARK HORSE COMICS
2.99
WILLOW
WONDERLAND

Illustration by Megan Lara

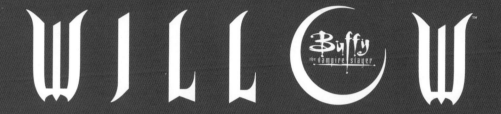

WILLOW™

Buffy the Vampire Slayer

SEASON 9 · WONDERLAND

SCRIPT
JEFF PARKER
CHRISTOS GAGE

PENCILS
BRIAN CHING

INKS
JASON GORDER

COLORS
MICHELLE MADSEN

LETTERS
RICHARD STARKINGS
& Comicraft's JIMMY BETANCOURT

COVER & CHAPTER BREAK ART
DAVID MACK

EXECUTIVE PRODUCER
JOSS WHEDON

DARK HORSE BOOKS

President & Publisher
MIKE RICHARDSON

Editors
SCOTT ALLIE & SIERRA HAHN

Assistant Editor
FREDDYE LINS

Collection Designer
JUSTIN COUCH

Willow #1 & 2 Script by Jeff Parker
Willow #3 Script by Jeff Parker & Christos Gage
Willow #4 & 5 Script by Christos Gage & Jeff Parker

Published by Dark Horse Books
A division of Dark Horse Comics, Inc.
10956 SE Main Street
Milwaukie, OR 97222

DarkHorse.com

International Licensing: (503) 905-2377
To find a comics shop in your area,
call the Comic Shop Locator Service toll-free at (888) 266-4226.

First edition: August 2013
ISBN 978-1-61655-145-2

10 9 8 7 6 5 4 3 2 1
Printed in China

This story takes place after the events in *Buffy the Vampire Slayer* Season 9 #5
and *Angel & Faith* #14.

Special thanks to Lauren Winarski at Twentieth Century Fox.

NEIL HANKERSON Executive Vice President • TOM WEDDLE Chief Financial Officer • RANDY STRADLEY Vice President of Publishing
• MICHAEL MARTENS Vice President of Book Trade Sales • ANITA NELSON Vice President of Business Affairs • SCOTT ALLIE Editor in
Chief • MATT PARKINSON Vice President of Marketing • DAVID SCROGGY Vice President of Product Development • DALE LAFOUNTAIN
Vice President of Information Technology • DARLENE VOGEL Senior Director of Print, Design, and Production • KEN LIZZI General
Counsel • DAVEY ESTRADA Editorial Director • CHRIS WARNER Senior Books Editor • DIANA SCHUTZ Executive Editor • CARY GRAZZINI
Director of Print and Development • LIA RIBACCHI Art Director • CARA NIECE Director of Scheduling • TIM WIESCH Director of Inter-
national Licensing • MARK BERNARDI Director of Digital Publishing

This volume reprints the comic-book series *Willow: Wonderland* #1–#5 from Dark Horse Comics.

WILLOW

Buffy the Vampire Slayer

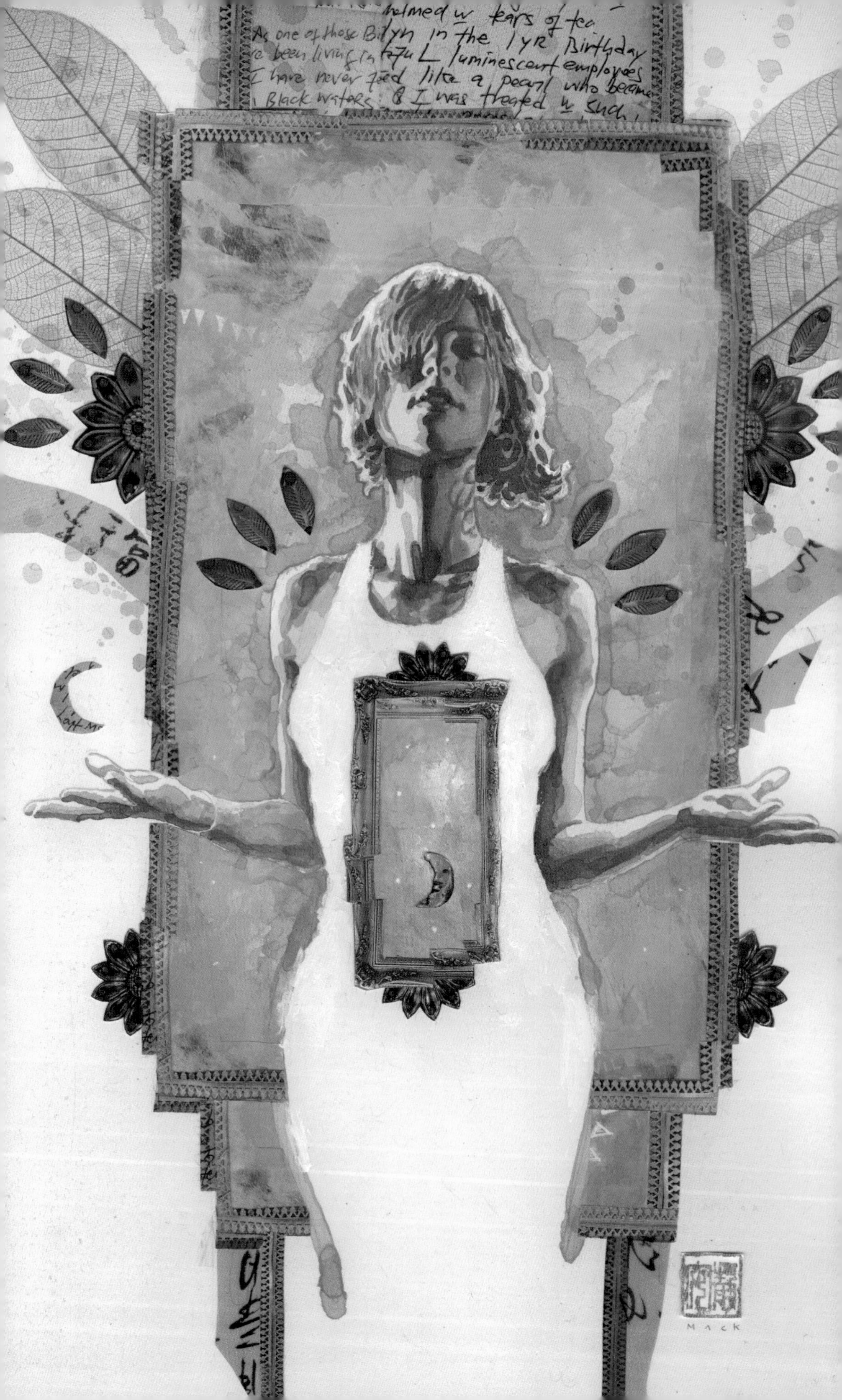

tears of tea
As one of those in the 1YR Birthday
luminescent employees
I have never like a pearl who became
Black waters & I was treated w such
MACK

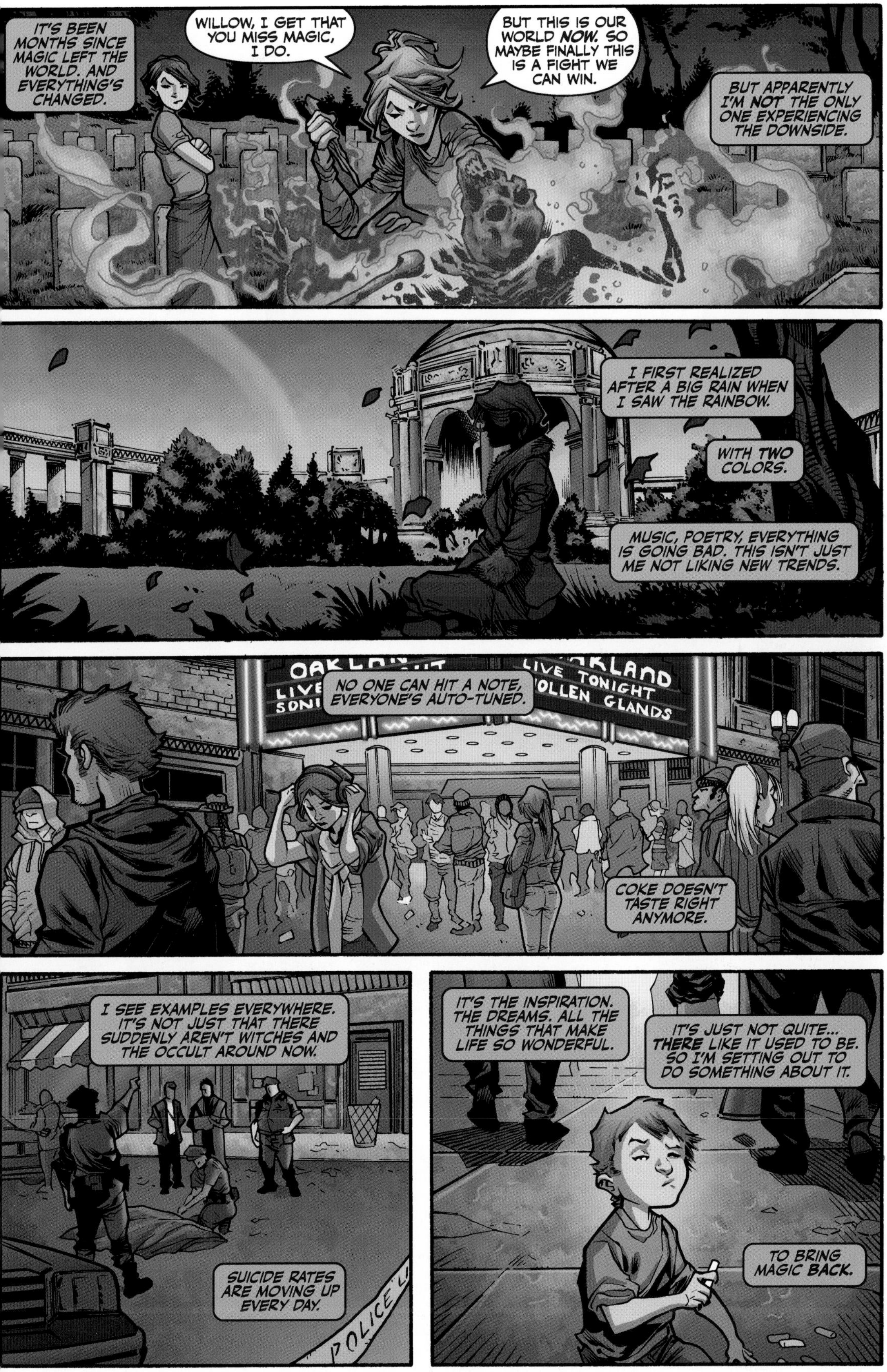

IT'S BEEN MONTHS SINCE MAGIC LEFT THE WORLD. AND EVERYTHING'S CHANGED.
WILLOW, I GET THAT YOU MISS MAGIC, I DO.
BUT THIS IS OUR WORLD NOW. SO MAYBE FINALLY THIS IS A FIGHT WE CAN WIN.
BUT APPARENTLY I'M NOT THE ONLY ONE EXPERIENCING THE DOWNSIDE.
I FIRST REALIZED AFTER A BIG RAIN WHEN I SAW THE RAINBOW.
WITH TWO COLORS.
MUSIC, POETRY, EVERYTHING IS GOING BAD. THIS ISN'T JUST ME NOT LIKING NEW TRENDS.
LIVE TONIGHT
NO ONE CAN HIT A NOTE, EVERYONE'S AUTO-TUNED.
COKE DOESN'T TASTE RIGHT ANYMORE.
I SEE EXAMPLES EVERYWHERE. IT'S NOT JUST THAT THERE SUDDENLY AREN'T WITCHES AND THE OCCULT AROUND NOW.
SUICIDE RATES ARE MOVING UP EVERY DAY.
IT'S THE INSPIRATION. THE DREAMS. ALL THE THINGS THAT MAKE LIFE SO WONDERFUL.
IT'S JUST NOT QUITE... THERE LIKE IT USED TO BE. SO I'M SETTING OUT TO DO SOMETHING ABOUT IT.
TO BRING MAGIC BACK.

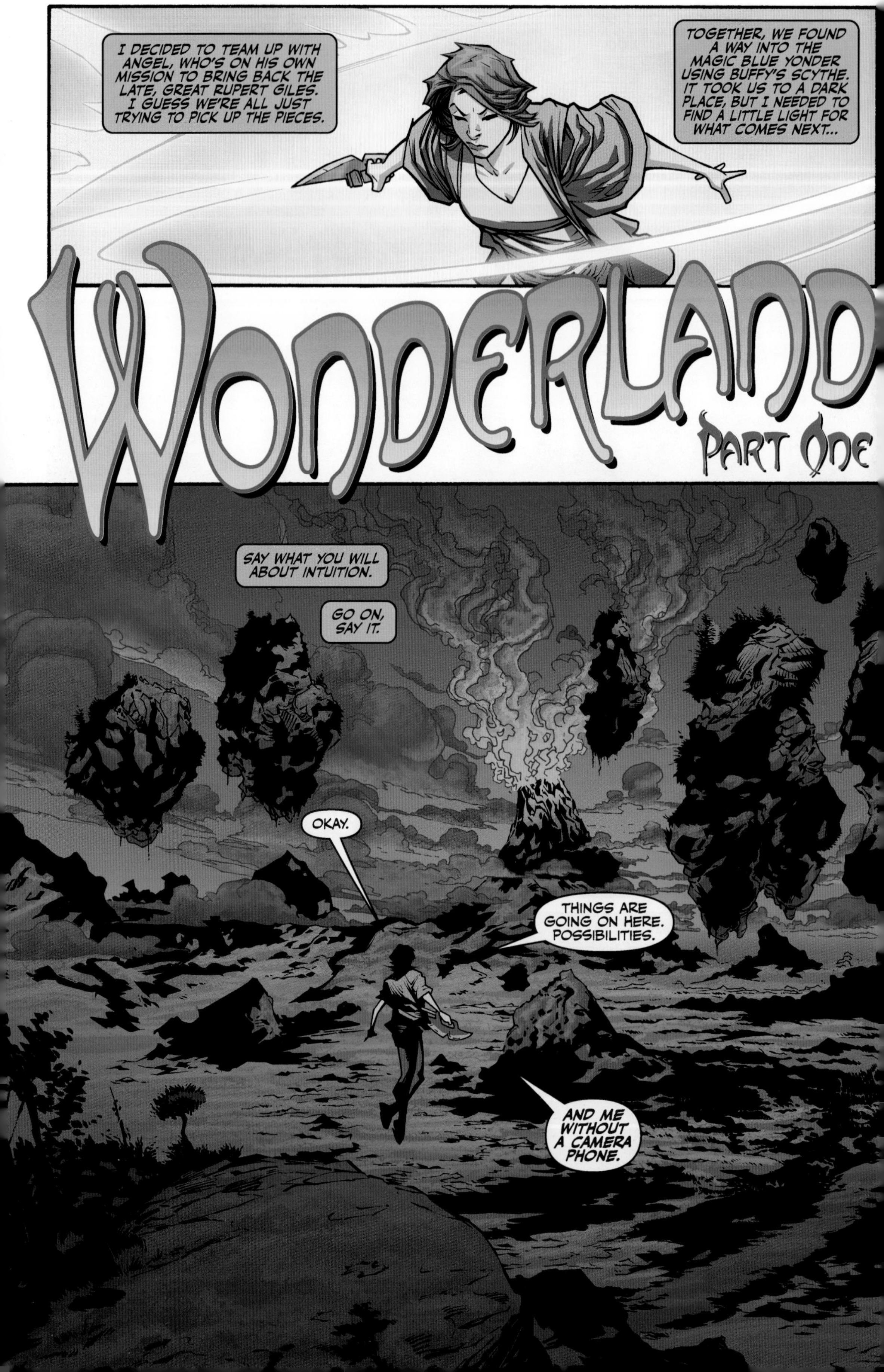
I DECIDED TO TEAM UP WITH ANGEL, WHO'S ON HIS OWN MISSION TO BRING BACK THE LATE, GREAT RUPERT GILES. I GUESS WE'RE ALL JUST TRYING TO PICK UP THE PIECES.
TOGETHER, WE FOUND A WAY INTO THE MAGIC BLUE YONDER USING BUFFY'S SCYTHE. IT TOOK US TO A DARK PLACE, BUT I NEEDED TO FIND A LITTLE LIGHT FOR WHAT COMES NEXT...
WONDERLAND
PART ONE
SAY WHAT YOU WILL ABOUT INTUITION.
GO ON, SAY IT.
OKAY.
THINGS ARE GOING ON HERE. POSSIBILITIES.
AND ME WITHOUT A CAMERA PHONE.

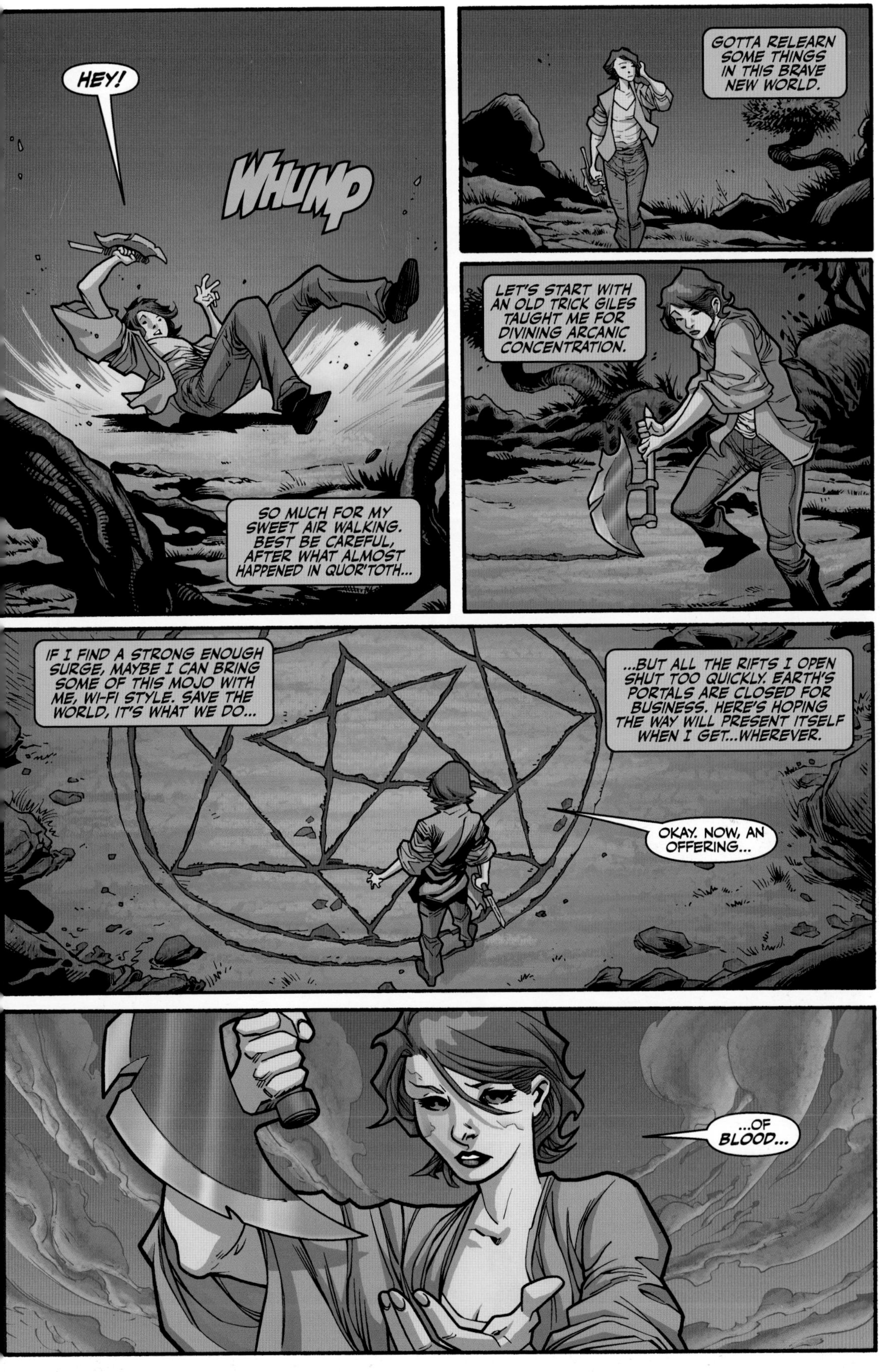
HEY!
WHUMP
SO MUCH FOR MY SWEET AIR WALKING. BEST BE CAREFUL, AFTER WHAT ALMOST HAPPENED IN QUOR'TOTH...
GOTTA RELEARN SOME THINGS IN THIS BRAVE NEW WORLD.
LET'S START WITH AN OLD TRICK GILES TAUGHT ME FOR DIVINING ARCANIC CONCENTRATION.
IF I FIND A STRONG ENOUGH SURGE, MAYBE I CAN BRING SOME OF THIS MOJO WITH ME, WI-FI STYLE. SAVE THE WORLD, IT'S WHAT WE DO...
...BUT ALL THE RIFTS I OPEN SHUT TOO QUICKLY. EARTH'S PORTALS ARE CLOSED FOR BUSINESS. HERE'S HOPING THE WAY WILL PRESENT ITSELF WHEN I GET...WHEREVER.
OKAY. NOW, AN OFFERING...
...OF BLOOD...

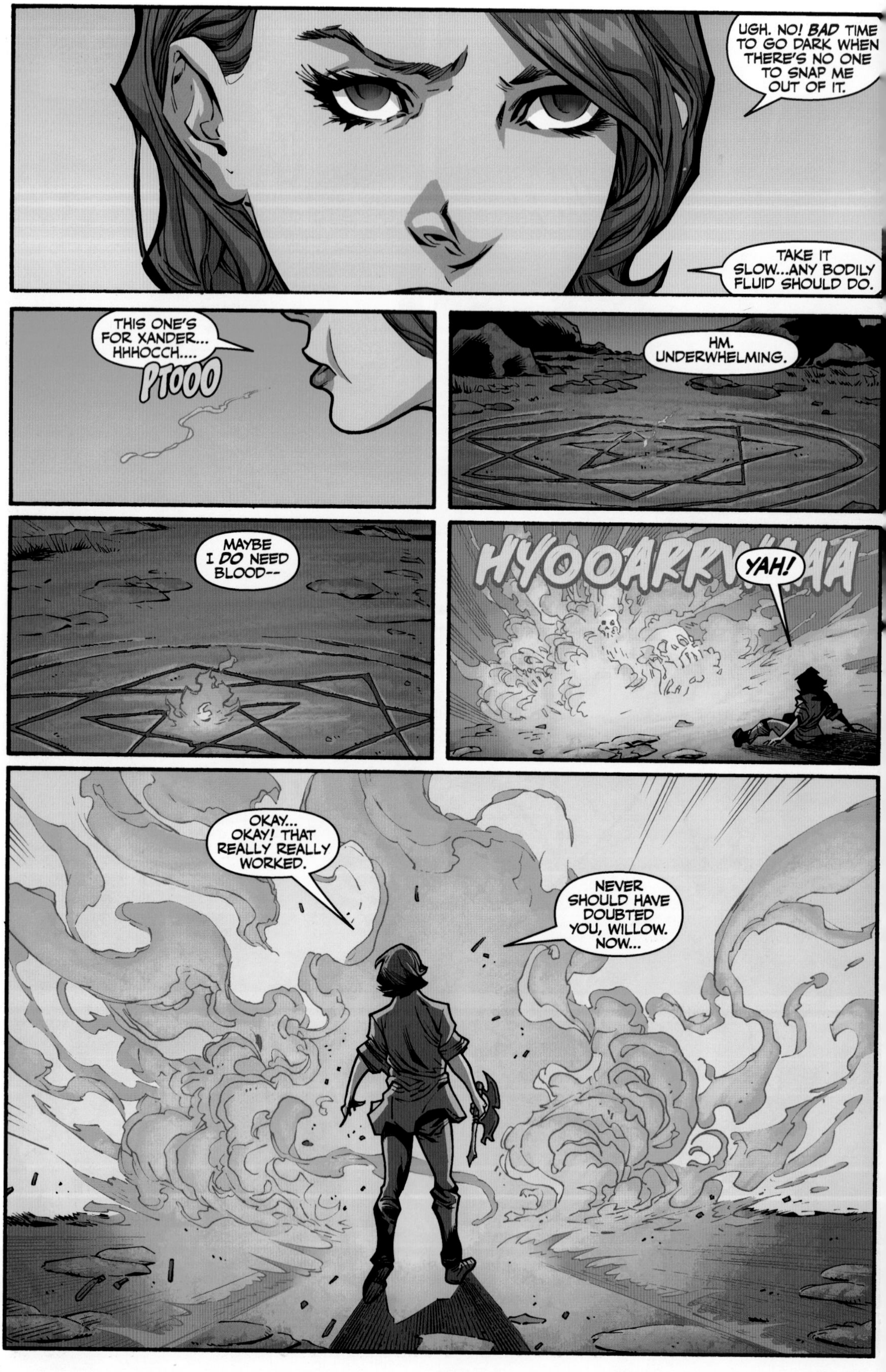
UGH. NO! BAD TIME TO GO DARK WHEN THERE'S NO ONE TO SNAP ME OUT OF IT.
TAKE IT SLOW...ANY BODILY FLUID SHOULD DO.
THIS ONE'S FOR XANDER... HHHOCCH....
PTOOO
HM. UNDERWHELMING.
MAYBE I DO NEED BLOOD--
HYOOARR
YAH!
OKAY... OKAY! THAT REALLY REALLY WORKED.
NEVER SHOULD HAVE DOUBTED YOU, WILLOW. NOW...

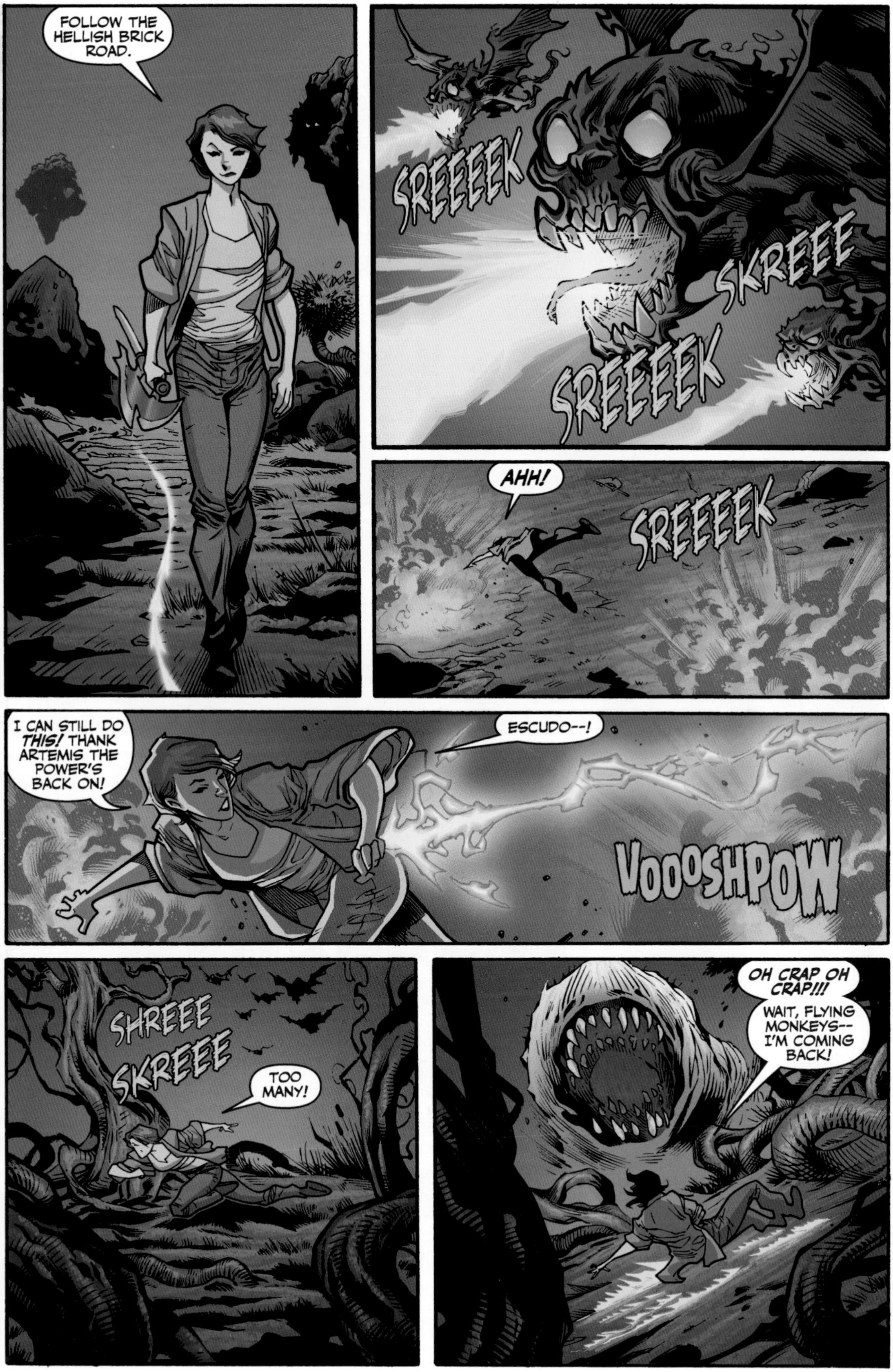
FOLLOW THE HELLISH BRICK ROAD.
SREEEEK
SKREEE
SREEEEK
AHH!
SREEEEK
I CAN STILL DO THIS! THANK ARTEMIS THE POWER'S BACK ON!
ESCUDO--!
VOOOSHPOW
SHREEE
SKREEE
TOO MANY!
OH CRAP OH CRAP!!!
WAIT, FLYING MONKEYS-- I'M COMING BACK!

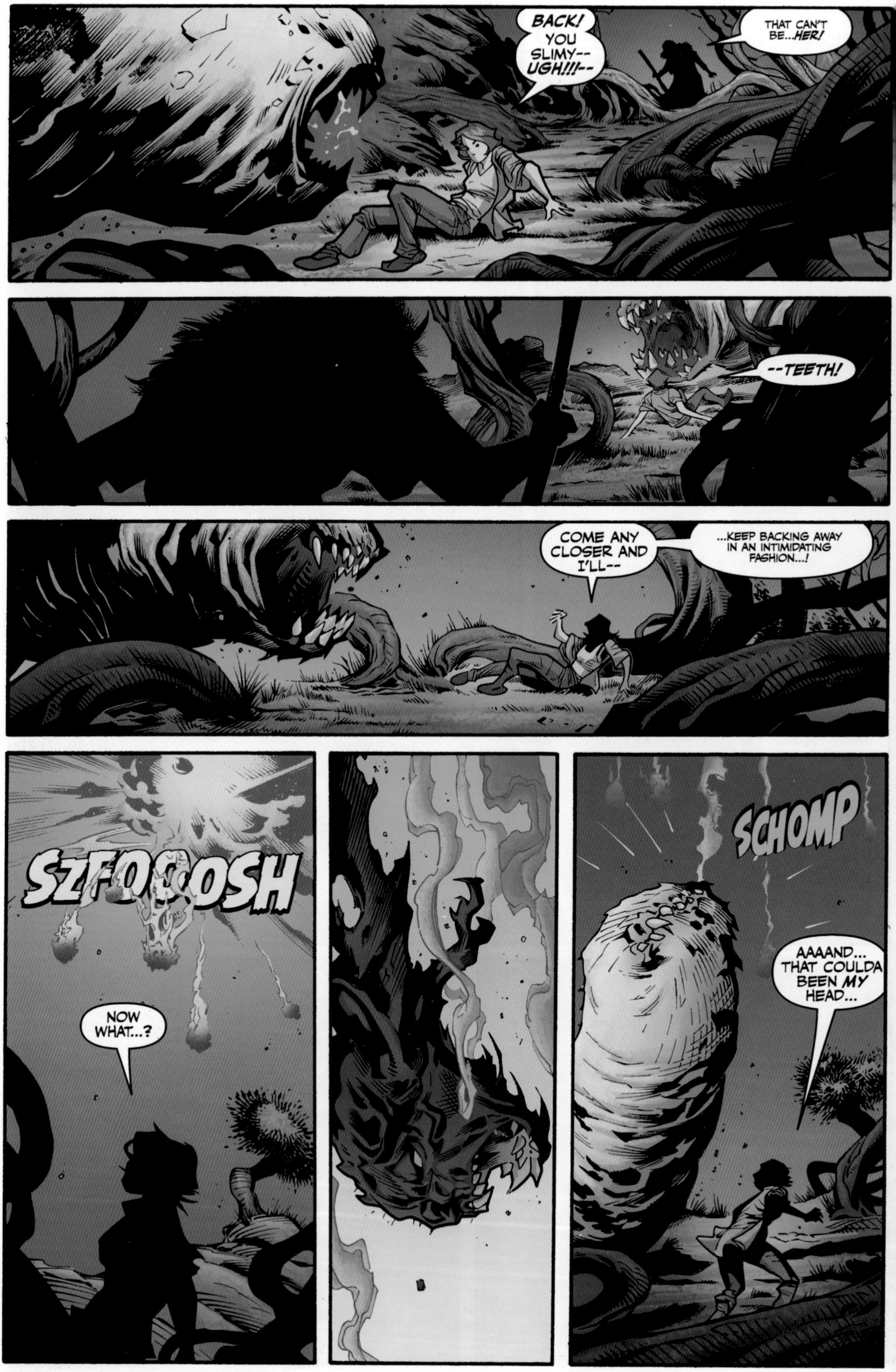
BACK! YOU SLIMY-- UGH!!!--
THAT CAN'T BE...HER!
--TEETH!
COME ANY CLOSER AND I'LL--
...KEEP BACKING AWAY IN AN INTIMIDATING FASHION...!
SZFOOOSH
NOW WHAT...?
SCHOMP
AAAAND... THAT COULDA BEEN MY HEAD...

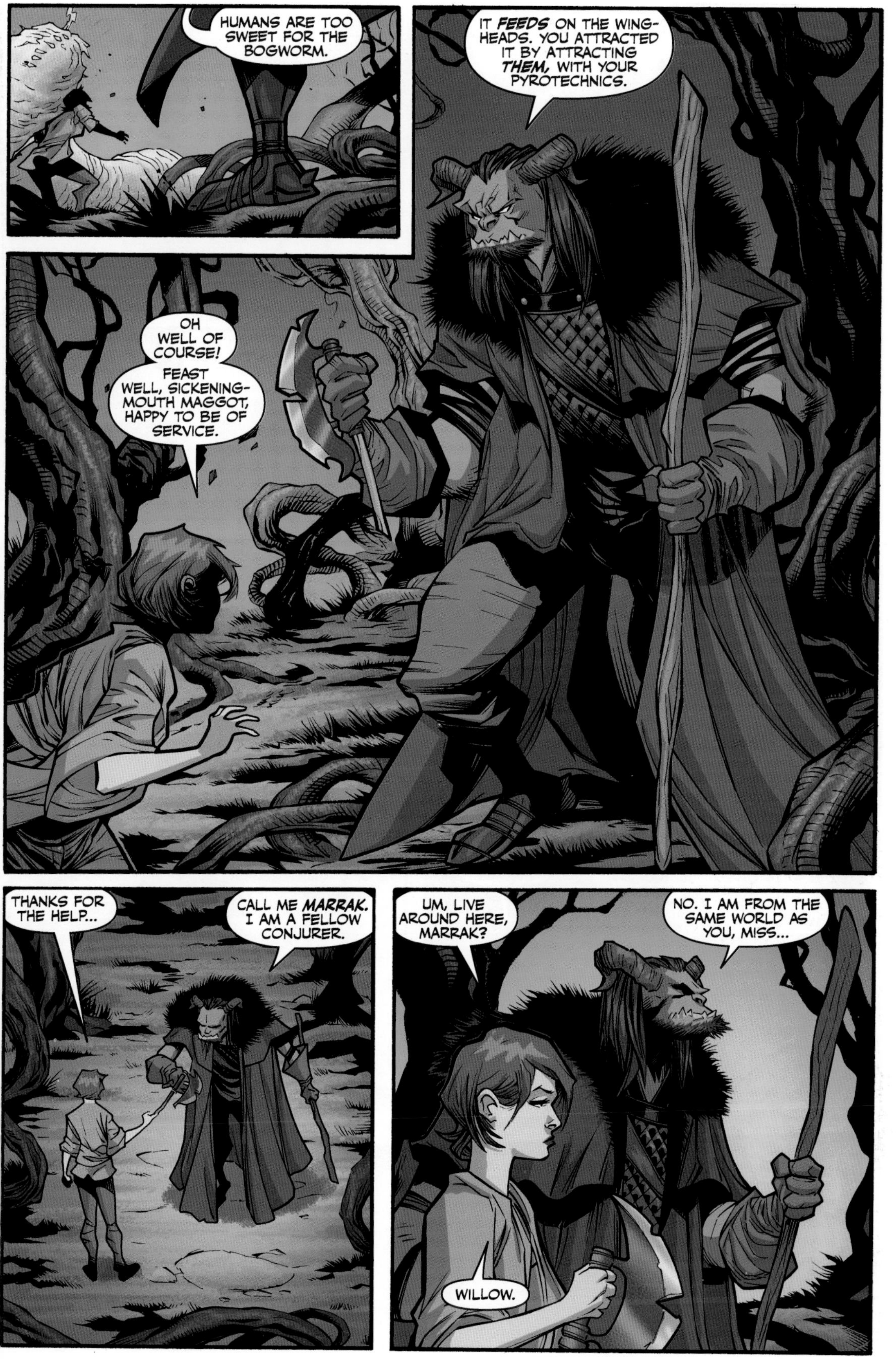
HUMANS ARE TOO SWEET FOR THE BOGWORM.
IT *FEEDS* ON THE WING-HEADS. YOU ATTRACTED IT BY ATTRACTING *THEM,* WITH YOUR PYROTECHNICS.
OH WELL OF COURSE!
FEAST WELL, SICKENING-MOUTH MAGGOT, HAPPY TO BE OF SERVICE.
THANKS FOR THE HELP...
CALL ME *MARRAK.* I AM A FELLOW CONJURER.
UM, LIVE AROUND HERE, MARRAK?
NO. I AM FROM THE SAME WORLD AS YOU, MISS...
WILLOW.

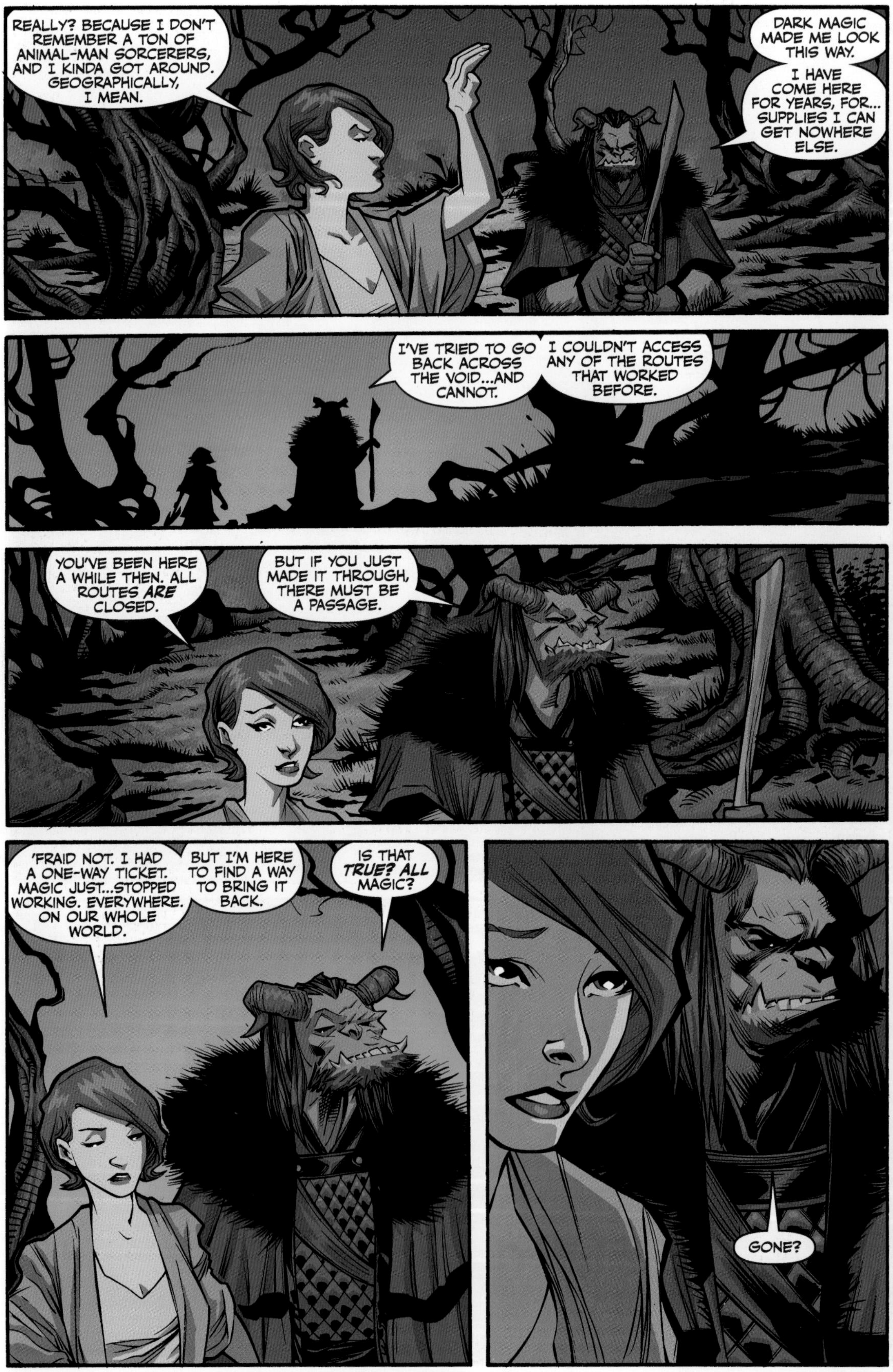
REALLY? BECAUSE I DON'T REMEMBER A TON OF ANIMAL-MAN SORCERERS, AND I KINDA GOT AROUND. GEOGRAPHICALLY, I MEAN.
DARK MAGIC MADE ME LOOK THIS WAY.
I HAVE COME HERE FOR YEARS, FOR... SUPPLIES I CAN GET NOWHERE ELSE.
I'VE TRIED TO GO BACK ACROSS THE VOID...AND CANNOT.
I COULDN'T ACCESS ANY OF THE ROUTES THAT WORKED BEFORE.
YOU'VE BEEN HERE A WHILE THEN. ALL ROUTES *ARE* CLOSED.
BUT IF YOU JUST MADE IT THROUGH, THERE MUST BE A PASSAGE.
'FRAID NOT. I HAD A ONE-WAY TICKET. MAGIC JUST...STOPPED WORKING. EVERYWHERE. ON OUR WHOLE WORLD.
BUT I'M HERE TO FIND A WAY TO BRING IT BACK.
IS THAT *TRUE? ALL* MAGIC?
GONE?

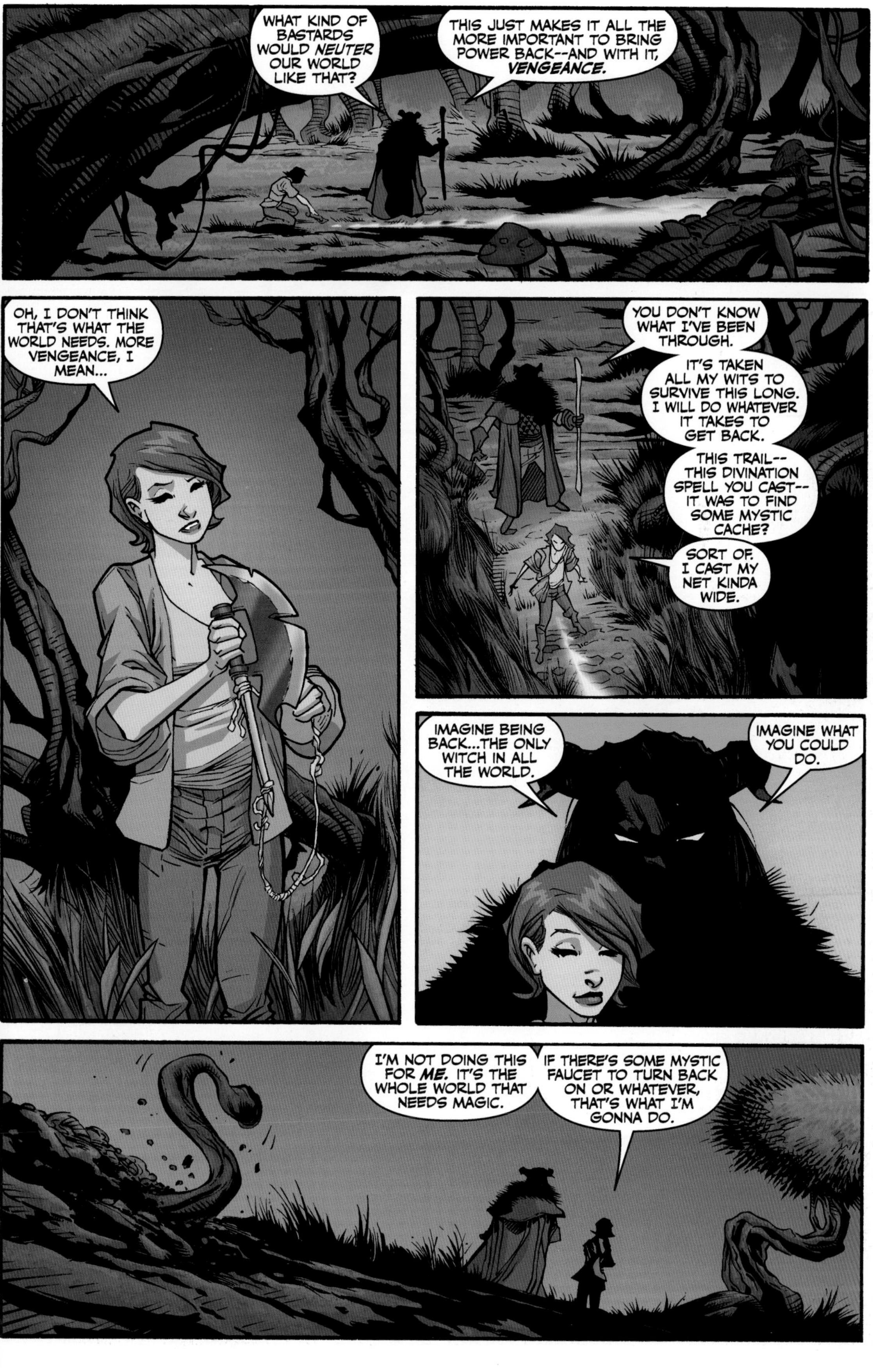
WHAT KIND OF BASTARDS WOULD *NEUTER* OUR WORLD LIKE THAT?
THIS JUST MAKES IT ALL THE MORE IMPORTANT TO BRING POWER BACK--AND WITH IT, ***VENGEANCE.***
OH, I DON'T THINK THAT'S WHAT THE WORLD NEEDS. MORE VENGEANCE, I MEAN...
YOU DON'T KNOW WHAT I'VE BEEN THROUGH.
IT'S TAKEN ALL MY WITS TO SURVIVE THIS LONG. I WILL DO WHATEVER IT TAKES TO GET BACK.
THIS TRAIL-- THIS DIVINATION SPELL YOU CAST-- IT WAS TO FIND SOME MYSTIC CACHE?
SORT OF. I CAST MY NET KINDA WIDE.
IMAGINE BEING BACK...THE ONLY WITCH IN ALL THE WORLD.
IMAGINE WHAT YOU COULD DO.
I'M NOT DOING THIS FOR ***ME.*** IT'S THE WHOLE WORLD THAT NEEDS MAGIC.
IF THERE'S SOME MYSTIC FAUCET TO TURN BACK ON OR WHATEVER, THAT'S WHAT I'M GONNA DO.

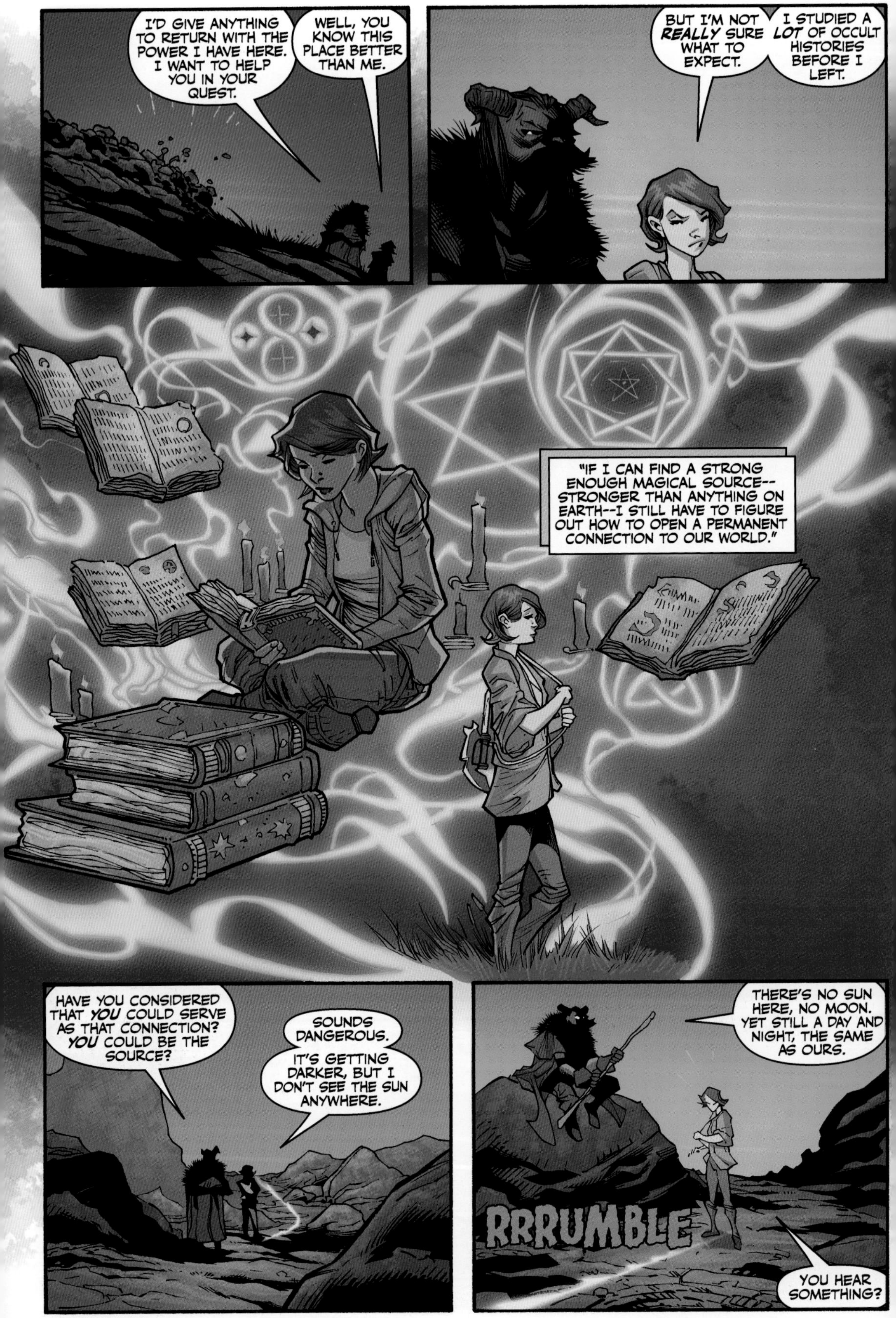

I'D GIVE ANYTHING TO RETURN WITH THE POWER I HAVE HERE. I WANT TO HELP YOU IN YOUR QUEST.
WELL, YOU KNOW THIS PLACE BETTER THAN ME.
BUT I'M NOT REALLY SURE WHAT TO EXPECT.
I STUDIED A LOT OF OCCULT HISTORIES BEFORE I LEFT.
"IF I CAN FIND A STRONG ENOUGH MAGICAL SOURCE--STRONGER THAN ANYTHING ON EARTH--I STILL HAVE TO FIGURE OUT HOW TO OPEN A PERMANENT CONNECTION TO OUR WORLD."
HAVE YOU CONSIDERED THAT YOU COULD SERVE AS THAT CONNECTION? YOU COULD BE THE SOURCE?
SOUNDS DANGEROUS.
IT'S GETTING DARKER, BUT I DON'T SEE THE SUN ANYWHERE.
THERE'S NO SUN HERE, NO MOON. YET STILL A DAY AND NIGHT, THE SAME AS OURS.
RRRUMBLE
YOU HEAR SOMETHING?

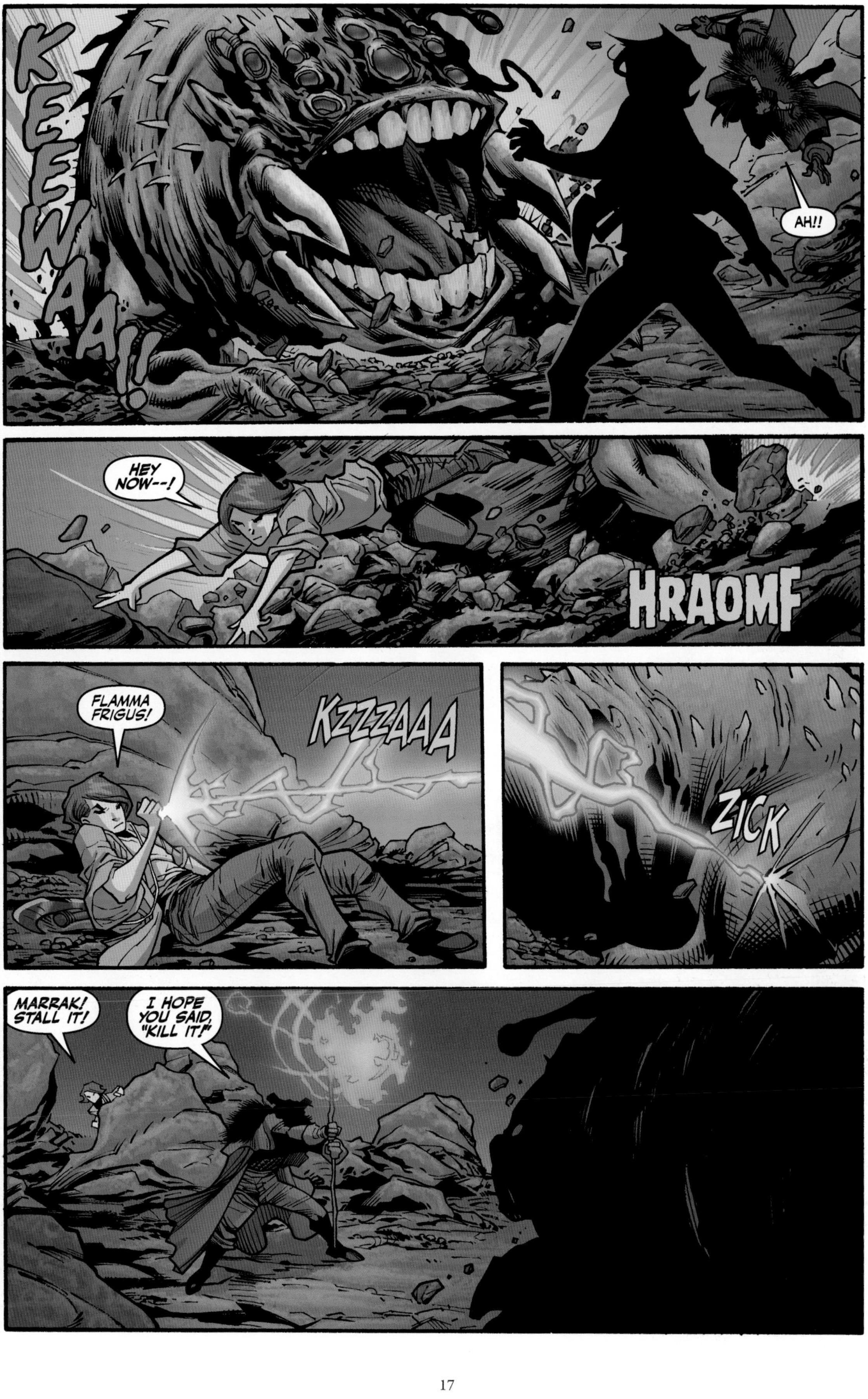
KEEWAA!!
AH!!
HEY NOW--!
HRAOMF
FLAMMA FRIGUS!
KZZZAAA
ZICK
MARRAK! STALL IT!
I HOPE YOU SAID, "KILL IT!"

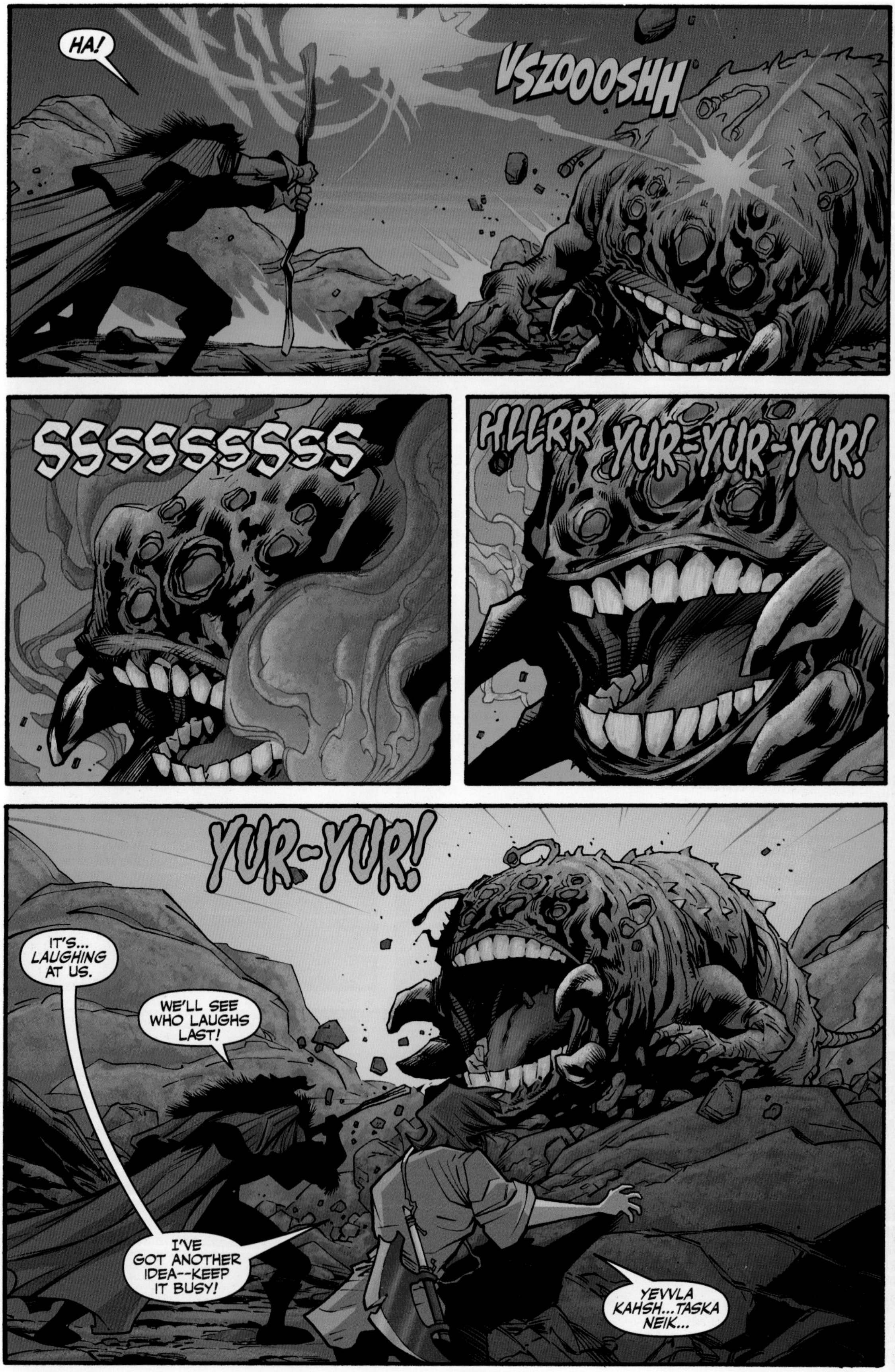
HA!
VSZOOOSHH
SSSSSSSSS
HLLRR YUR-YUR-YUR!
YUR-YUR!
IT'S... LAUGHING AT US.
WE'LL SEE WHO LAUGHS LAST!
I'VE GOT ANOTHER IDEA--KEEP IT BUSY!
YEVVLA KAHSH...TASKA NEIK...

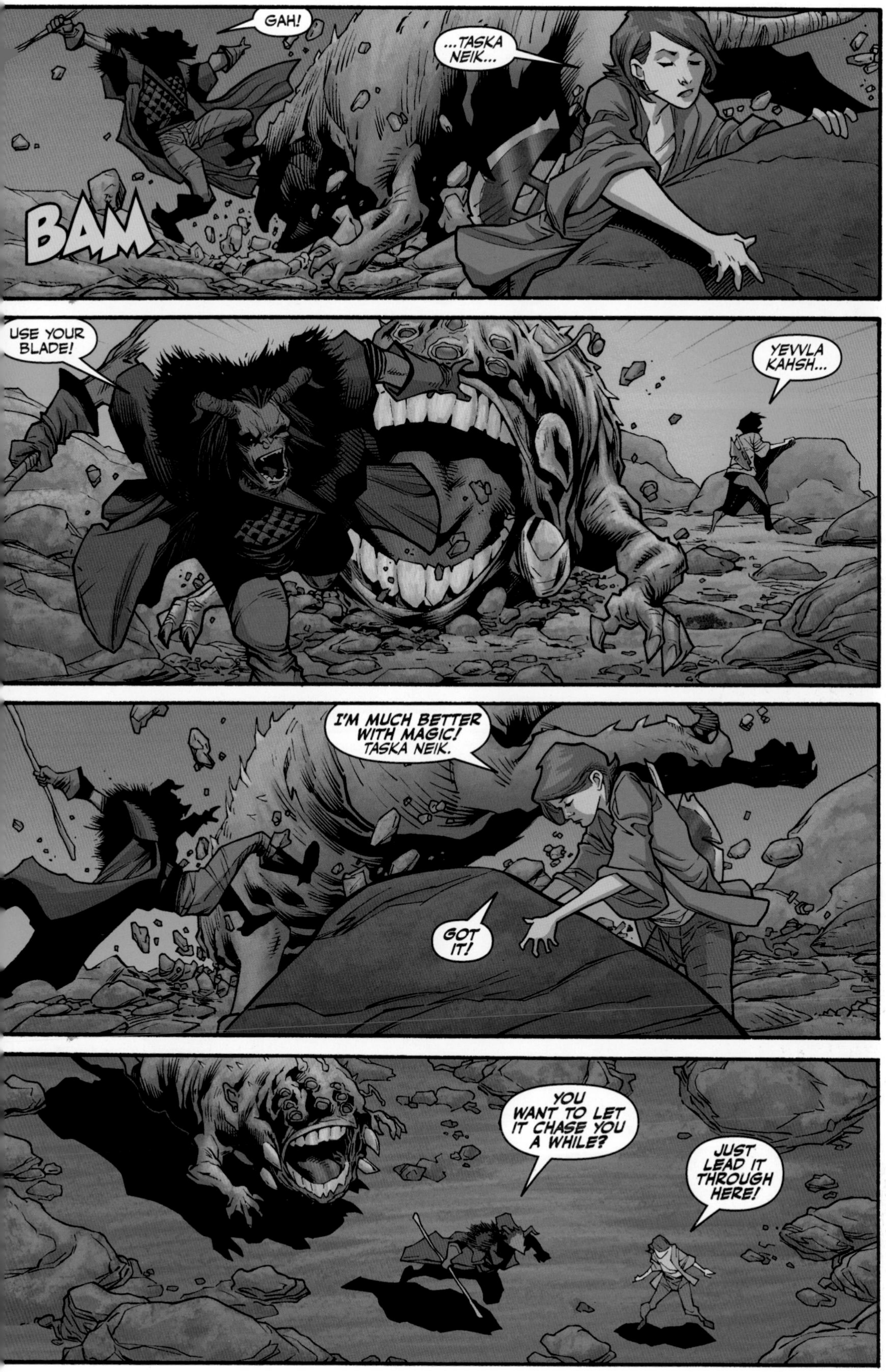
GAH!
...TASKA NEIK...
BAM
USE YOUR BLADE!
YEVVLA KAHSH...
I'M MUCH BETTER WITH MAGIC! TASKA NEIK.
GOT IT!
YOU WANT TO LET IT CHASE YOU A WHILE?
JUST LEAD IT THROUGH HERE!

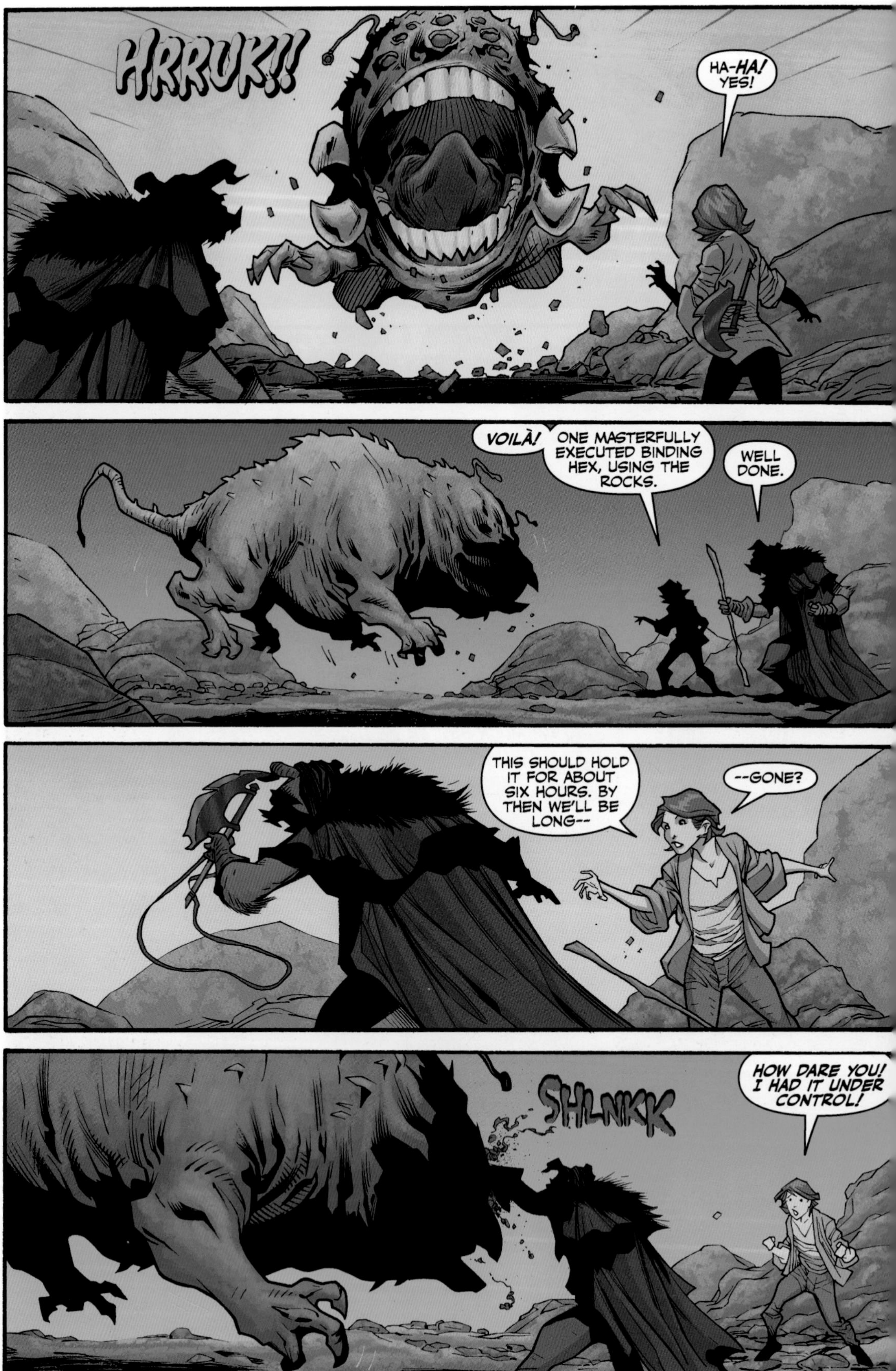
HRRUK!!
HA-HA! YES!
VOILÀ!
ONE MASTERFULLY EXECUTED BINDING HEX, USING THE ROCKS.
WELL DONE.
THIS SHOULD HOLD IT FOR ABOUT SIX HOURS. BY THEN WE'LL BE LONG--
--GONE?
SHLNKK
HOW DARE YOU! I HAD IT UNDER CONTROL!

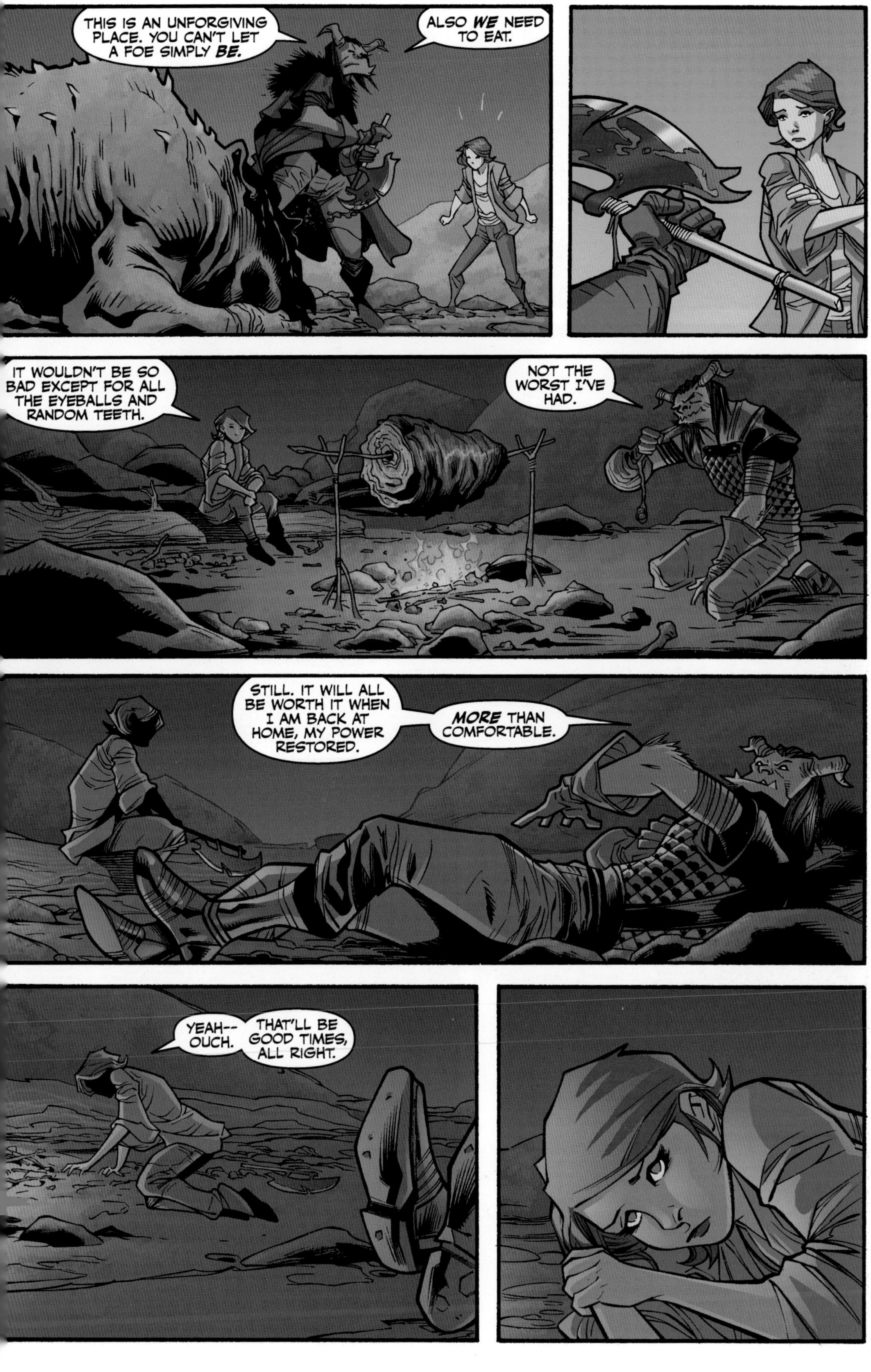
THIS IS AN UNFORGIVING PLACE. YOU CAN'T LET A FOE SIMPLY *BE.*
ALSO *WE* NEED TO EAT.
IT WOULDN'T BE SO BAD EXCEPT FOR ALL THE EYEBALLS AND RANDOM TEETH.
NOT THE WORST I'VE HAD.
STILL. IT WILL ALL BE WORTH IT WHEN I AM BACK AT HOME, MY POWER RESTORED.
MORE THAN COMFORTABLE.
YEAH-- OUCH.
THAT'LL BE GOOD TIMES, ALL RIGHT.

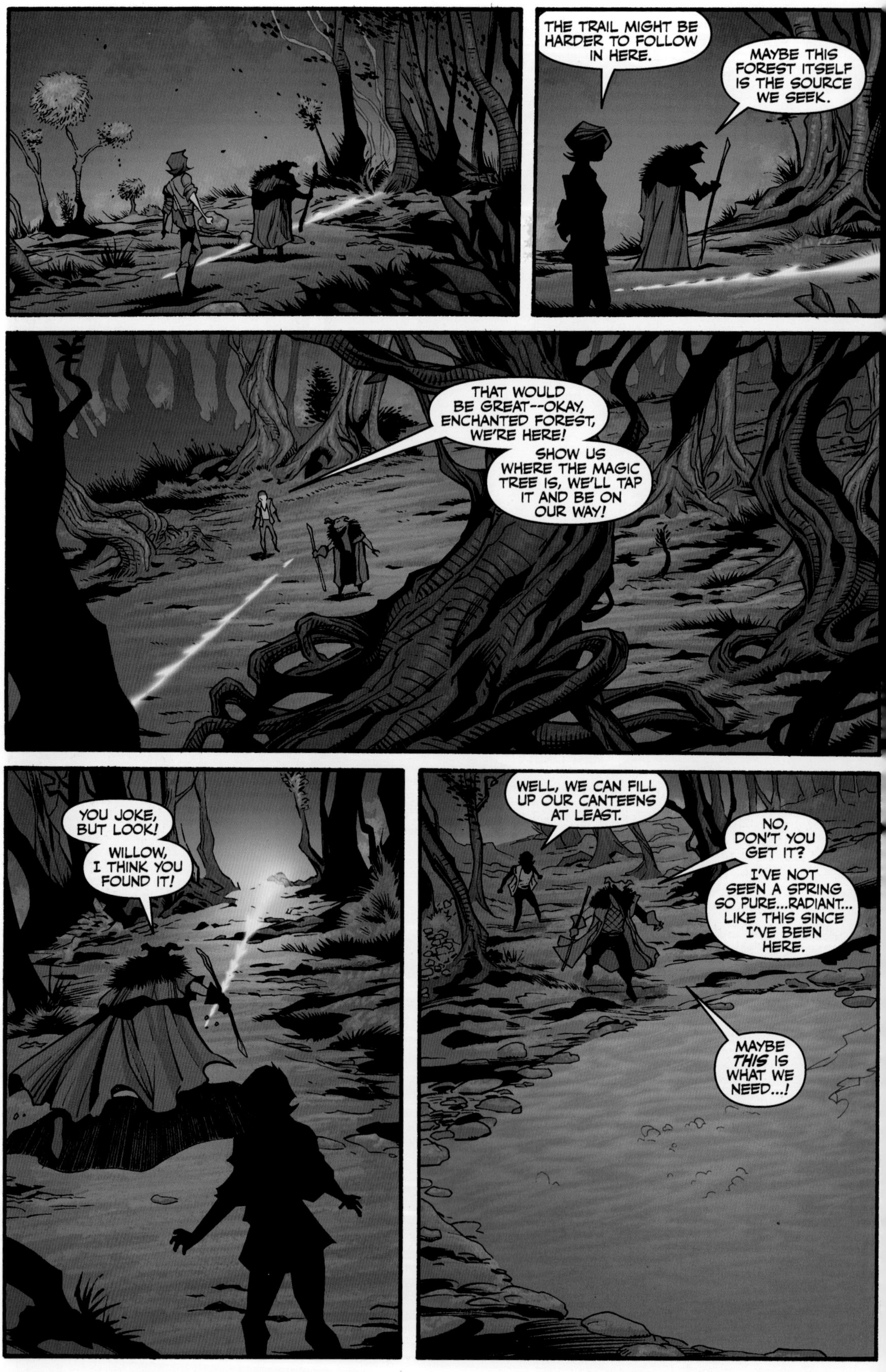
THE TRAIL MIGHT BE HARDER TO FOLLOW IN HERE.
MAYBE THIS FOREST ITSELF IS THE SOURCE WE SEEK.
THAT WOULD BE GREAT--OKAY, ENCHANTED FOREST, WE'RE HERE!
SHOW US WHERE THE MAGIC TREE IS, WE'LL TAP IT AND BE ON OUR WAY!
YOU JOKE, BUT LOOK!
WILLOW, I THINK YOU FOUND IT!
WELL, WE CAN FILL UP OUR CANTEENS AT LEAST.
NO, DON'T YOU GET IT?
I'VE NOT SEEN A SPRING SO PURE...RADIANT... LIKE THIS SINCE I'VE BEEN HERE.
MAYBE *THIS* IS WHAT WE NEED...!

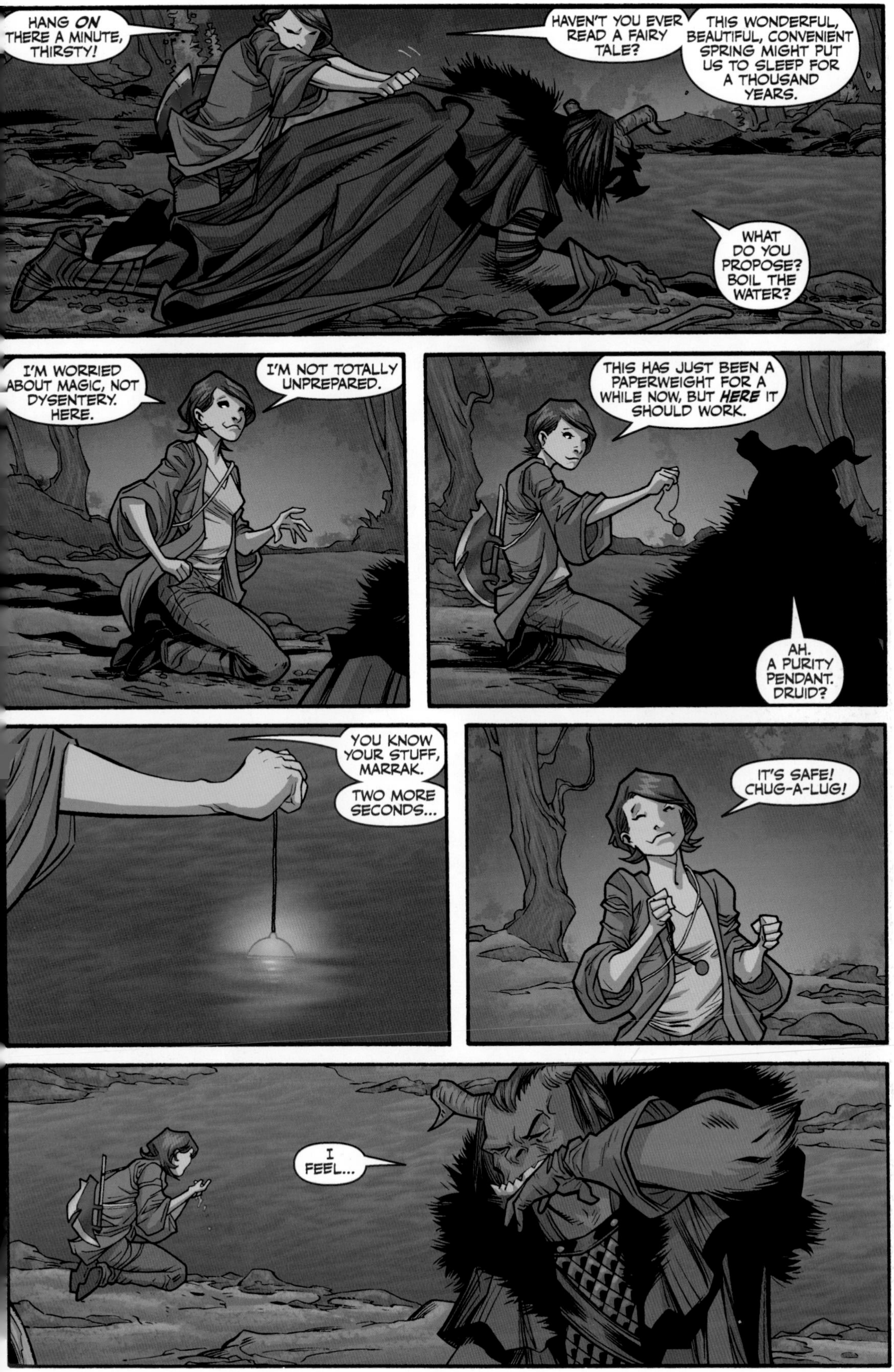
HANG ON THERE A MINUTE, THIRSTY!
HAVEN'T YOU EVER READ A FAIRY TALE?
THIS WONDERFUL, BEAUTIFUL, CONVENIENT SPRING MIGHT PUT US TO SLEEP FOR A THOUSAND YEARS.
WHAT DO YOU PROPOSE? BOIL THE WATER?
I'M WORRIED ABOUT MAGIC, NOT DYSENTERY. HERE.
I'M NOT TOTALLY UNPREPARED.
THIS HAS JUST BEEN A PAPERWEIGHT FOR A WHILE NOW, BUT HERE IT SHOULD WORK.
AH. A PURITY PENDANT. DRUID?
YOU KNOW YOUR STUFF, MARRAK.
TWO MORE SECONDS...
IT'S SAFE! CHUG-A-LUG!
I FEEL...

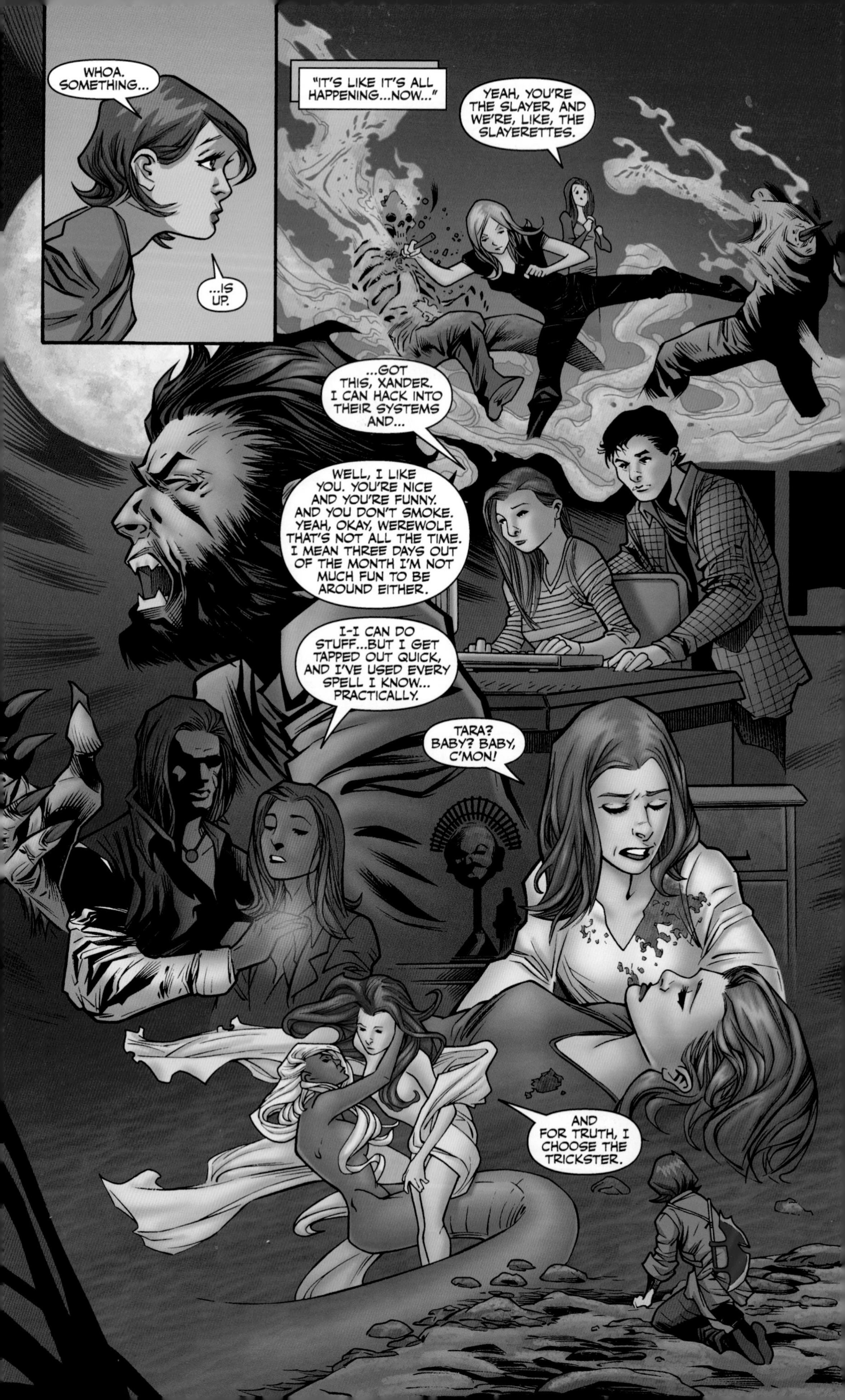
WHOA. SOMETHING...
...IS UP.
"IT'S LIKE IT'S ALL HAPPENING...NOW..."
YEAH, YOU'RE THE SLAYER, AND WE'RE, LIKE, THE SLAYERETTES.
...GOT THIS, XANDER. I CAN HACK INTO THEIR SYSTEMS AND...
WELL, I LIKE YOU. YOU'RE NICE AND YOU'RE FUNNY. AND YOU DON'T SMOKE. YEAH, OKAY, WEREWOLF. THAT'S NOT ALL THE TIME. I MEAN THREE DAYS OUT OF THE MONTH I'M NOT MUCH FUN TO BE AROUND EITHER.
I-I CAN DO STUFF...BUT I GET TAPPED OUT QUICK, AND I'VE USED EVERY SPELL I KNOW... PRACTICALLY.
TARA? BABY? BABY, C'MON!
AND FOR TRUTH, I CHOOSE THE TRICKSTER.

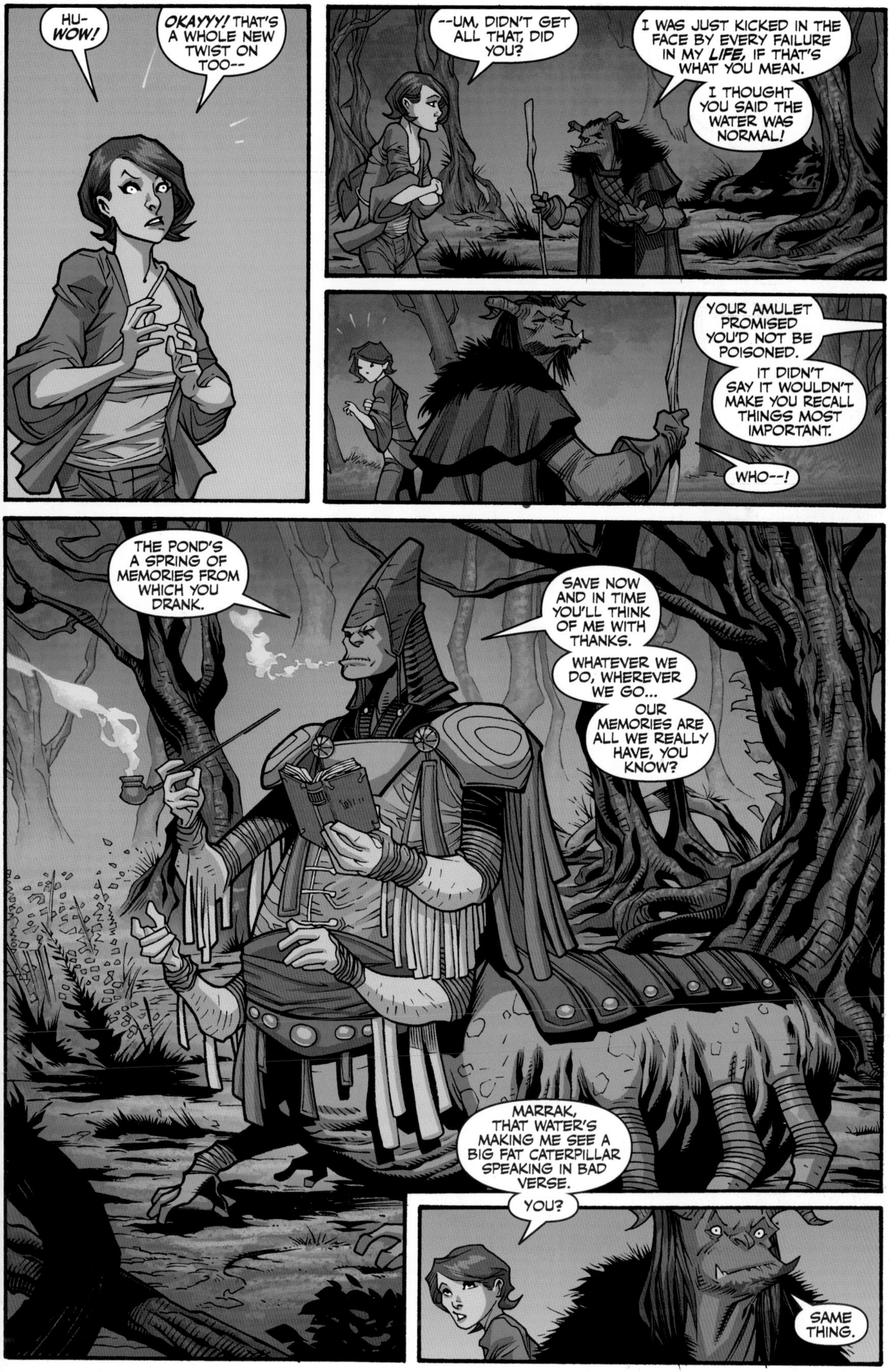
HU-WOW!
OKAYYY! THAT'S A WHOLE NEW TWIST ON TOO--
--UM, DIDN'T GET ALL THAT, DID YOU?
I WAS JUST KICKED IN THE FACE BY EVERY FAILURE IN MY LIFE, IF THAT'S WHAT YOU MEAN.
I THOUGHT YOU SAID THE WATER WAS NORMAL!
YOUR AMULET PROMISED YOU'D NOT BE POISONED.
IT DIDN'T SAY IT WOULDN'T MAKE YOU RECALL THINGS MOST IMPORTANT.
WHO--!
THE POND'S A SPRING OF MEMORIES FROM WHICH YOU DRANK.
SAVE NOW AND IN TIME YOU'LL THINK OF ME WITH THANKS.
WHATEVER WE DO, WHEREVER WE GO...
OUR MEMORIES ARE ALL WE REALLY HAVE, YOU KNOW?
MARRAK, THAT WATER'S MAKING ME SEE A BIG FAT CATERPILLAR SPEAKING IN BAD VERSE.
YOU?
SAME THING.

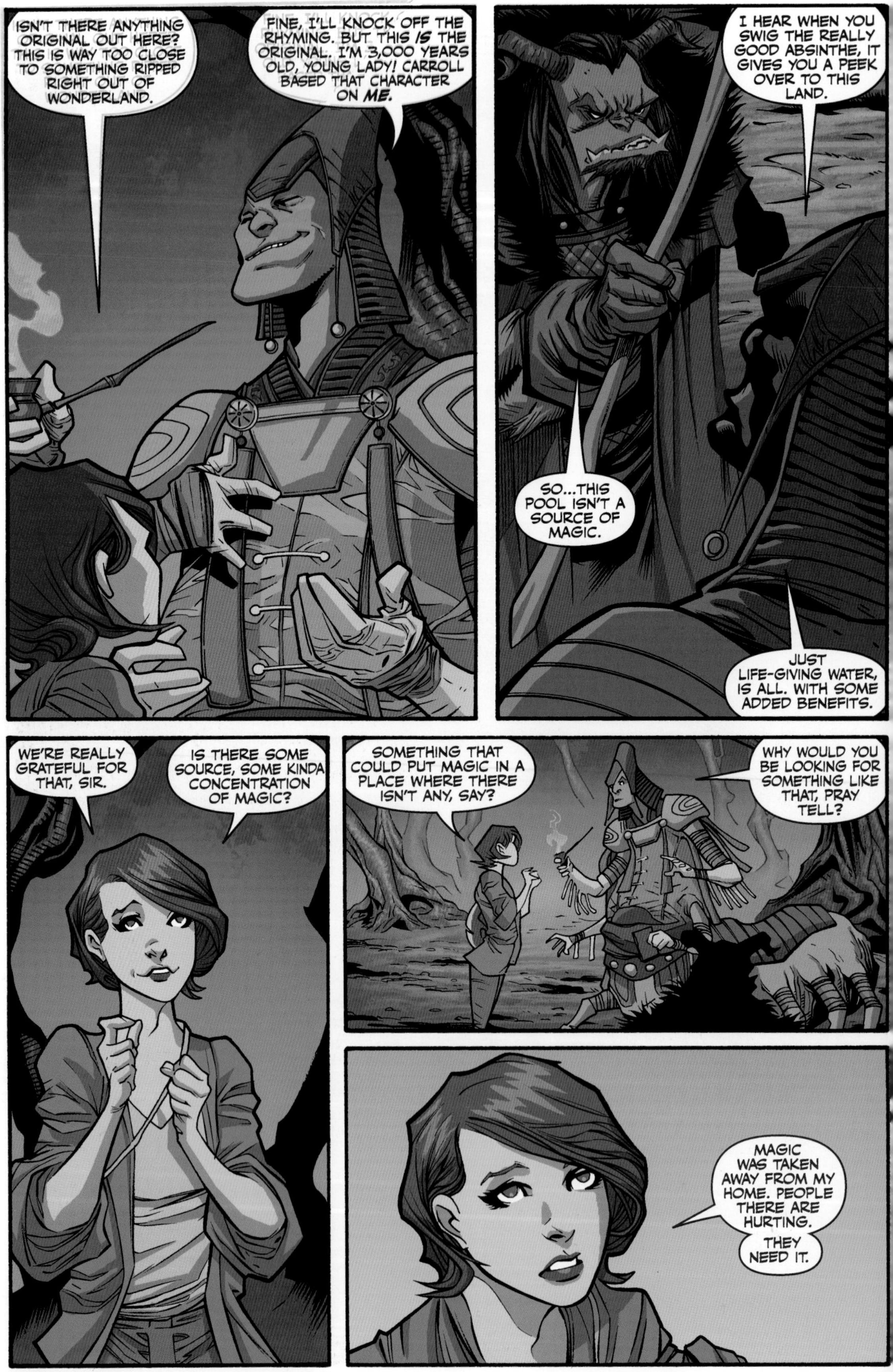
ISN'T THERE ANYTHING ORIGINAL OUT HERE? THIS IS WAY TOO CLOSE TO SOMETHING RIPPED RIGHT OUT OF WONDERLAND.
FINE, I'LL KNOCK OFF THE RHYMING. BUT THIS *IS* THE ORIGINAL. I'M 3,000 YEARS OLD, YOUNG LADY! CARROLL BASED THAT CHARACTER ON *ME*.
I HEAR WHEN YOU SWIG THE REALLY GOOD ABSINTHE, IT GIVES YOU A PEEK OVER TO THIS LAND.
SO...THIS POOL ISN'T A SOURCE OF MAGIC.
JUST LIFE-GIVING WATER, IS ALL. WITH SOME ADDED BENEFITS.
WE'RE REALLY GRATEFUL FOR THAT, SIR.
IS THERE SOME SOURCE, SOME KINDA CONCENTRATION OF MAGIC?
SOMETHING THAT COULD PUT MAGIC IN A PLACE WHERE THERE ISN'T ANY, SAY?
WHY WOULD YOU BE LOOKING FOR SOMETHING LIKE THAT, PRAY TELL?
MAGIC WAS TAKEN AWAY FROM MY HOME. PEOPLE THERE ARE HURTING.
THEY NEED IT.

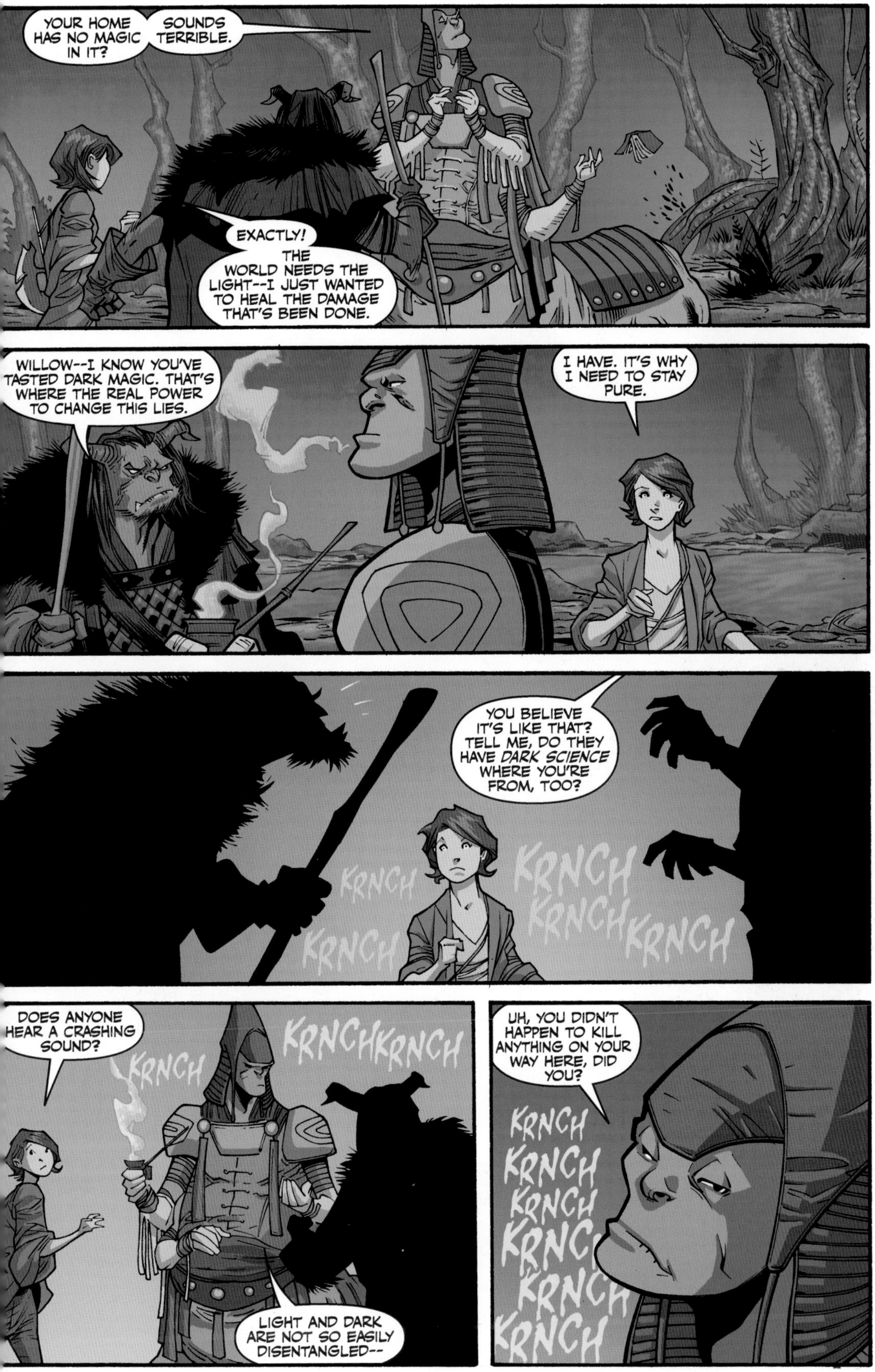
YOUR HOME HAS NO MAGIC IN IT?
SOUNDS TERRIBLE.
EXACTLY! THE WORLD NEEDS THE LIGHT--I JUST WANTED TO HEAL THE DAMAGE THAT'S BEEN DONE.
WILLOW--I KNOW YOU'VE TASTED DARK MAGIC. THAT'S WHERE THE REAL POWER TO CHANGE THIS LIES.
I HAVE. IT'S WHY I NEED TO STAY PURE.
YOU BELIEVE IT'S LIKE THAT? TELL ME, DO THEY HAVE *DARK SCIENCE* WHERE YOU'RE FROM, TOO?
KRNCH
KRNCH
KRNCH
KRNCH
KRNCH
DOES ANYONE HEAR A CRASHING SOUND?
KRNCH
KRNCHKRNCH
LIGHT AND DARK ARE NOT SO EASILY DISENTANGLED--
UH, YOU DIDN'T HAPPEN TO KILL ANYTHING ON YOUR WAY HERE, DID YOU?
KRNCH
KRNCH
KRNCH
KRNCH
KRNCH
KRNCH

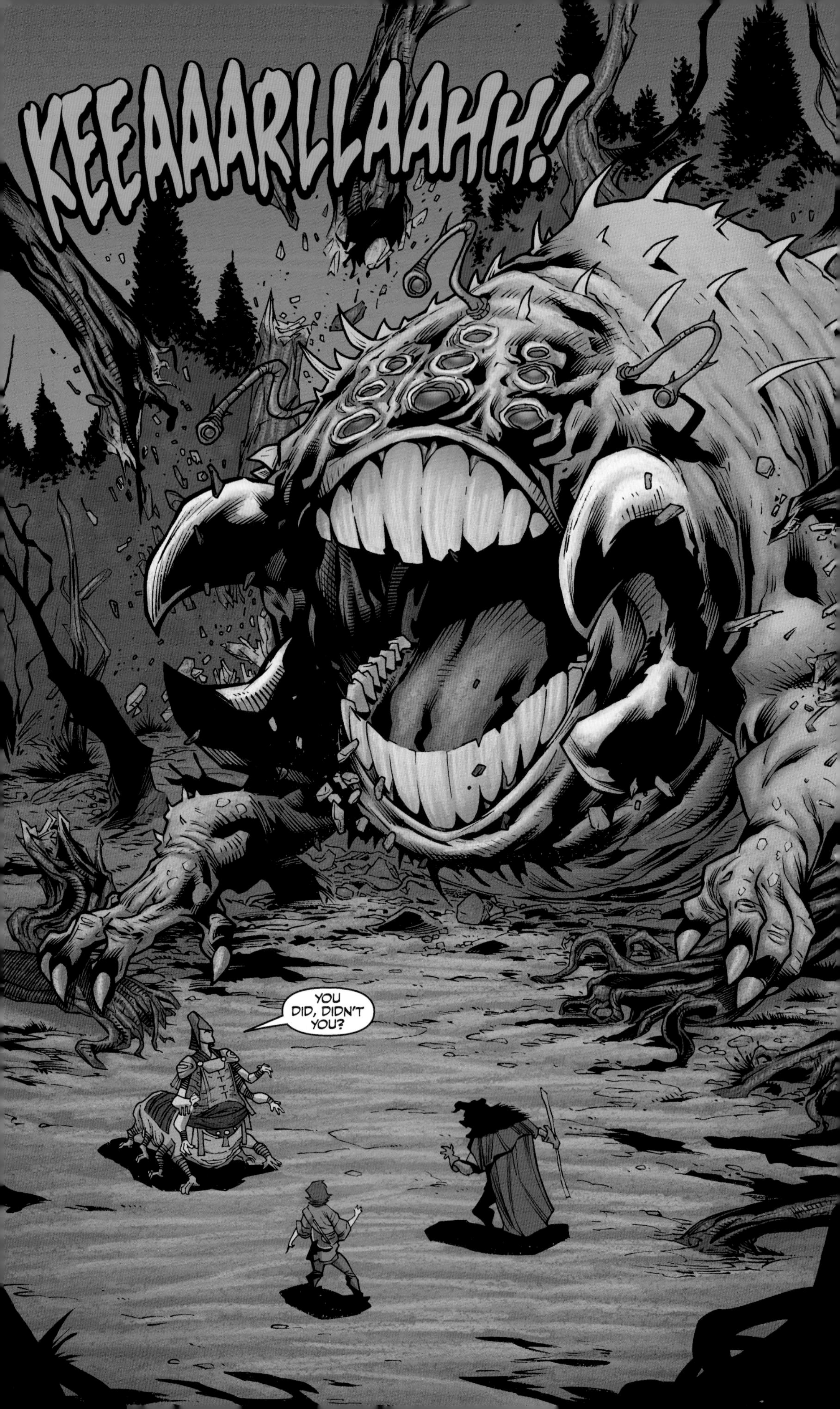
KEEAAARLLAAHH!
YOU DID, DIDN'T YOU?

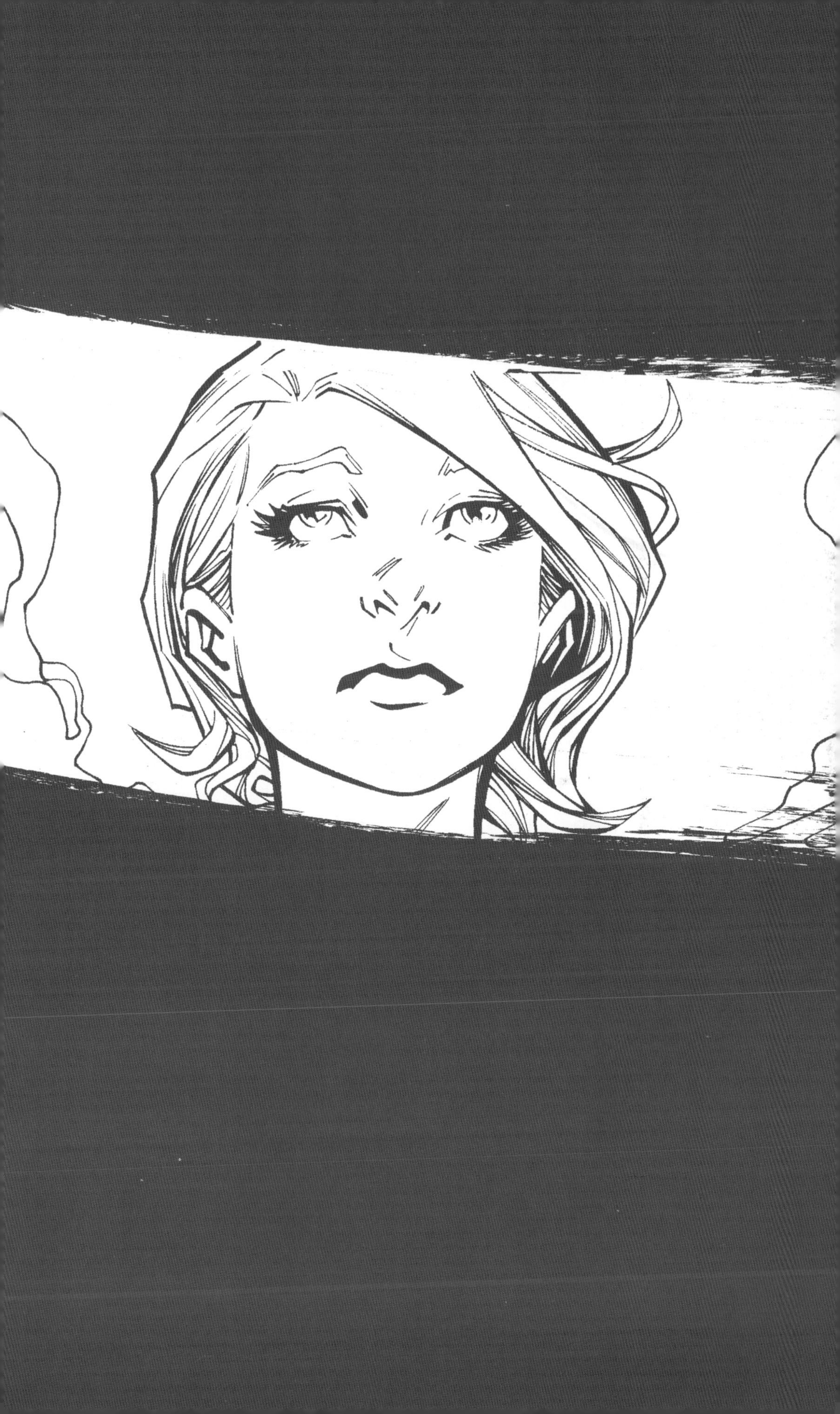

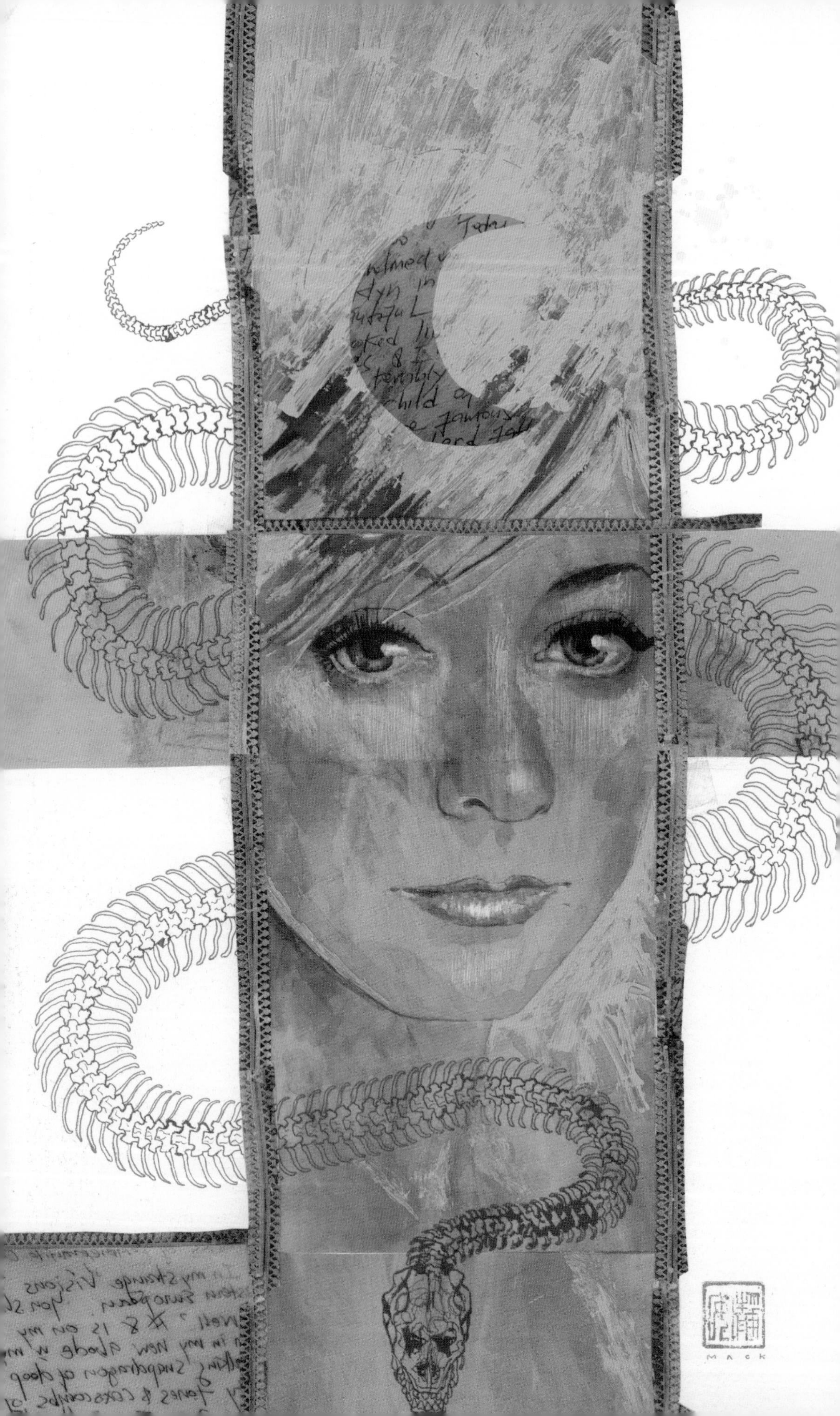
MACK

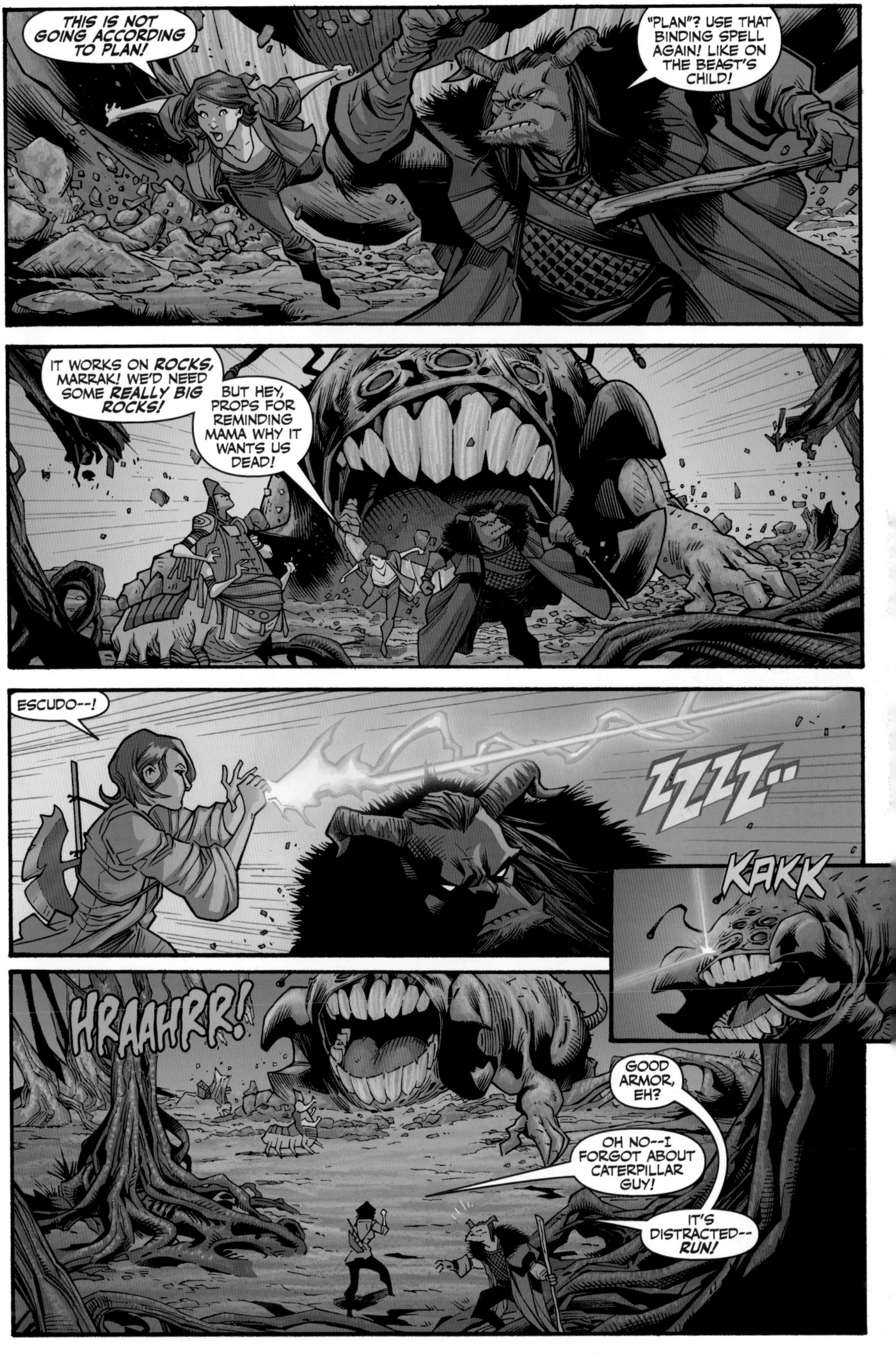
THIS IS NOT GOING ACCORDING TO PLAN!
"PLAN"? USE THAT BINDING SPELL AGAIN! LIKE ON THE BEAST'S CHILD!
IT WORKS ON ROCKS, MARRAK! WE'D NEED SOME REALLY BIG ROCKS!
BUT HEY, PROPS FOR REMINDING MAMA WHY IT WANTS US DEAD!
ESCUDO--!
ZZZZ..
KAKK
HRAAHRR!
GOOD ARMOR, EH?
OH NO--I FORGOT ABOUT CATERPILLAR GUY!
IT'S DISTRACTED-- RUN!

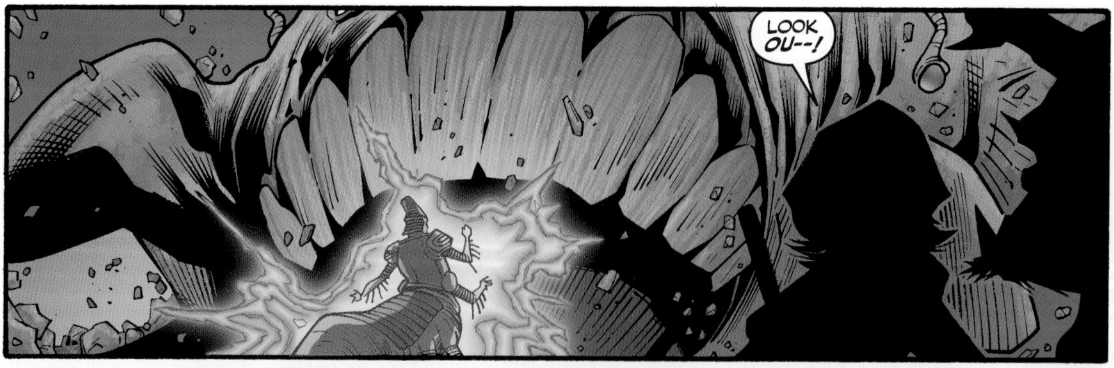
LOOK OU--!

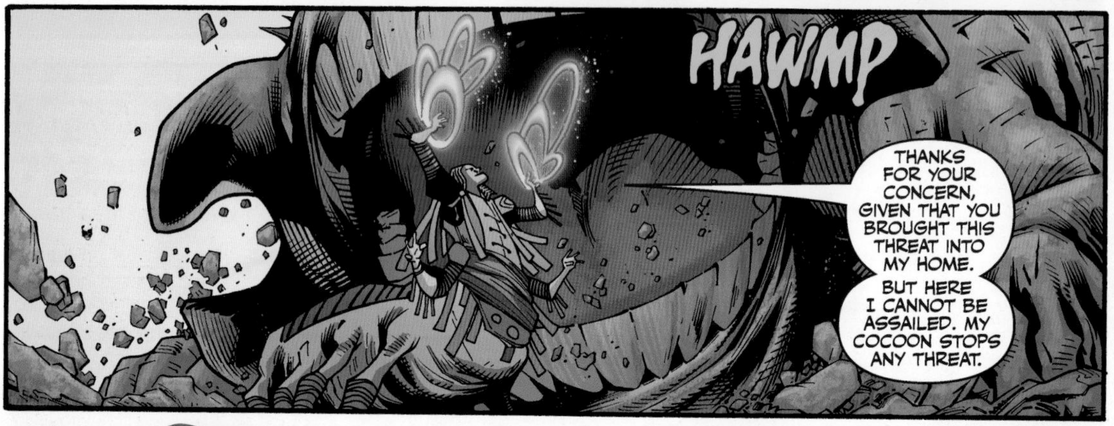
HAWMP
THANKS FOR YOUR CONCERN, GIVEN THAT YOU BROUGHT THIS THREAT INTO MY HOME.
BUT HERE I CANNOT BE ASSAILED. MY COCOON STOPS ANY THREAT.

WONDERLAND

PART TWO

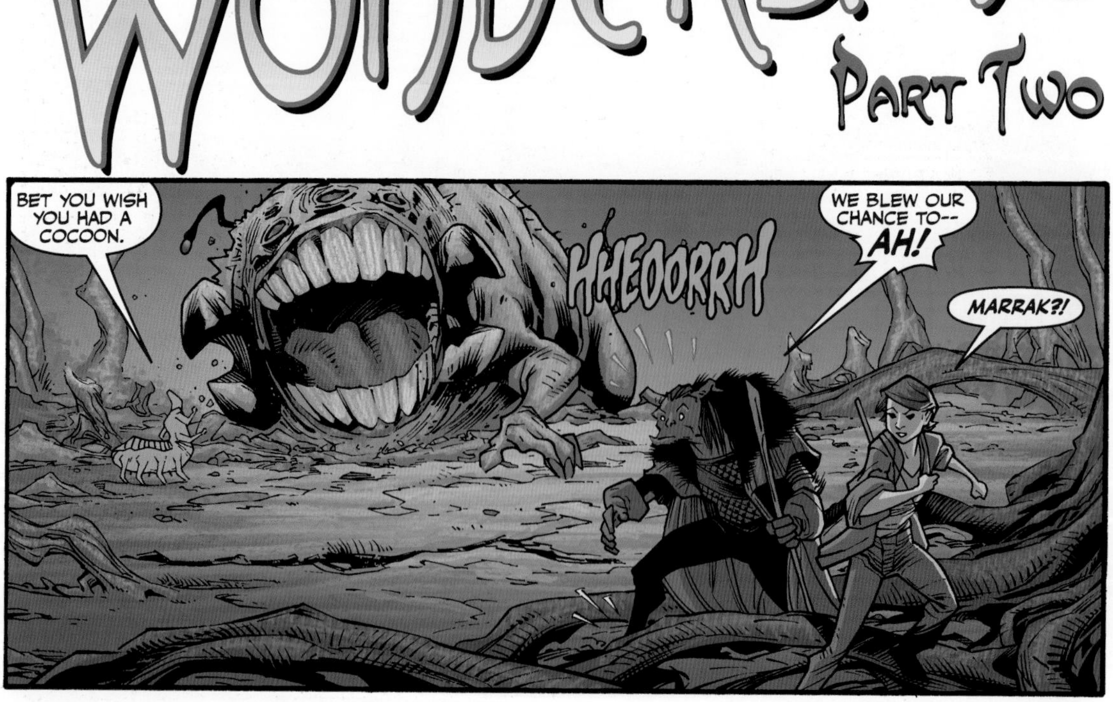
BET YOU WISH YOU HAD A COCOON.
HHEOORRH
WE BLEW OUR CHANCE TO-- AH!
MARRAK?!

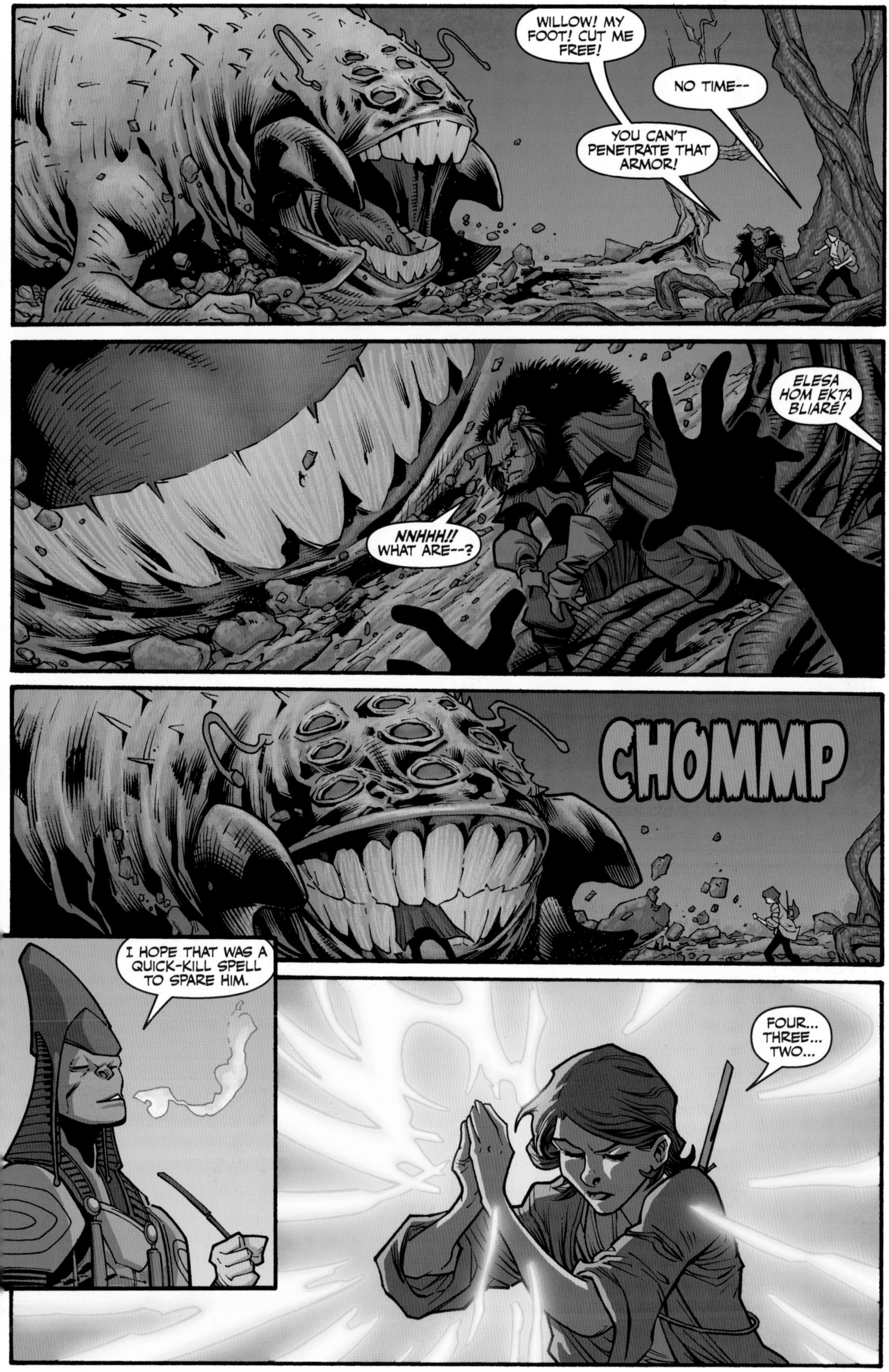
WILLOW! MY FOOT! CUT ME FREE!
NO TIME--
YOU CAN'T PENETRATE THAT ARMOR!
ELESA HOM EKTA BLIARÉ!
NNHHH!! WHAT ARE--?
CHOMMP
I HOPE THAT WAS A QUICK-KILL SPELL TO SPARE HIM.
FOUR... THREE... TWO...

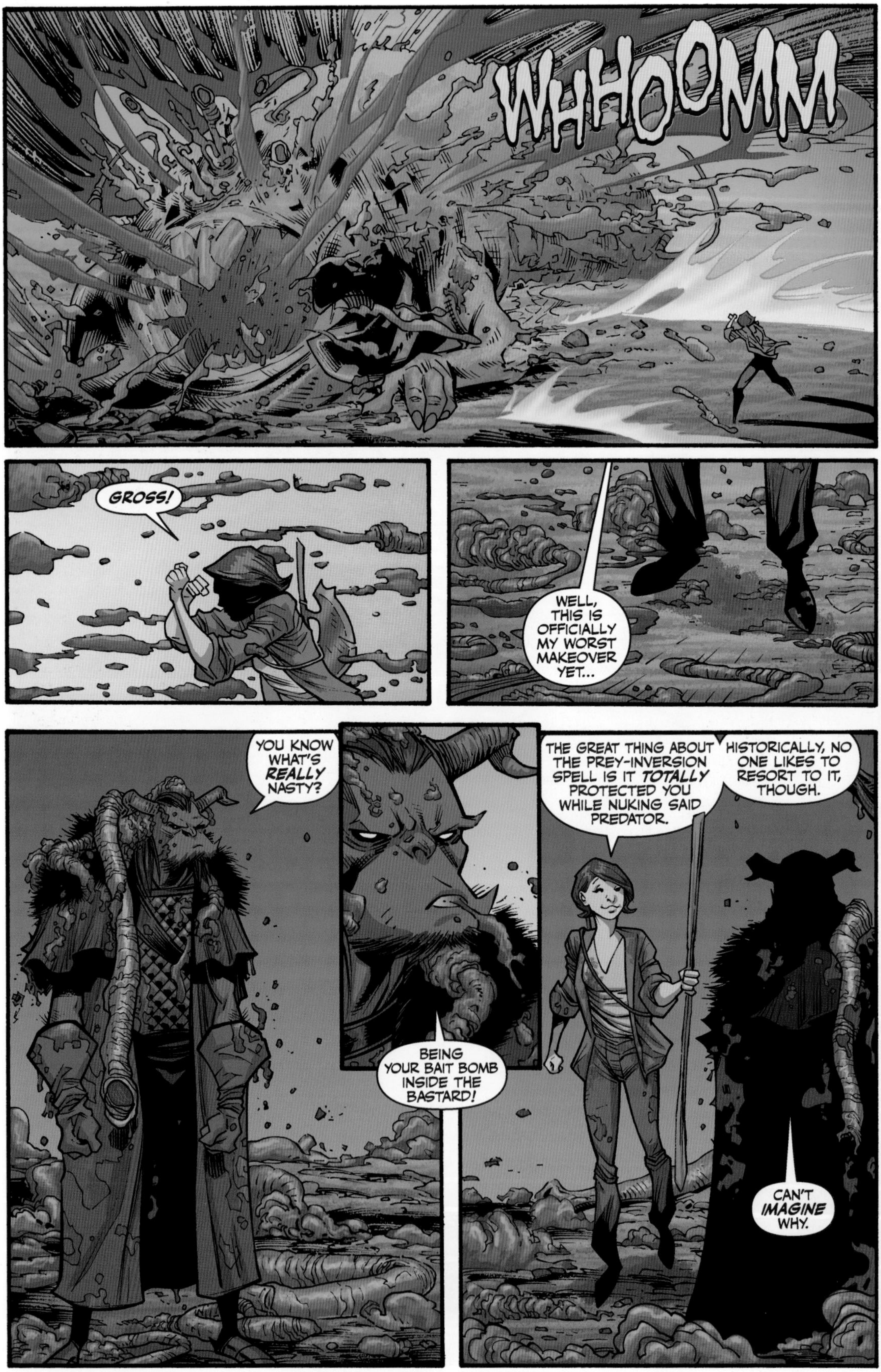
WHHOOMM
GROSS!
WELL, THIS IS OFFICIALLY MY WORST MAKEOVER YET...
YOU KNOW WHAT'S *REALLY* NASTY?
BEING YOUR BAIT BOMB INSIDE THE BASTARD!
THE GREAT THING ABOUT THE PREY-INVERSION SPELL IS IT *TOTALLY* PROTECTED YOU WHILE NUKING SAID PREDATOR.
HISTORICALLY, NO ONE LIKES TO RESORT TO IT, THOUGH.
CAN'T *IMAGINE* WHY.

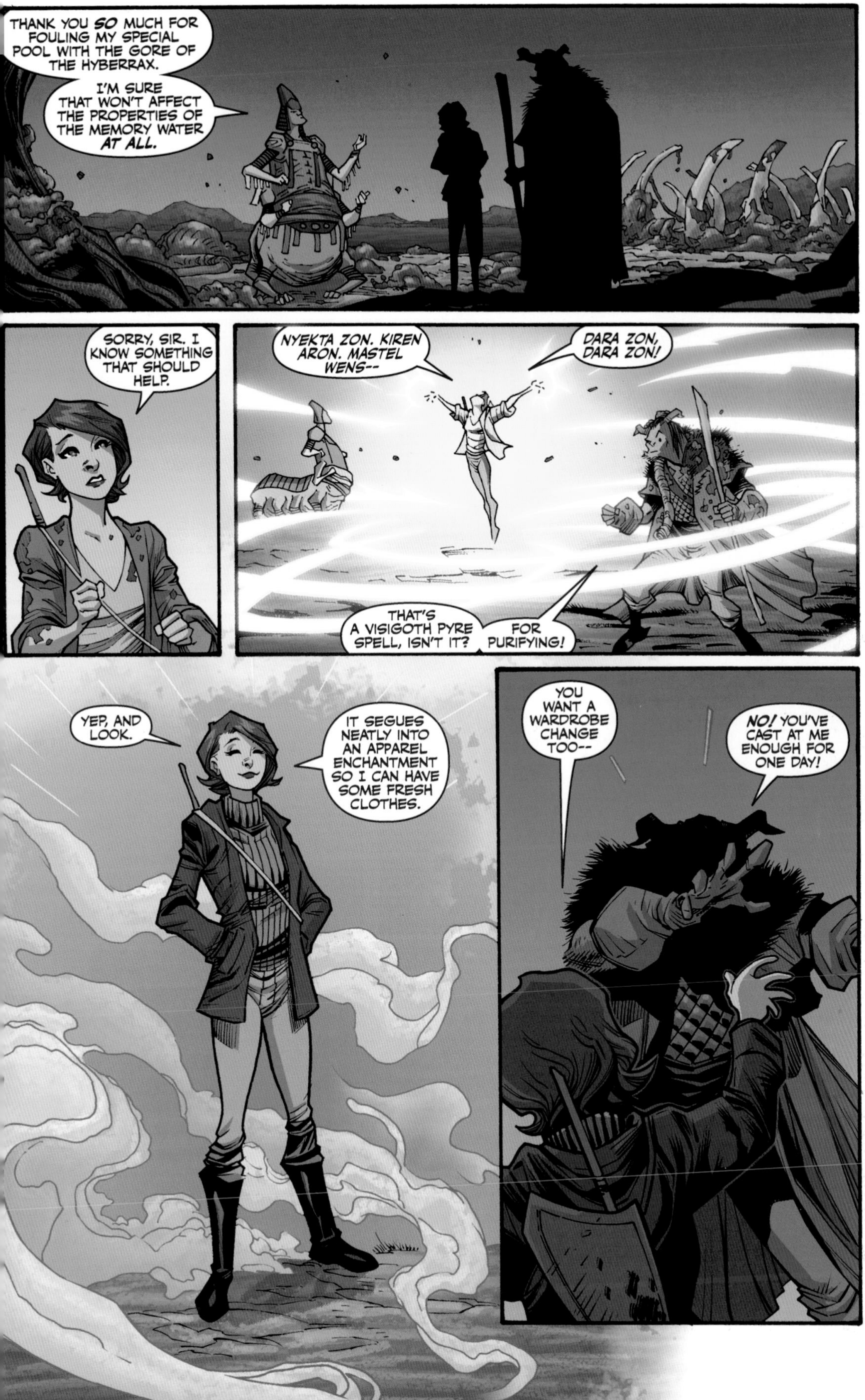
THANK YOU SO MUCH FOR FOULING MY SPECIAL POOL WITH THE GORE OF THE HYBERRAX.
I'M SURE THAT WON'T AFFECT THE PROPERTIES OF THE MEMORY WATER AT ALL.
SORRY, SIR. I KNOW SOMETHING THAT SHOULD HELP.
NYEKTA ZON. KIREN ARON. MASTEL WENS--
DARA ZON, DARA ZON!
THAT'S A VISIGOTH PYRE SPELL, ISN'T IT?
FOR PURIFYING!
YEP, AND LOOK.
IT SEGUES NEATLY INTO AN APPAREL ENCHANTMENT SO I CAN HAVE SOME FRESH CLOTHES.
YOU WANT A WARDROBE CHANGE TOO--
NO! YOU'VE CAST AT ME ENOUGH FOR ONE DAY!

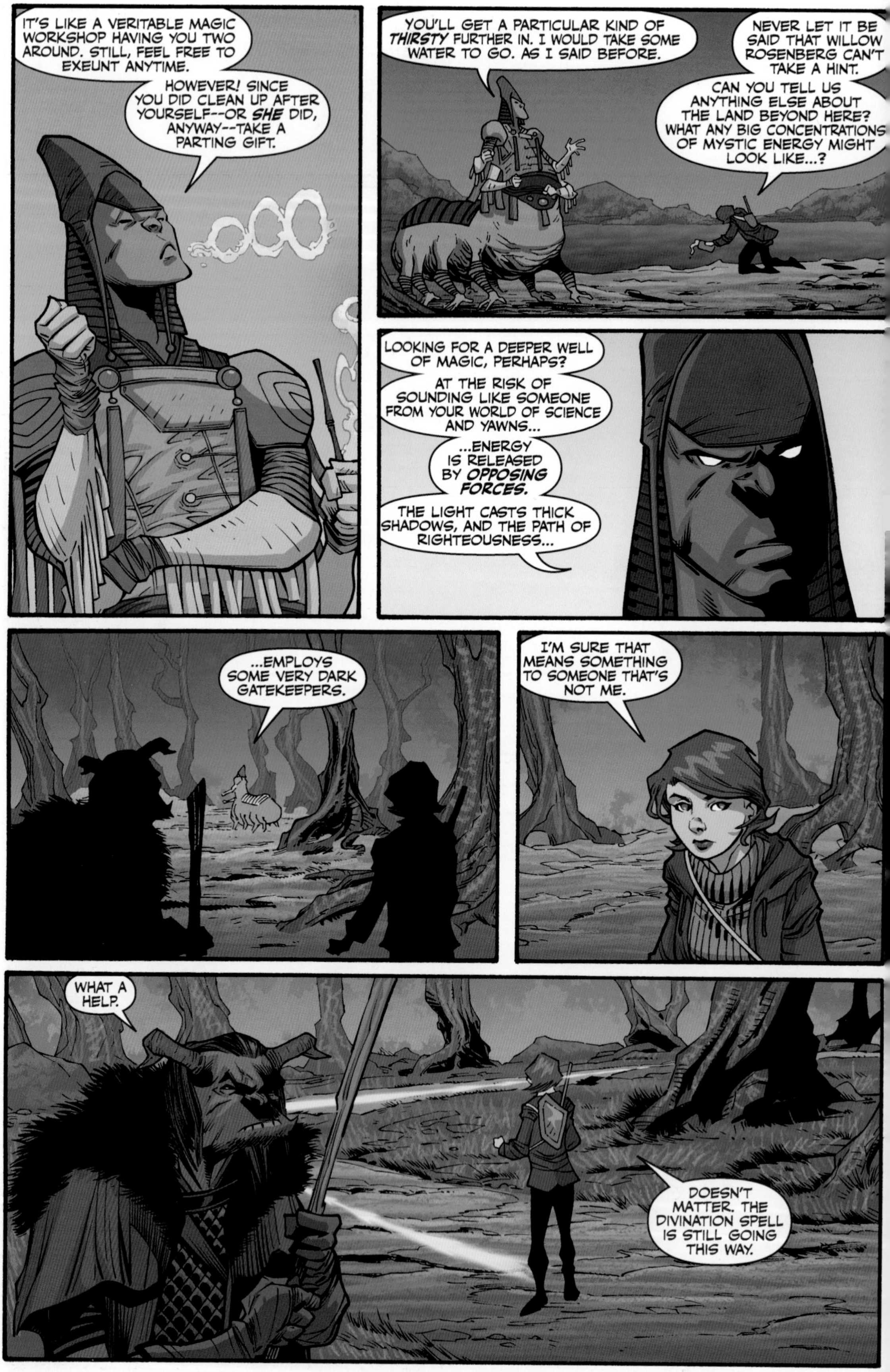

IT'S LIKE A VERITABLE MAGIC WORKSHOP HAVING YOU TWO AROUND. STILL, FEEL FREE TO EXEUNT ANYTIME.
HOWEVER! SINCE YOU DID CLEAN UP AFTER YOURSELF--OR SHE DID, ANYWAY--TAKE A PARTING GIFT.
YOU'LL GET A PARTICULAR KIND OF THIRSTY FURTHER IN. I WOULD TAKE SOME WATER TO GO. AS I SAID BEFORE.
NEVER LET IT BE SAID THAT WILLOW ROSENBERG CAN'T TAKE A HINT.
CAN YOU TELL US ANYTHING ELSE ABOUT THE LAND BEYOND HERE? WHAT ANY BIG CONCENTRATIONS OF MYSTIC ENERGY MIGHT LOOK LIKE...?
LOOKING FOR A DEEPER WELL OF MAGIC, PERHAPS?
AT THE RISK OF SOUNDING LIKE SOMEONE FROM YOUR WORLD OF SCIENCE AND YAWNS...
...ENERGY IS RELEASED BY OPPOSING FORCES.
THE LIGHT CASTS THICK SHADOWS, AND THE PATH OF RIGHTEOUSNESS...
...EMPLOYS SOME VERY DARK GATEKEEPERS.
I'M SURE THAT MEANS SOMETHING TO SOMEONE THAT'S NOT ME.
WHAT A HELP.
DOESN'T MATTER. THE DIVINATION SPELL IS STILL GOING THIS WAY.

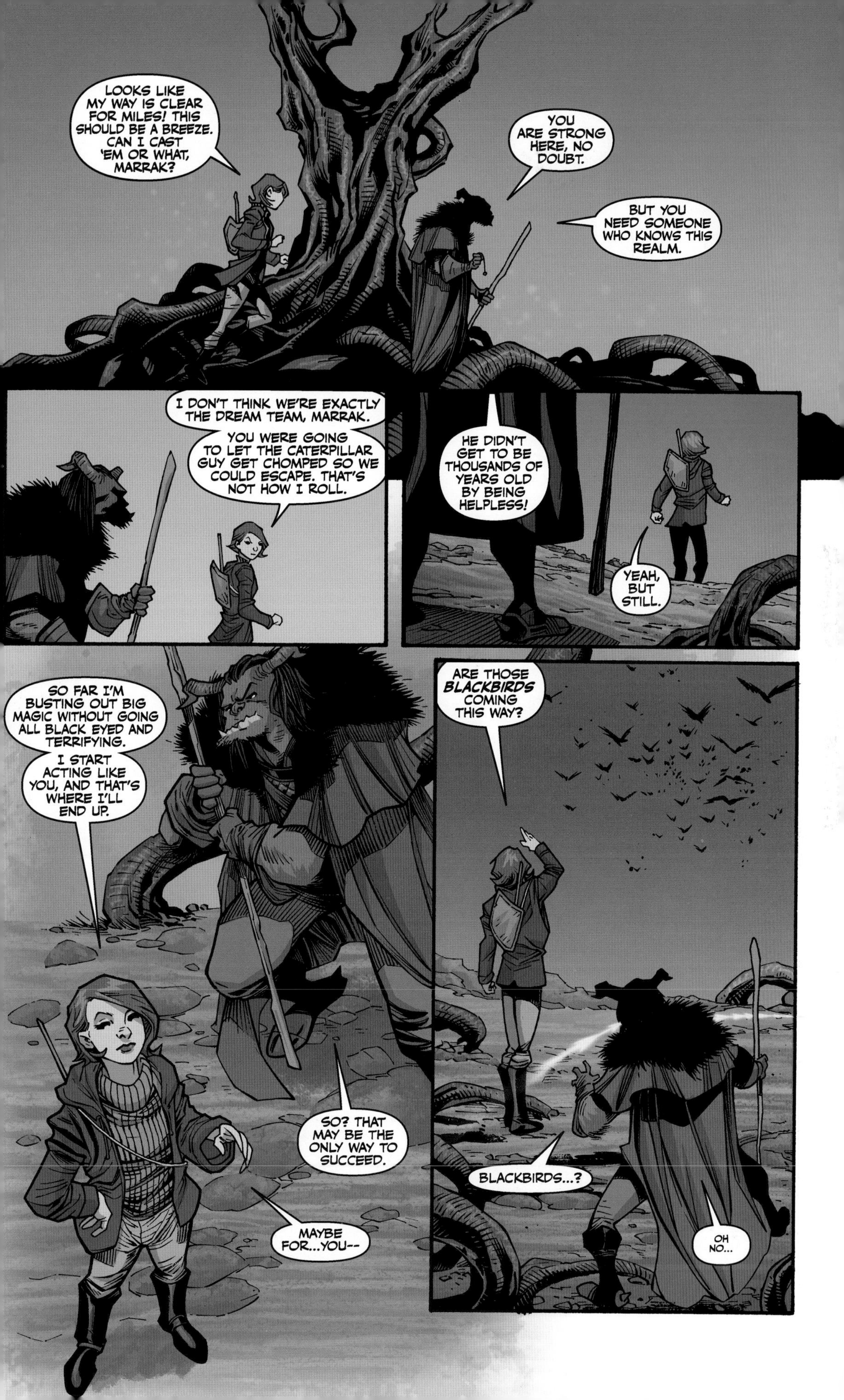
LOOKS LIKE MY WAY IS CLEAR FOR MILES! THIS SHOULD BE A BREEZE. CAN I CAST 'EM OR WHAT, MARRAK?
YOU ARE STRONG HERE, NO DOUBT.
BUT YOU NEED SOMEONE WHO KNOWS THIS REALM.
I DON'T THINK WE'RE EXACTLY THE DREAM TEAM, MARRAK.
YOU WERE GOING TO LET THE CATERPILLAR GUY GET CHOMPED SO WE COULD ESCAPE. THAT'S NOT HOW I ROLL.
HE DIDN'T GET TO BE THOUSANDS OF YEARS OLD BY BEING HELPLESS!
YEAH, BUT STILL.
SO FAR I'M BUSTING OUT BIG MAGIC WITHOUT GOING ALL BLACK EYED AND TERRIFYING.
I START ACTING LIKE YOU, AND THAT'S WHERE I'LL END UP.
SO? THAT MAY BE THE ONLY WAY TO SUCCEED.
MAYBE FOR...YOU--
ARE THOSE *BLACKBIRDS* COMING THIS WAY?
BLACKBIRDS...?
OH NO...

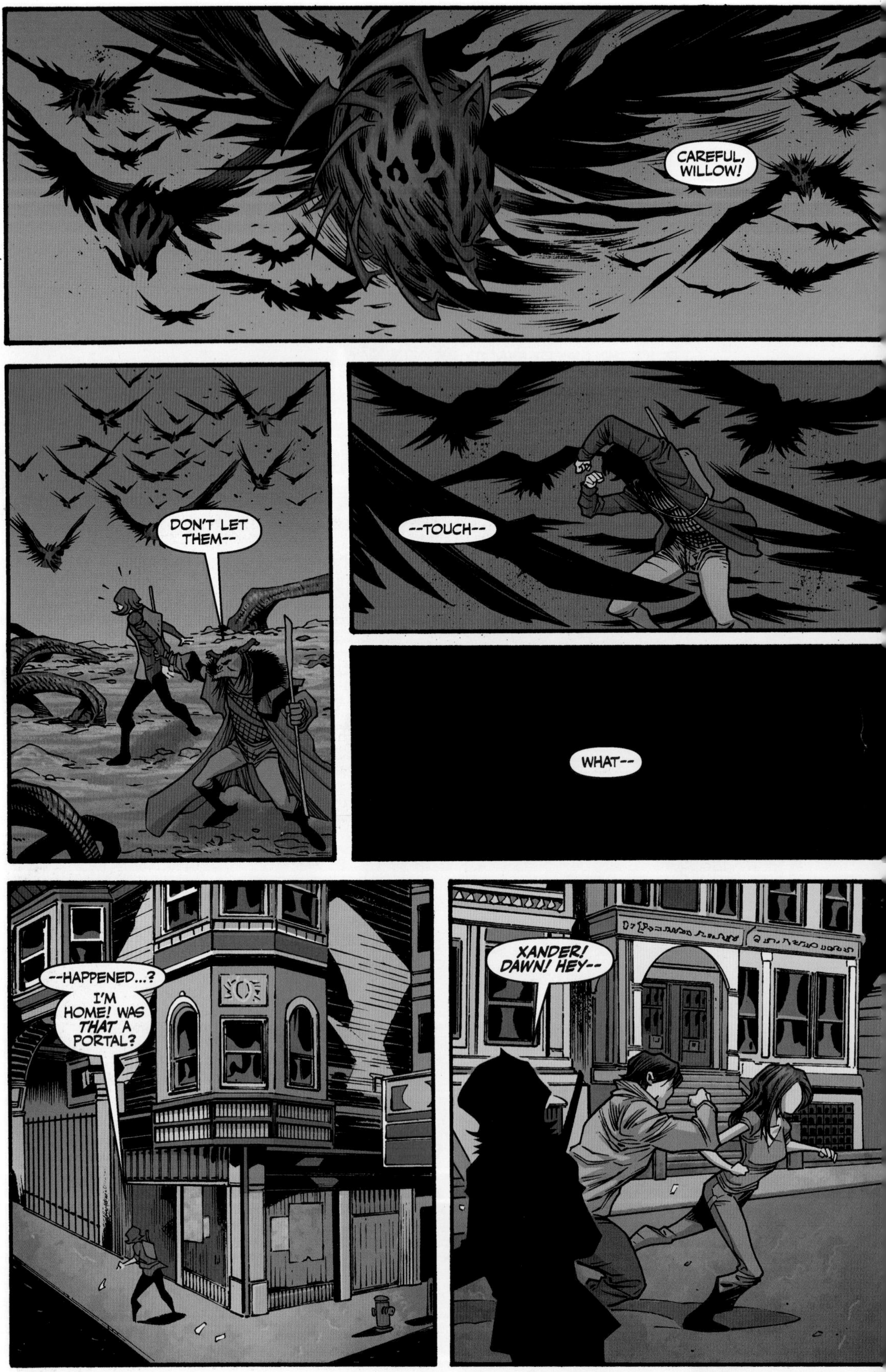
CAREFUL, WILLOW!
DON'T LET THEM--
--TOUCH--
WHAT--
--HAPPENED...?
I'M HOME! WAS THAT A PORTAL?
XANDER! DAWN! HEY--

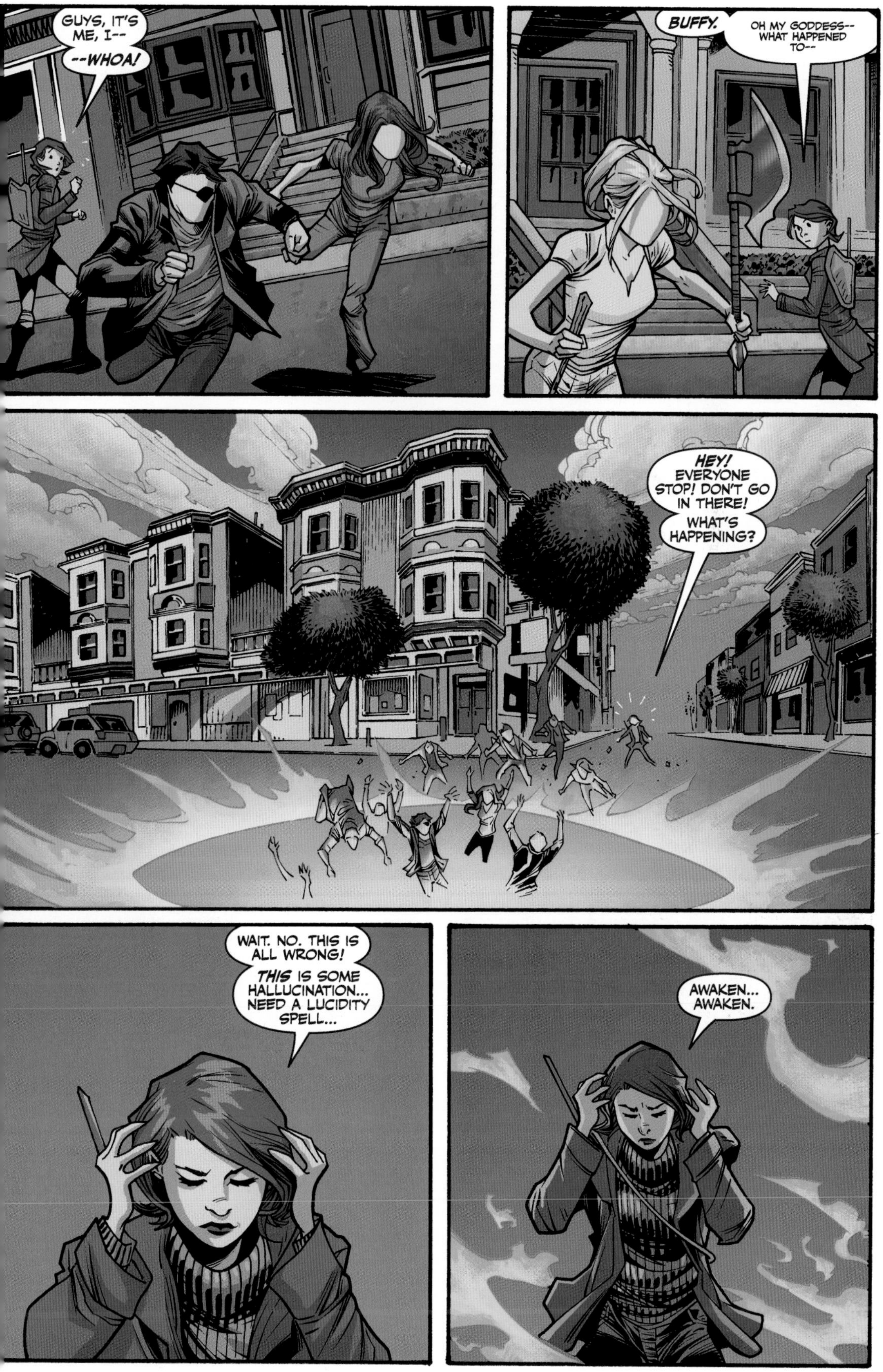
GUYS, IT'S ME, I--
--WHOA!
BUFFY.
OH MY GODDESS-- WHAT HAPPENED TO--
HEY! EVERYONE STOP! DON'T GO IN THERE!
WHAT'S HAPPENING?
WAIT. NO. THIS IS ALL WRONG!
THIS IS SOME HALLUCINATION... NEED A LUCIDITY SPELL...
AWAKEN... AWAKEN.

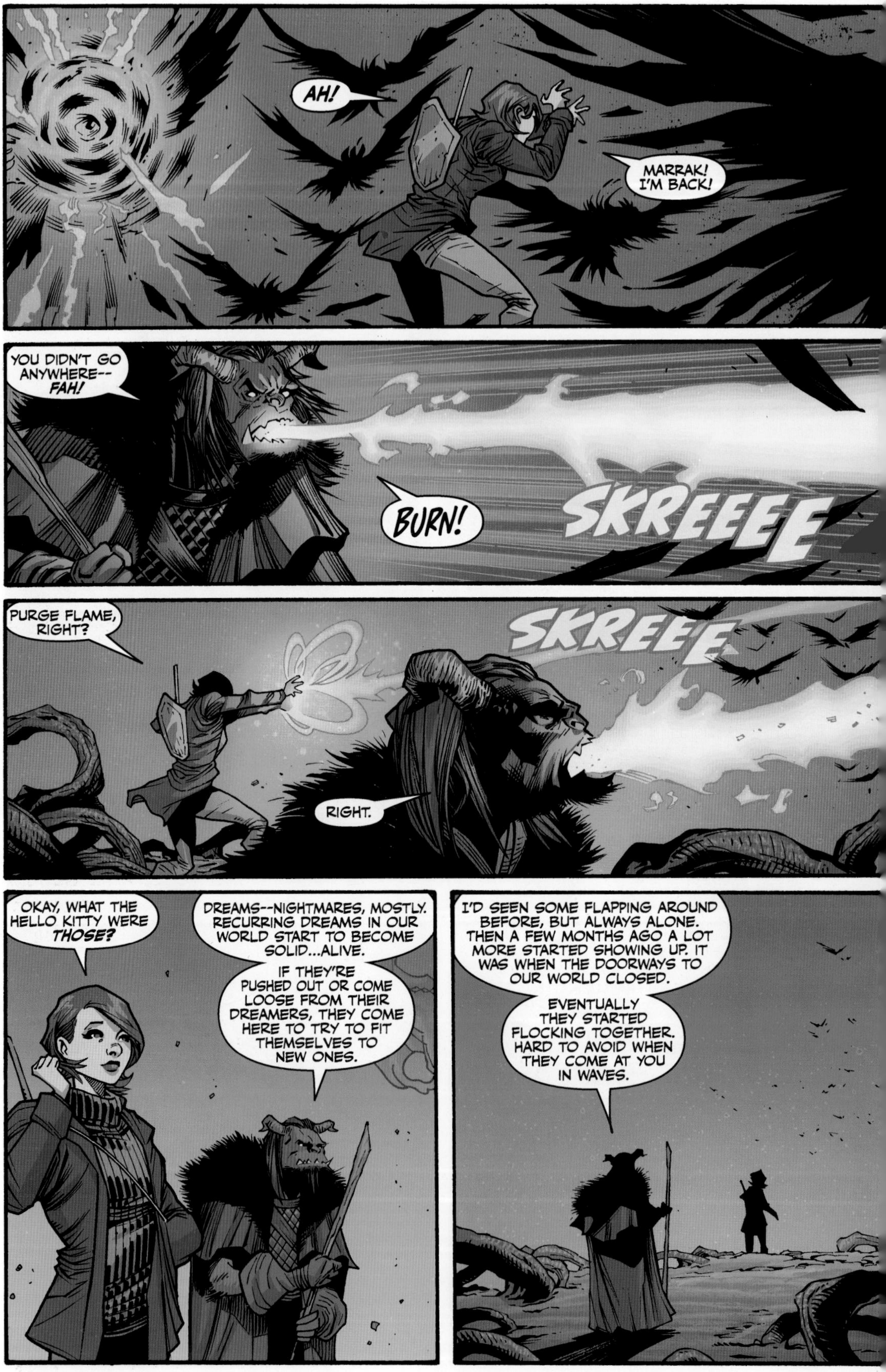
AH!
MARRAK! I'M BACK!
YOU DIDN'T GO ANYWHERE-- FAH!
BURN!
SKREEEEE
PURGE FLAME, RIGHT?
SKREEE
RIGHT.
OKAY, WHAT THE HELLO KITTY WERE THOSE?
DREAMS--NIGHTMARES, MOSTLY. RECURRING DREAMS IN OUR WORLD START TO BECOME SOLID...ALIVE.
IF THEY'RE PUSHED OUT OR COME LOOSE FROM THEIR DREAMERS, THEY COME HERE TO TRY TO FIT THEMSELVES TO NEW ONES.
I'D SEEN SOME FLAPPING AROUND BEFORE, BUT ALWAYS ALONE. THEN A FEW MONTHS AGO A LOT MORE STARTED SHOWING UP. IT WAS WHEN THE DOORWAYS TO OUR WORLD CLOSED.
EVENTUALLY THEY STARTED FLOCKING TOGETHER. HARD TO AVOID WHEN THEY COME AT YOU IN WAVES.

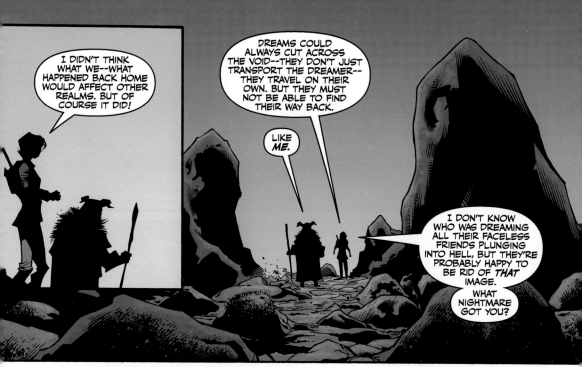

I DIDN'T THINK WHAT WE--WHAT HAPPENED BACK HOME WOULD AFFECT OTHER REALMS. BUT OF COURSE IT DID!

DREAMS COULD ALWAYS CUT ACROSS THE VOID--THEY DON'T JUST TRANSPORT THE DREAMER-- THEY TRAVEL ON THEIR OWN. BUT THEY MUST NOT BE ABLE TO FIND THEIR WAY BACK.

LIKE *ME.*

I DON'T KNOW WHO WAS DREAMING ALL THEIR FACELESS FRIENDS PLUNGING INTO HELL, BUT THEY'RE PROBABLY HAPPY TO BE RID OF *THAT* IMAGE.

WHAT NIGHTMARE GOT YOU?

ACTUALLY, I GOT HIT BY SOMEONE'S DREAM ABOUT... *NURSES.*

NOT SO BAD--BUT I STILL FREED MYSELF.

MAN.

WHY COULDN'T I HAVE GOTTEN THAT *NURSE* DREAM?

YEAH. THE DREAMER PROBABLY WANTS THAT ONE *BACK.*

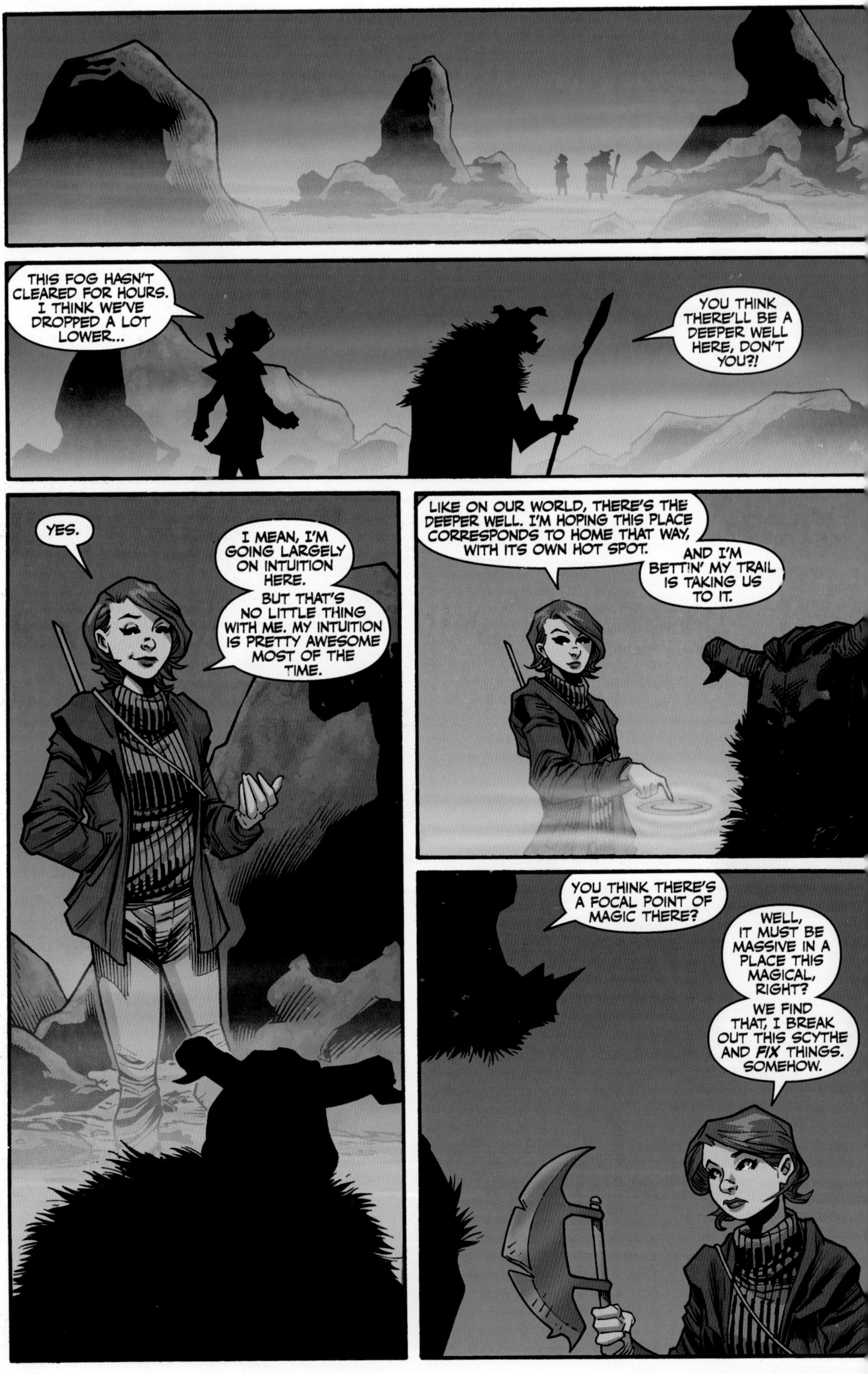
THIS FOG HASN'T CLEARED FOR HOURS. I THINK WE'VE DROPPED A LOT LOWER...
YOU THINK THERE'LL BE A DEEPER WELL HERE, DON'T YOU?!
YES.
I MEAN, I'M GOING LARGELY ON INTUITION HERE.
BUT THAT'S NO LITTLE THING WITH ME. MY INTUITION IS PRETTY AWESOME MOST OF THE TIME.
LIKE ON OUR WORLD, THERE'S THE DEEPER WELL. I'M HOPING THIS PLACE CORRESPONDS TO HOME THAT WAY, WITH ITS OWN HOT SPOT.
AND I'M BETTIN' MY TRAIL IS TAKING US TO IT.
YOU THINK THERE'S A FOCAL POINT OF MAGIC THERE?
WELL, IT MUST BE MASSIVE IN A PLACE THIS MAGICAL, RIGHT?
WE FIND THAT, I BREAK OUT THIS SCYTHE AND *FIX* THINGS. SOMEHOW.

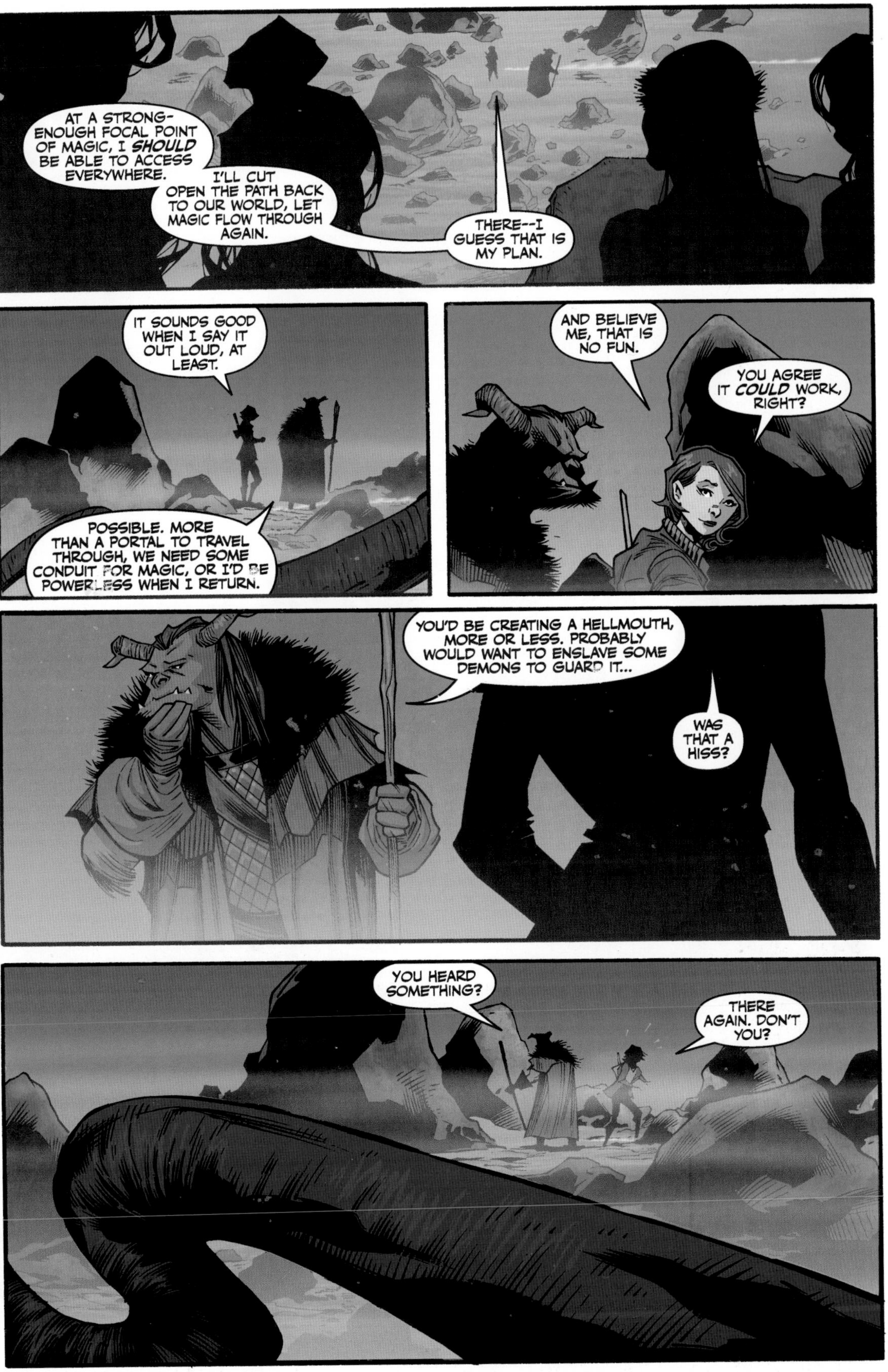
AT A STRONG-ENOUGH FOCAL POINT OF MAGIC, I *SHOULD* BE ABLE TO ACCESS EVERYWHERE.
I'LL CUT OPEN THE PATH BACK TO OUR WORLD, LET MAGIC FLOW THROUGH AGAIN.
THERE--I GUESS THAT IS MY PLAN.
IT SOUNDS GOOD WHEN I SAY IT OUT LOUD, AT LEAST.
POSSIBLE. MORE THAN A PORTAL TO TRAVEL THROUGH, WE NEED SOME CONDUIT FOR MAGIC, OR I'D BE POWERLESS WHEN I RETURN.
AND BELIEVE ME, THAT IS NO FUN.
YOU AGREE IT *COULD* WORK, RIGHT?
YOU'D BE CREATING A HELLMOUTH, MORE OR LESS. PROBABLY WOULD WANT TO ENSLAVE SOME DEMONS TO GUARD IT...
WAS THAT A HISS?
YOU HEARD SOMETHING?
THERE AGAIN. DON'T YOU?

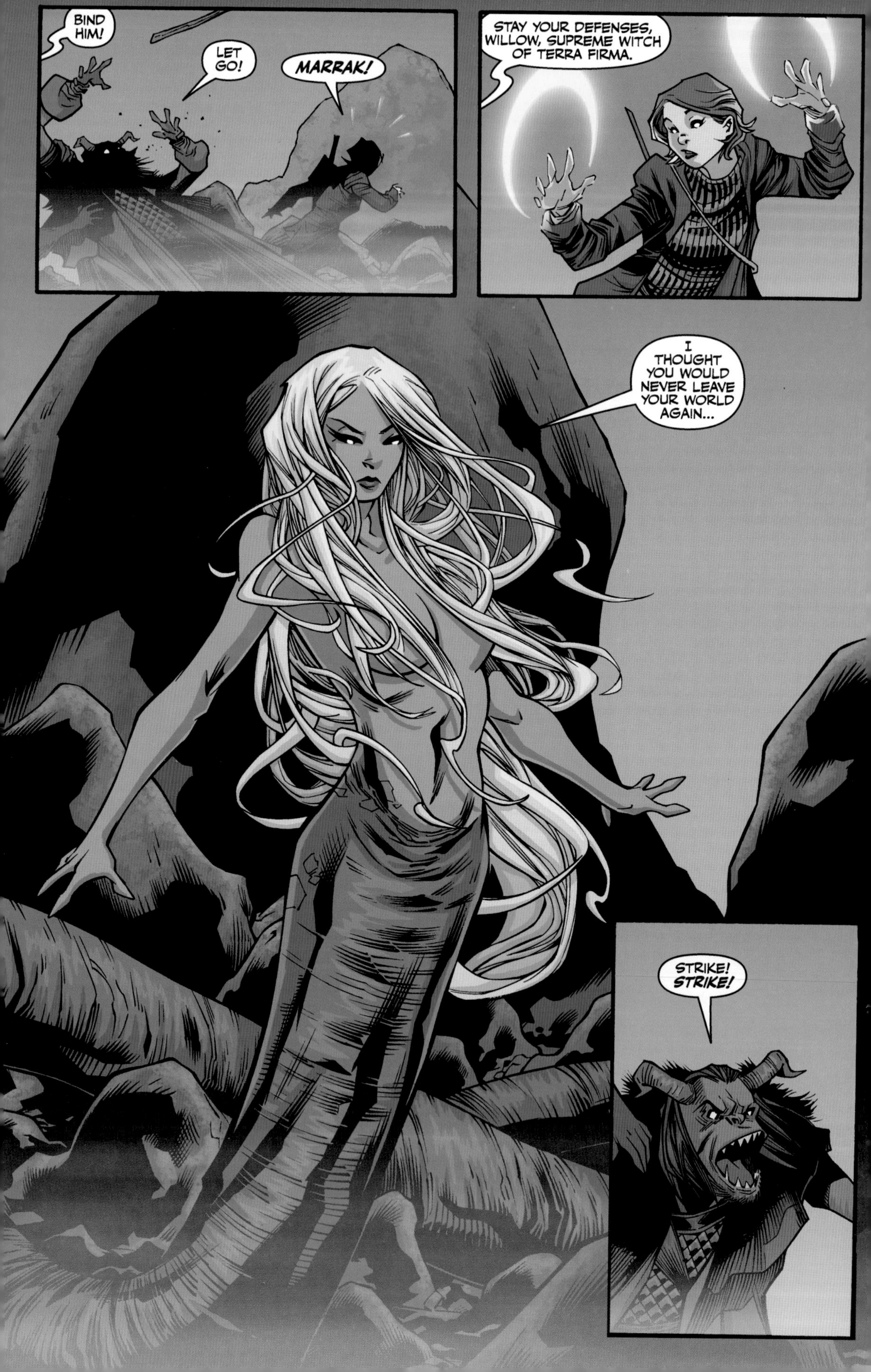
BIND HIM!
LET GO!
MARRAK!
STAY YOUR DEFENSES, WILLOW, SUPREME WITCH OF TERRA FIRMA.
I THOUGHT YOU WOULD NEVER LEAVE YOUR WORLD AGAIN...
STRIKE! STRIKE!

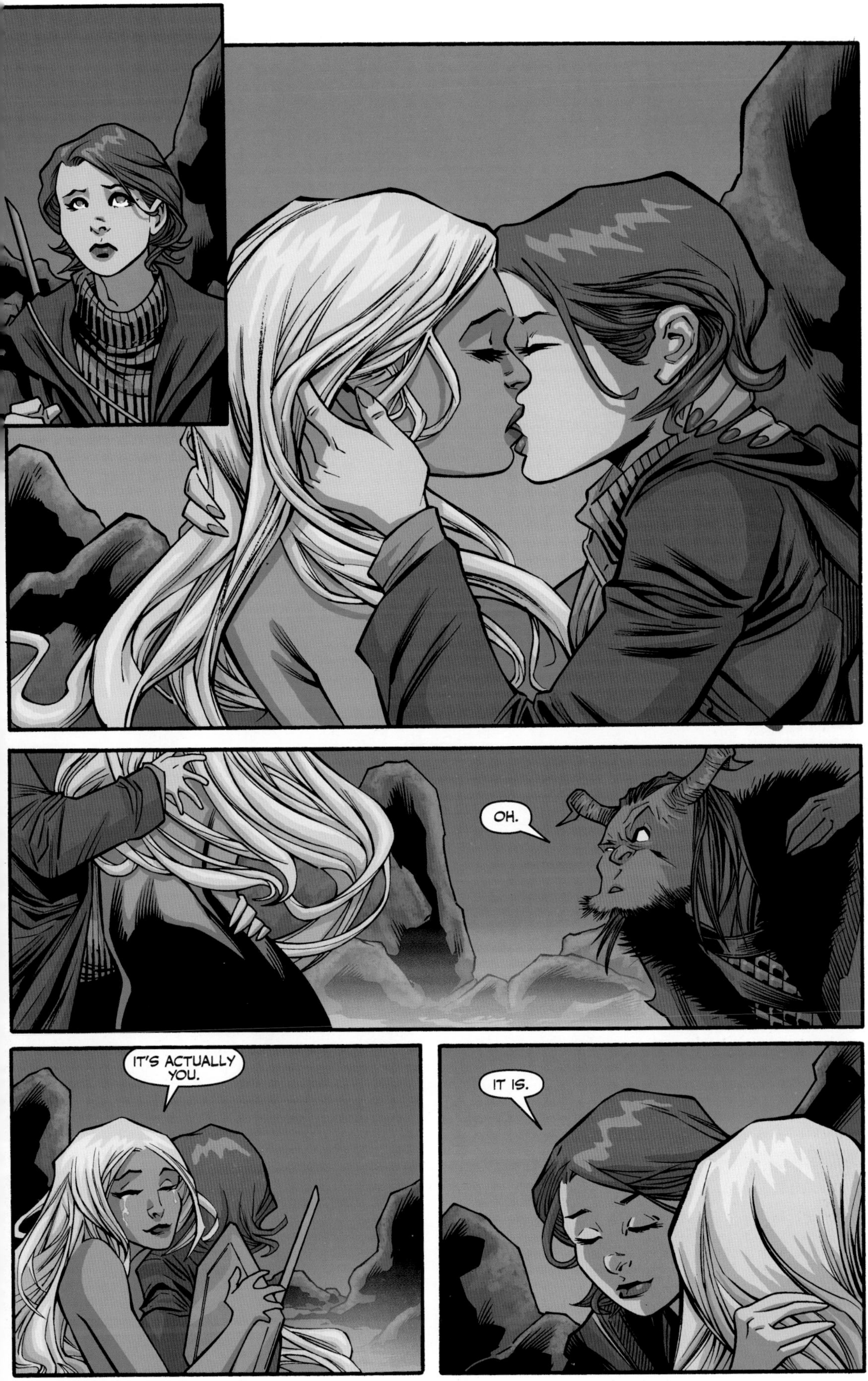
OH.
IT'S ACTUALLY YOU.
IT IS.

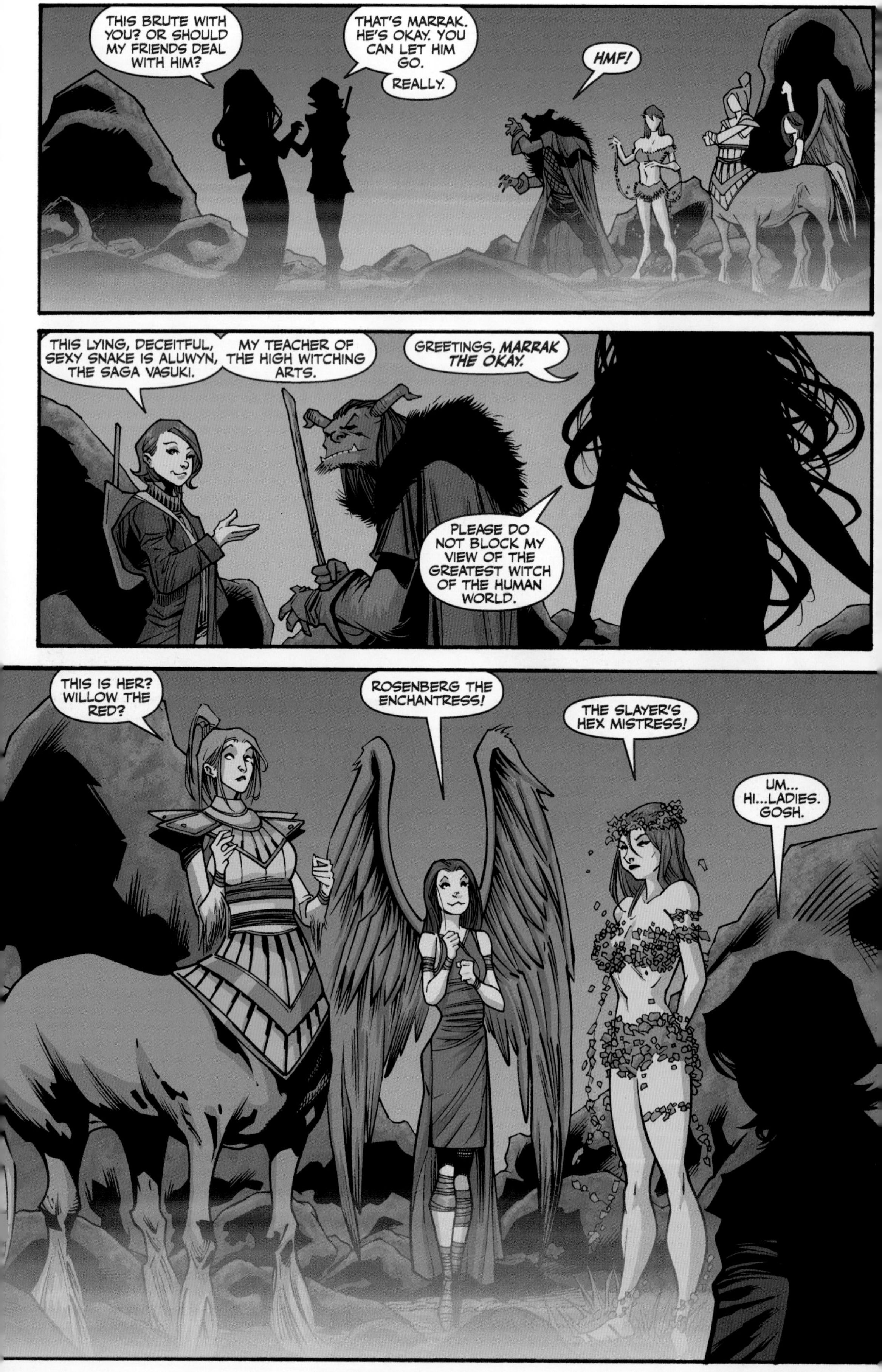
THIS BRUTE WITH YOU? OR SHOULD MY FRIENDS DEAL WITH HIM?
THAT'S MARRAK. HE'S OKAY. YOU CAN LET HIM GO.
REALLY.
HMF!
THIS LYING, DECEITFUL, SEXY SNAKE IS ALUWYN, THE SAGA VASUKI.
MY TEACHER OF THE HIGH WITCHING ARTS.
GREETINGS, MARRAK THE OKAY.
PLEASE DO NOT BLOCK MY VIEW OF THE GREATEST WITCH OF THE HUMAN WORLD.
THIS IS HER? WILLOW THE RED?
ROSENBERG THE ENCHANTRESS!
THE SLAYER'S HEX MISTRESS!
UM... HI...LADIES. GOSH.

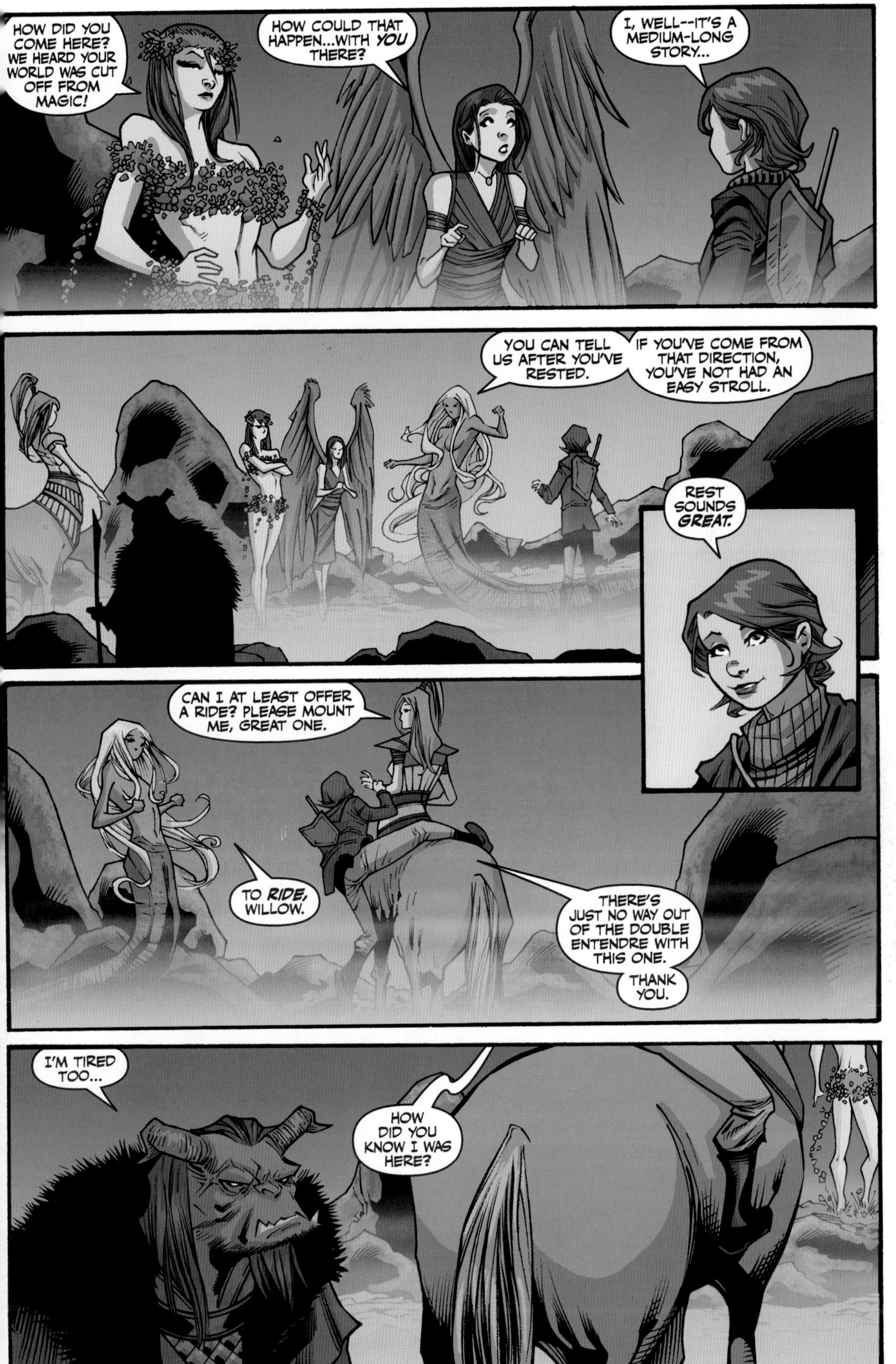
HOW DID YOU COME HERE? WE HEARD YOUR WORLD WAS CUT OFF FROM MAGIC!
HOW COULD THAT HAPPEN...WITH YOU THERE?
I, WELL--IT'S A MEDIUM-LONG STORY...
YOU CAN TELL US AFTER YOU'VE RESTED.
IF YOU'VE COME FROM THAT DIRECTION, YOU'VE NOT HAD AN EASY STROLL.
REST SOUNDS GREAT.
CAN I AT LEAST OFFER A RIDE? PLEASE MOUNT ME, GREAT ONE.
TO RIDE, WILLOW.
THERE'S JUST NO WAY OUT OF THE DOUBLE ENTENDRE WITH THIS ONE.
THANK YOU.
I'M TIRED TOO...
HOW DID YOU KNOW I WAS HERE?

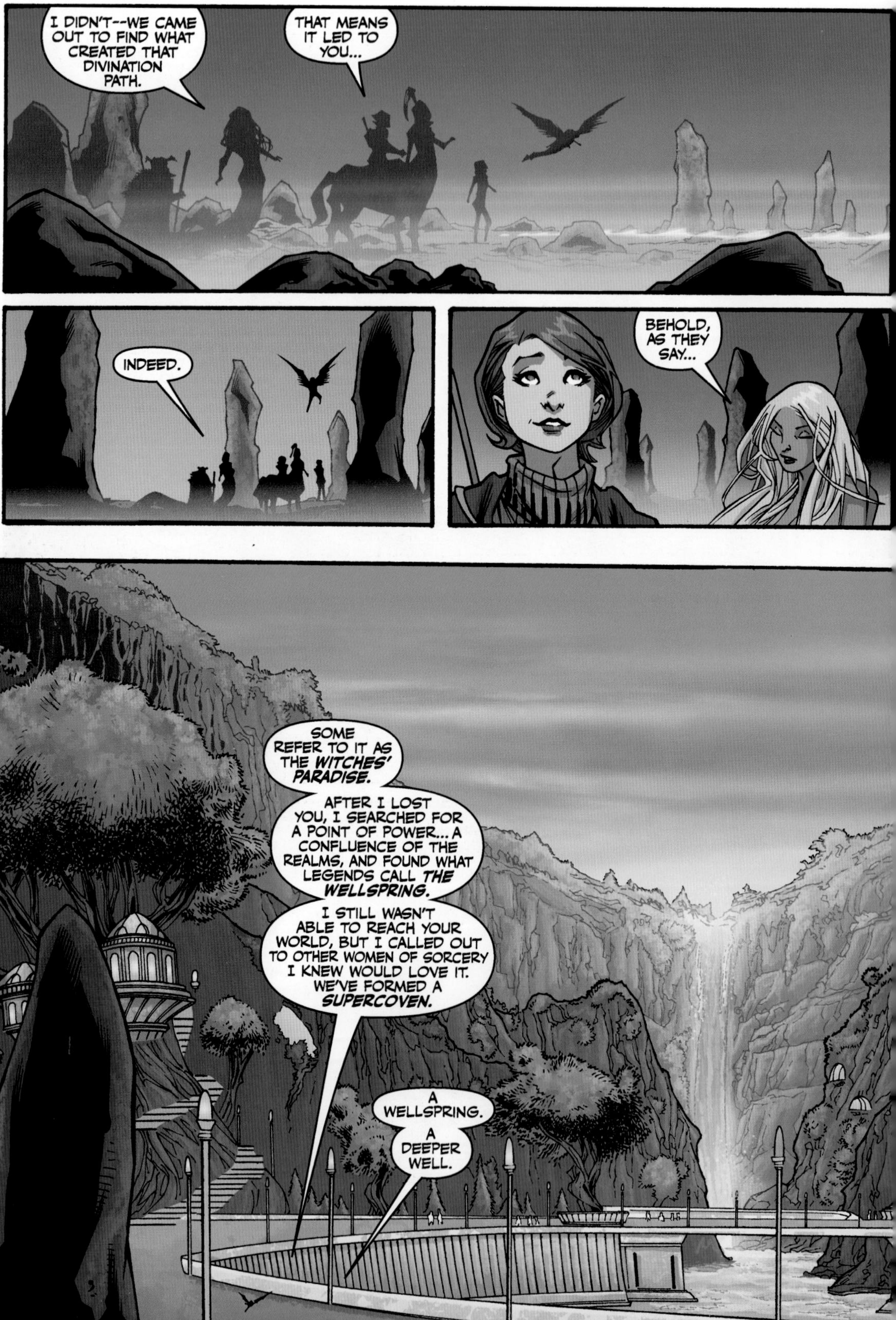
I DIDN'T--WE CAME OUT TO FIND WHAT CREATED THAT DIVINATION PATH.
THAT MEANS IT LED TO YOU...
INDEED.
BEHOLD, AS THEY SAY...
SOME REFER TO IT AS THE WITCHES' PARADISE.
AFTER I LOST YOU, I SEARCHED FOR A POINT OF POWER... A CONFLUENCE OF THE REALMS, AND FOUND WHAT LEGENDS CALL THE WELLSPRING.
I STILL WASN'T ABLE TO REACH YOUR WORLD, BUT I CALLED OUT TO OTHER WOMEN OF SORCERY I KNEW WOULD LOVE IT. WE'VE FORMED A SUPERCOVEN.
A WELLSPRING. A DEEPER WELL.

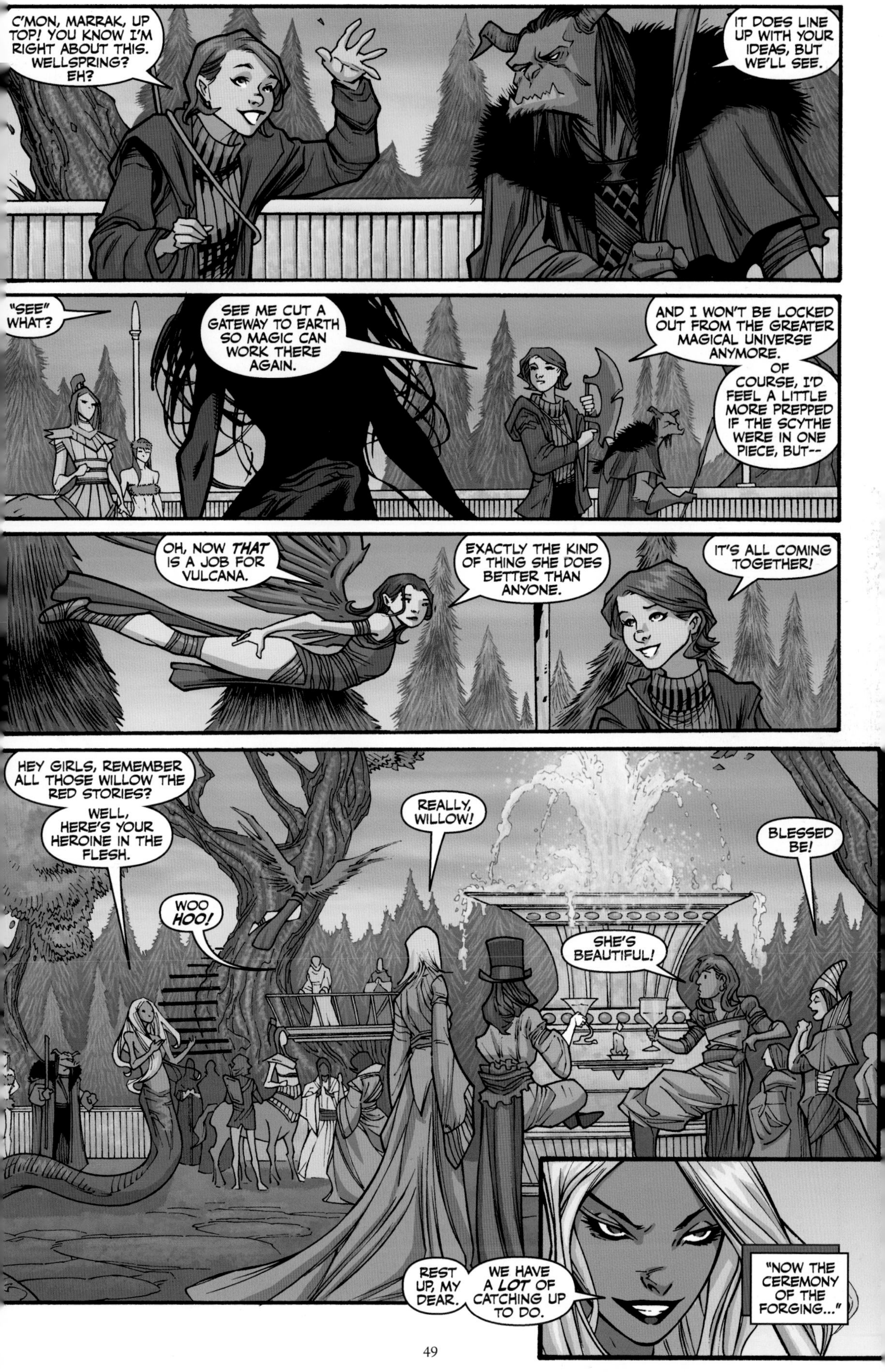
C'MON, MARRAK, UP TOP! YOU KNOW I'M RIGHT ABOUT THIS. WELLSPRING? EH?
IT DOES LINE UP WITH YOUR IDEAS, BUT WE'LL SEE.
"SEE" WHAT?
SEE ME CUT A GATEWAY TO EARTH SO MAGIC CAN WORK THERE AGAIN.
AND I WON'T BE LOCKED OUT FROM THE GREATER MAGICAL UNIVERSE ANYMORE.
OF COURSE, I'D FEEL A LITTLE MORE PREPPED IF THE SCYTHE WERE IN ONE PIECE, BUT--
OH, NOW *THAT* IS A JOB FOR VULCANA.
EXACTLY THE KIND OF THING SHE DOES BETTER THAN ANYONE.
IT'S ALL COMING TOGETHER!
HEY GIRLS, REMEMBER ALL THOSE WILLOW THE RED STORIES?
WELL, HERE'S YOUR HEROINE IN THE FLESH.
REALLY, WILLOW!
BLESSED BE!
WOO *HOO!*
SHE'S BEAUTIFUL!
REST UP, MY DEAR.
WE HAVE A *LOT* OF CATCHING UP TO DO.
"NOW THE CEREMONY OF THE FORGING..."

A WEAPON BLESSED AS ITS COUNTERPART EXCALIBUR! A BLADE THAT HOLDS ITS POWER EVEN IN A MAGICLESS WORLD.

A WEAPON SO MADE CAN NEVER BE BROKEN!

A PERFECT DESIGN IS ETERNAL! STEP FORWARD, MIGHTY WILLOW THE RED!

COVEN, CHANNEL YOUR WHOLE! FOCUS ON US! USE YOUR HEALING POWER... CAST!

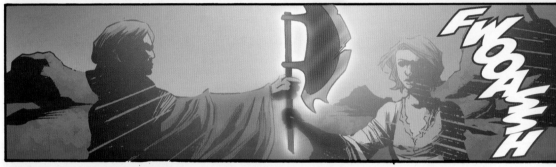

FWOOAWH

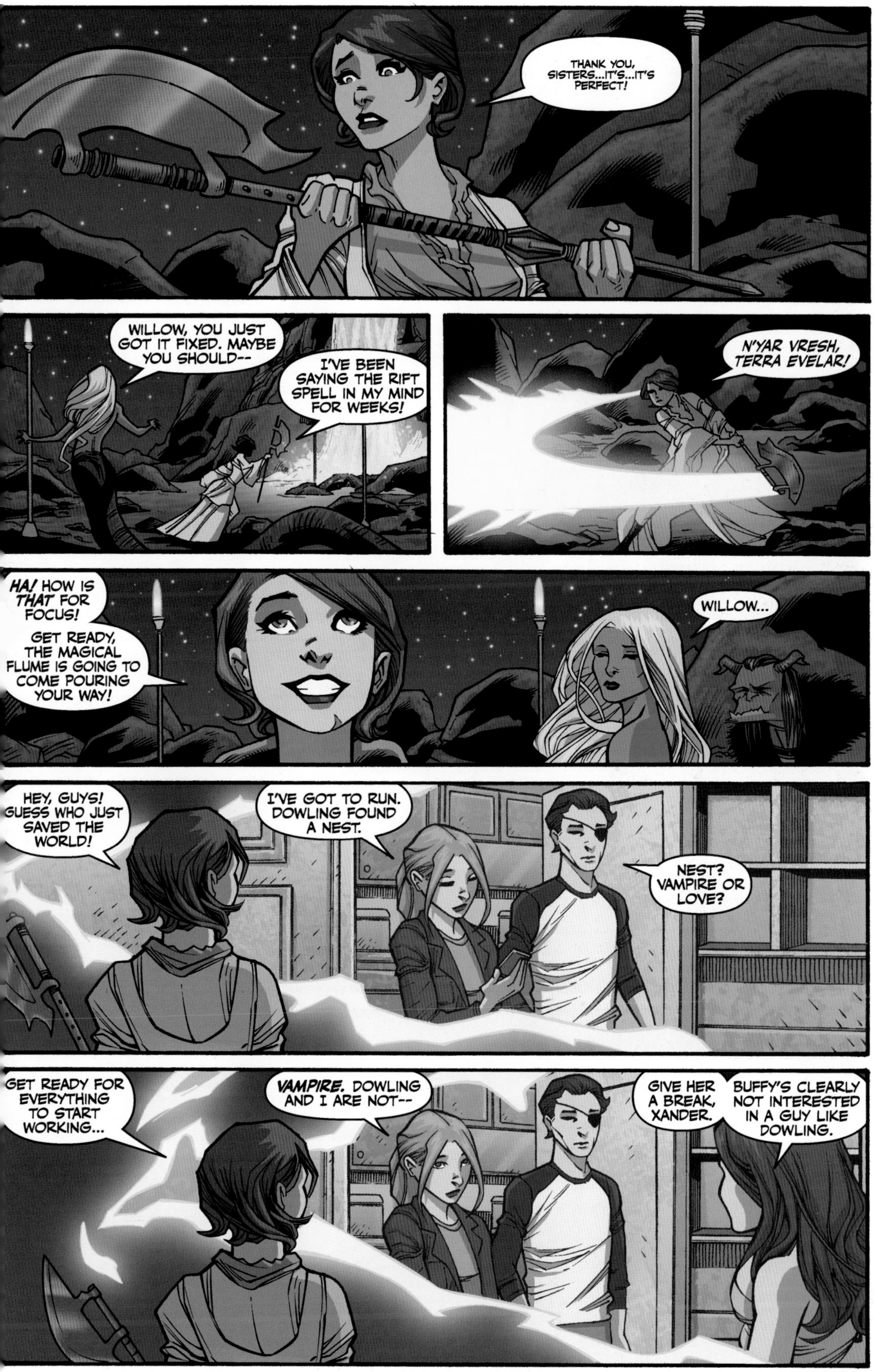
THANK YOU, SISTERS...IT'S...IT'S PERFECT!
WILLOW, YOU JUST GOT IT FIXED. MAYBE YOU SHOULD--
I'VE BEEN SAYING THE RIFT SPELL IN MY MIND FOR WEEKS!
N'YAR VRESH, TERRA EVELAR!
HA! HOW IS THAT FOR FOCUS!
GET READY, THE MAGICAL FLUME IS GOING TO COME POURING YOUR WAY!
WILLOW...
HEY, GUYS! GUESS WHO JUST SAVED THE WORLD!
I'VE GOT TO RUN. DOWLING FOUND A NEST.
NEST? VAMPIRE OR LOVE?
GET READY FOR EVERYTHING TO START WORKING...
VAMPIRE. DOWLING AND I ARE NOT--
GIVE HER A BREAK, XANDER.
BUFFY'S CLEARLY NOT INTERESTED IN A GUY LIKE DOWLING.

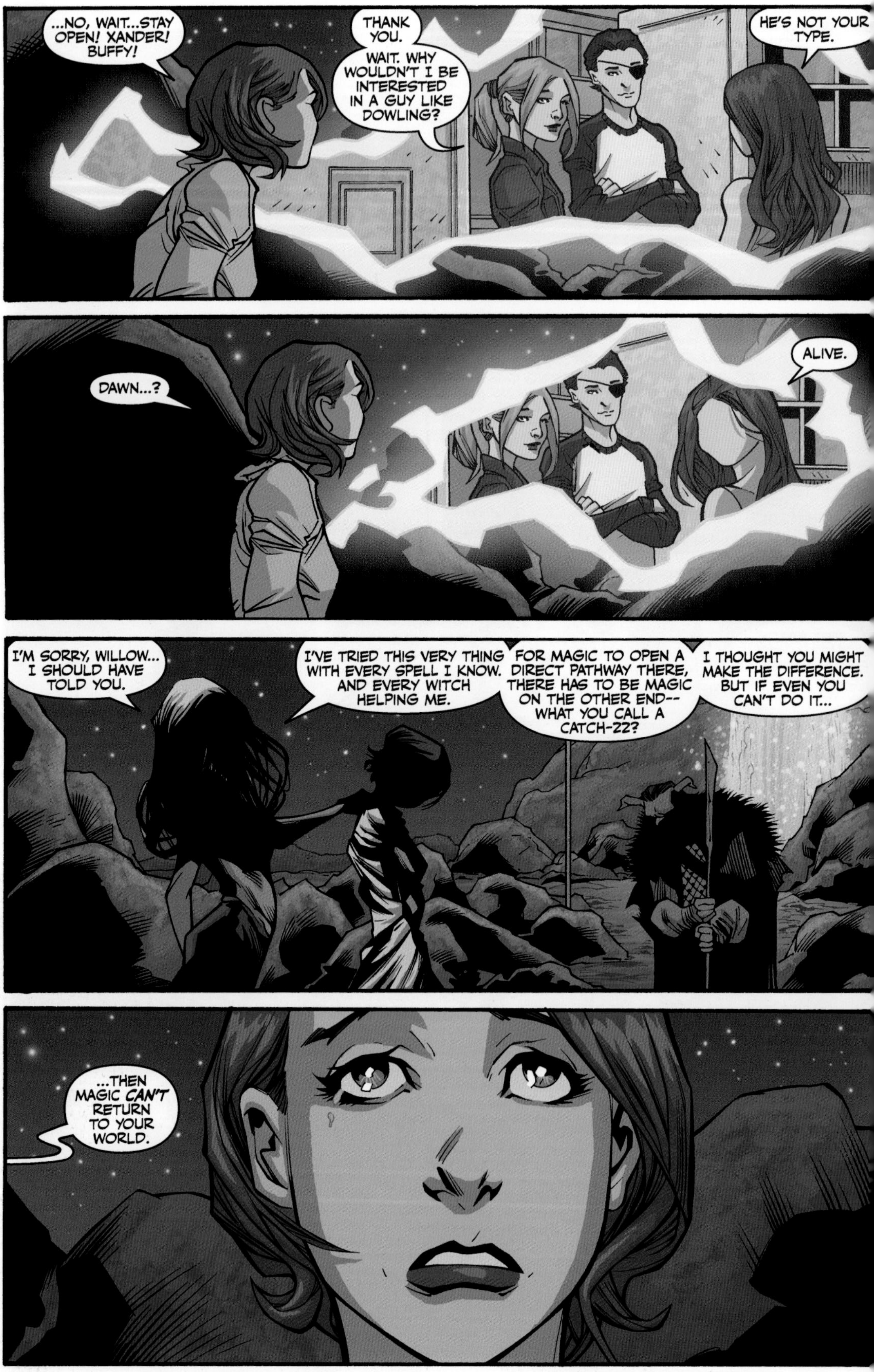
...NO, WAIT...STAY OPEN! XANDER! BUFFY!
THANK YOU.
WAIT. WHY WOULDN'T I BE INTERESTED IN A GUY LIKE DOWLING?
HE'S NOT YOUR TYPE.
DAWN...?
ALIVE.
I'M SORRY, WILLOW... I SHOULD HAVE TOLD YOU.
I'VE TRIED THIS VERY THING WITH EVERY SPELL I KNOW. AND EVERY WITCH HELPING ME.
FOR MAGIC TO OPEN A DIRECT PATHWAY THERE, THERE HAS TO BE MAGIC ON THE OTHER END-- WHAT YOU CALL A CATCH-22?
I THOUGHT YOU MIGHT MAKE THE DIFFERENCE. BUT IF EVEN YOU CAN'T DO IT...
...THEN MAGIC *CAN'T* RETURN TO YOUR WORLD.

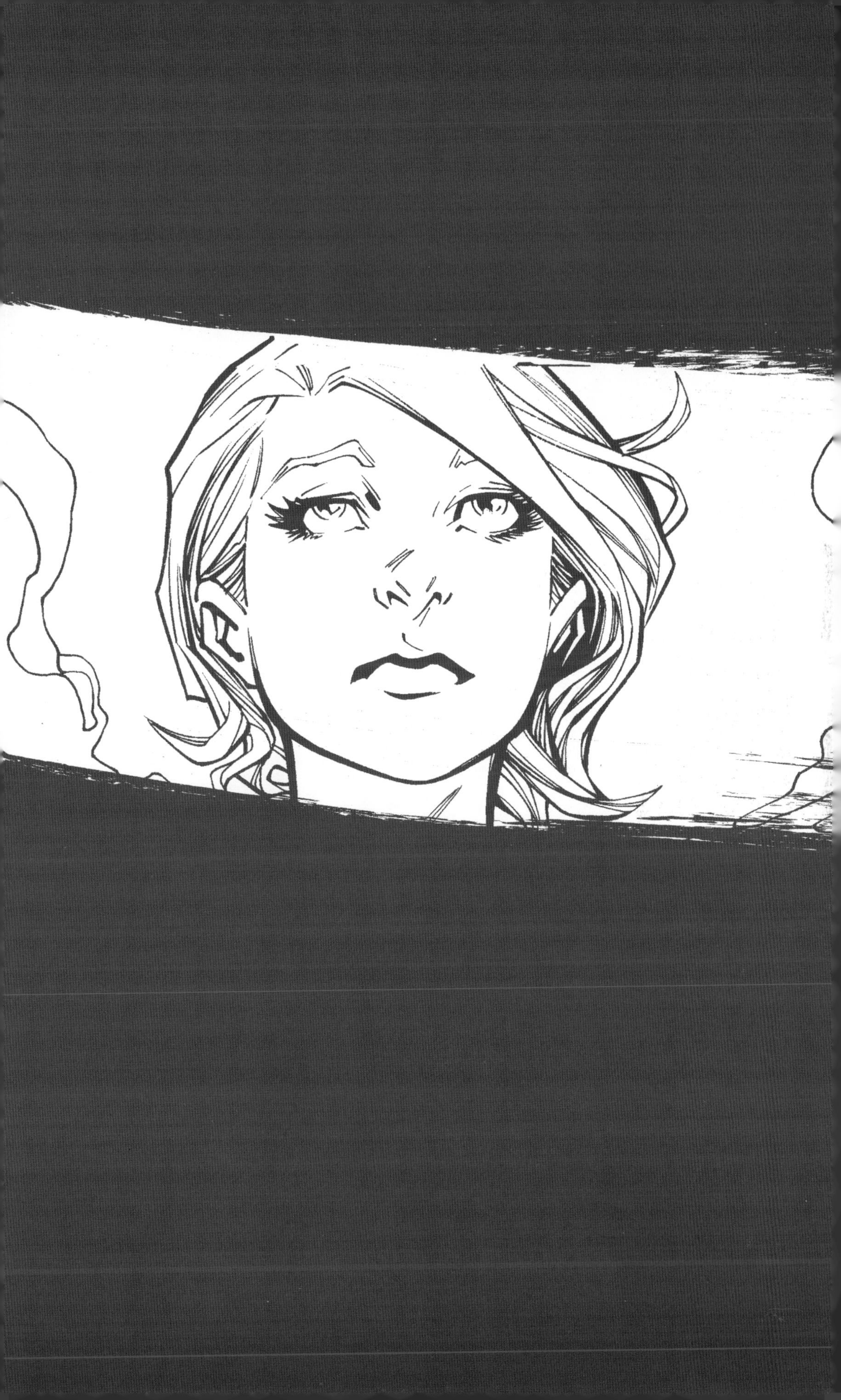

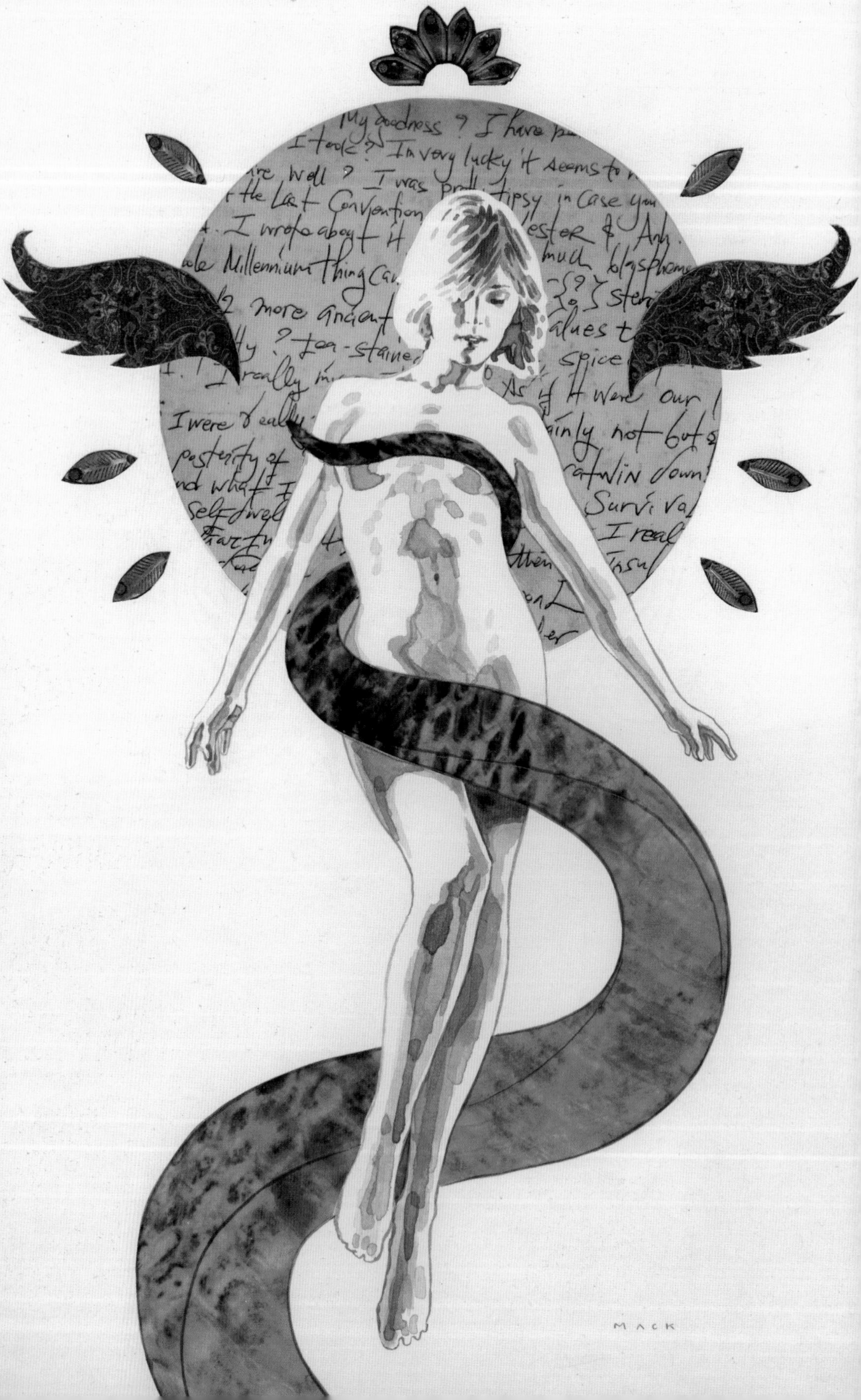
My goodness ? I have
I took ? I'm very lucky it seems to
well ? I was
tipsy in case you
the Last Convention
I wrote about it
Millennium thing
blasphem
more ancient
alues t
Tea-stained
spice
As if it were our
I were really
ainly not but
posterity of
Survival
MACK

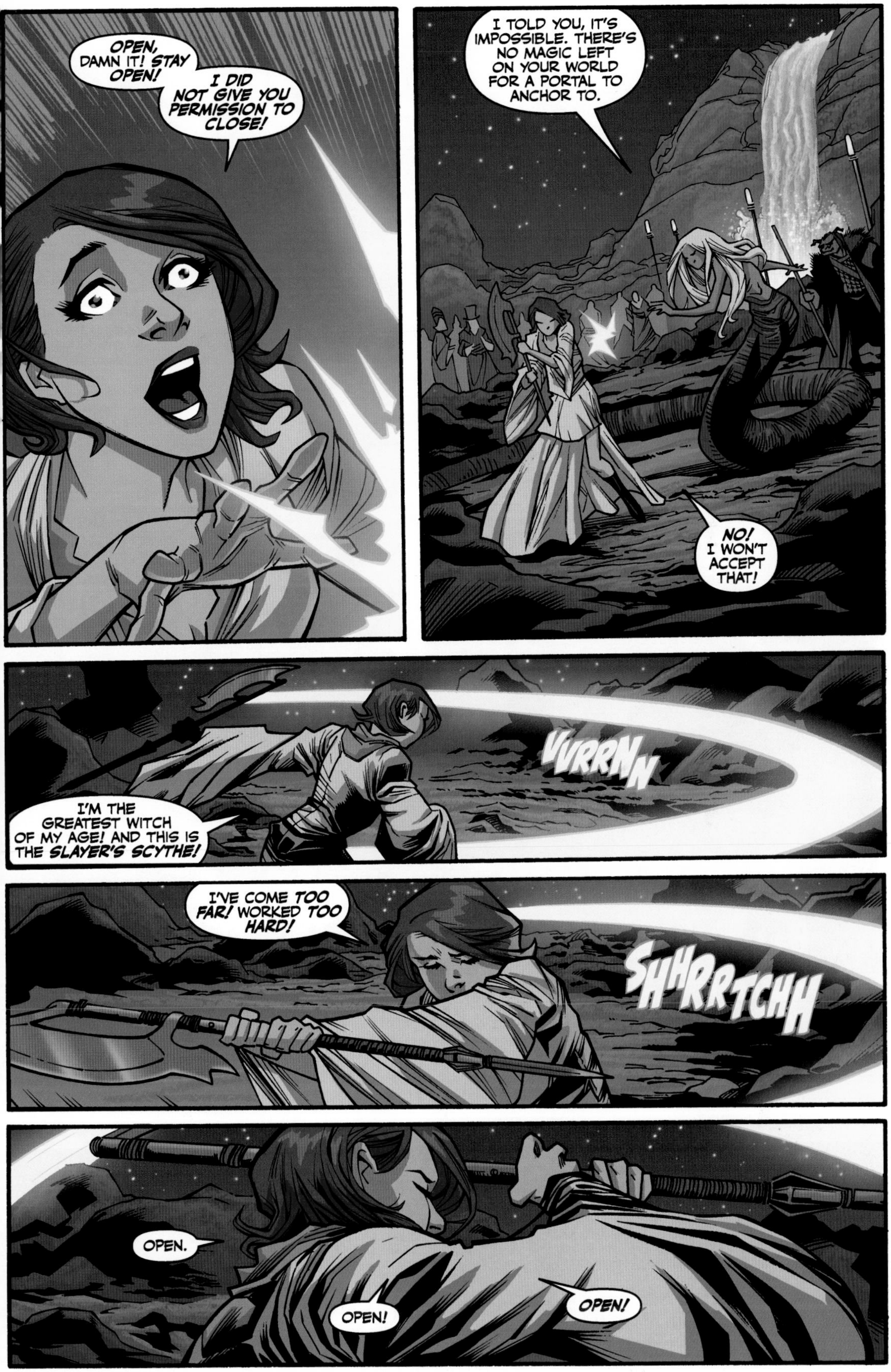
OPEN, DAMN IT! STAY OPEN!
I DID NOT GIVE YOU PERMISSION TO CLOSE!
I TOLD YOU, IT'S IMPOSSIBLE. THERE'S NO MAGIC LEFT ON YOUR WORLD FOR A PORTAL TO ANCHOR TO.
NO! I WON'T ACCEPT THAT!
VVRRNN
I'M THE GREATEST WITCH OF MY AGE! AND THIS IS THE SLAYER'S SCYTHE!
I'VE COME TOO FAR! WORKED TOO HARD!
SHHRRTCHH
OPEN.
OPEN!
OPEN!

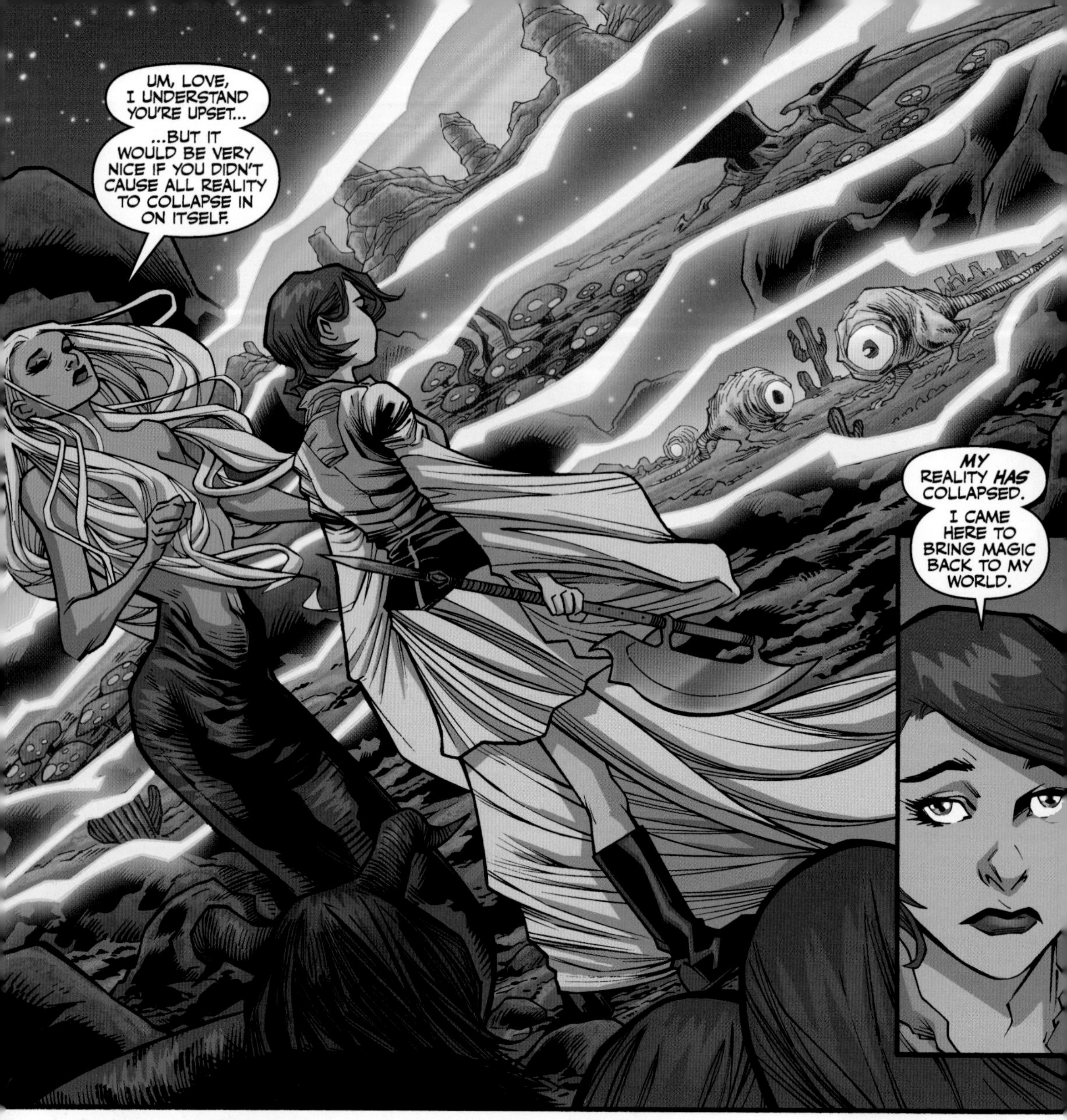
UM, LOVE, I UNDERSTAND YOU'RE UPSET...
...BUT IT WOULD BE VERY NICE IF YOU DIDN'T CAUSE ALL REALITY TO COLLAPSE IN ON ITSELF.
MY REALITY HAS COLLAPSED.
I CAME HERE TO BRING MAGIC BACK TO MY WORLD.

WONDERLAND
PART THREE

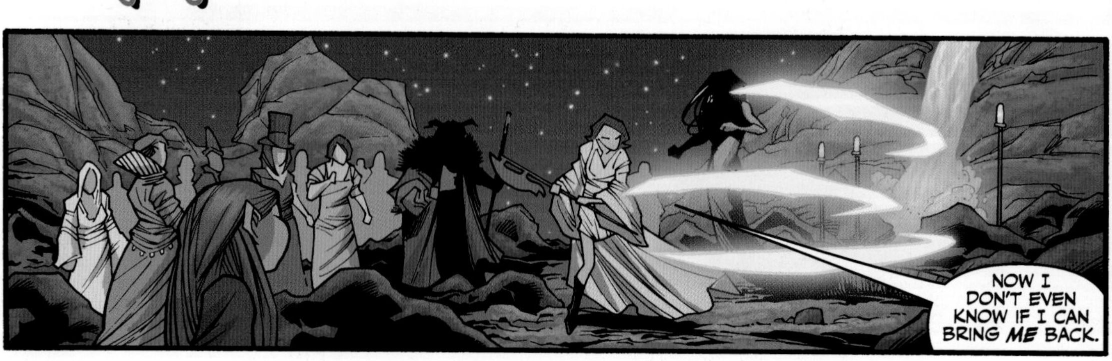
NOW I DON'T EVEN KNOW IF I CAN BRING ME BACK.

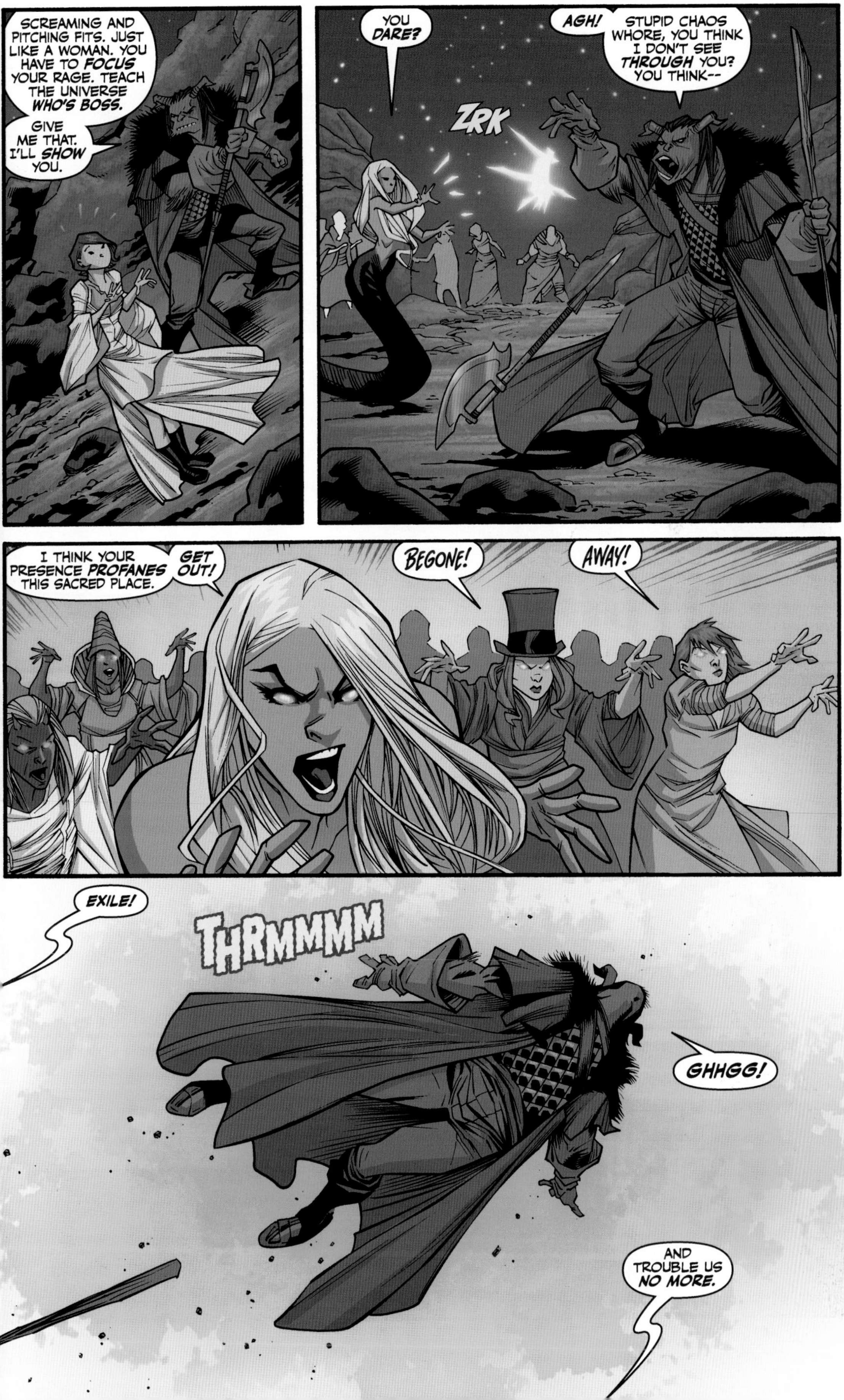
SCREAMING AND PITCHING FITS. JUST LIKE A WOMAN. YOU HAVE TO FOCUS YOUR RAGE. TEACH THE UNIVERSE WHO'S BOSS.
GIVE ME THAT. I'LL SHOW YOU.
YOU DARE?
AGH!
STUPID CHAOS WHORE, YOU THINK I DON'T SEE THROUGH YOU? YOU THINK--
ZRK
I THINK YOUR PRESENCE PROFANES THIS SACRED PLACE.
GET OUT!
BEGONE!
AWAY!
EXILE!
THRMMMM
GHHGG!
AND TROUBLE US NO MORE.

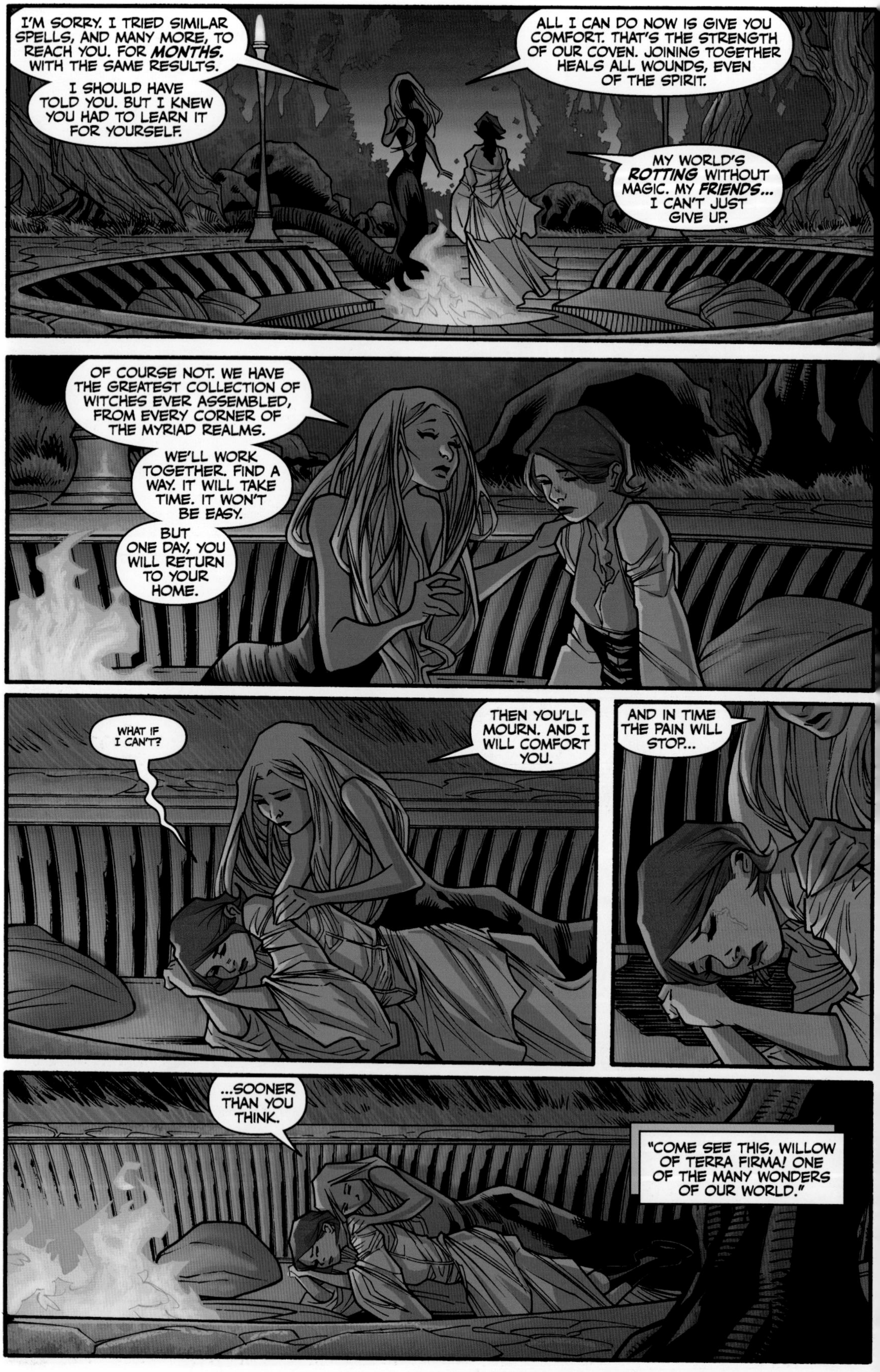

I'M SORRY. I TRIED SIMILAR SPELLS, AND MANY MORE, TO REACH YOU. FOR *MONTHS.* WITH THE SAME RESULTS.
I SHOULD HAVE TOLD YOU. BUT I KNEW YOU HAD TO LEARN IT FOR YOURSELF.
ALL I CAN DO NOW IS GIVE YOU COMFORT. THAT'S THE STRENGTH OF OUR COVEN. JOINING TOGETHER HEALS ALL WOUNDS, EVEN OF THE SPIRIT.
MY WORLD'S *ROTTING* WITHOUT MAGIC. MY *FRIENDS...* I CAN'T JUST GIVE UP.
OF COURSE NOT. WE HAVE THE GREATEST COLLECTION OF WITCHES EVER ASSEMBLED, FROM EVERY CORNER OF THE MYRIAD REALMS.
WE'LL WORK TOGETHER. FIND A WAY. IT WILL TAKE TIME. IT WON'T BE EASY.
BUT ONE DAY, YOU WILL RETURN TO YOUR HOME.
WHAT IF I CAN'T?
THEN YOU'LL MOURN. AND I WILL COMFORT YOU.
AND IN TIME THE PAIN WILL STOP...
...SOONER THAN YOU THINK.
"COME SEE THIS, WILLOW OF TERRA FIRMA! ONE OF THE MANY WONDERS OF OUR WORLD."

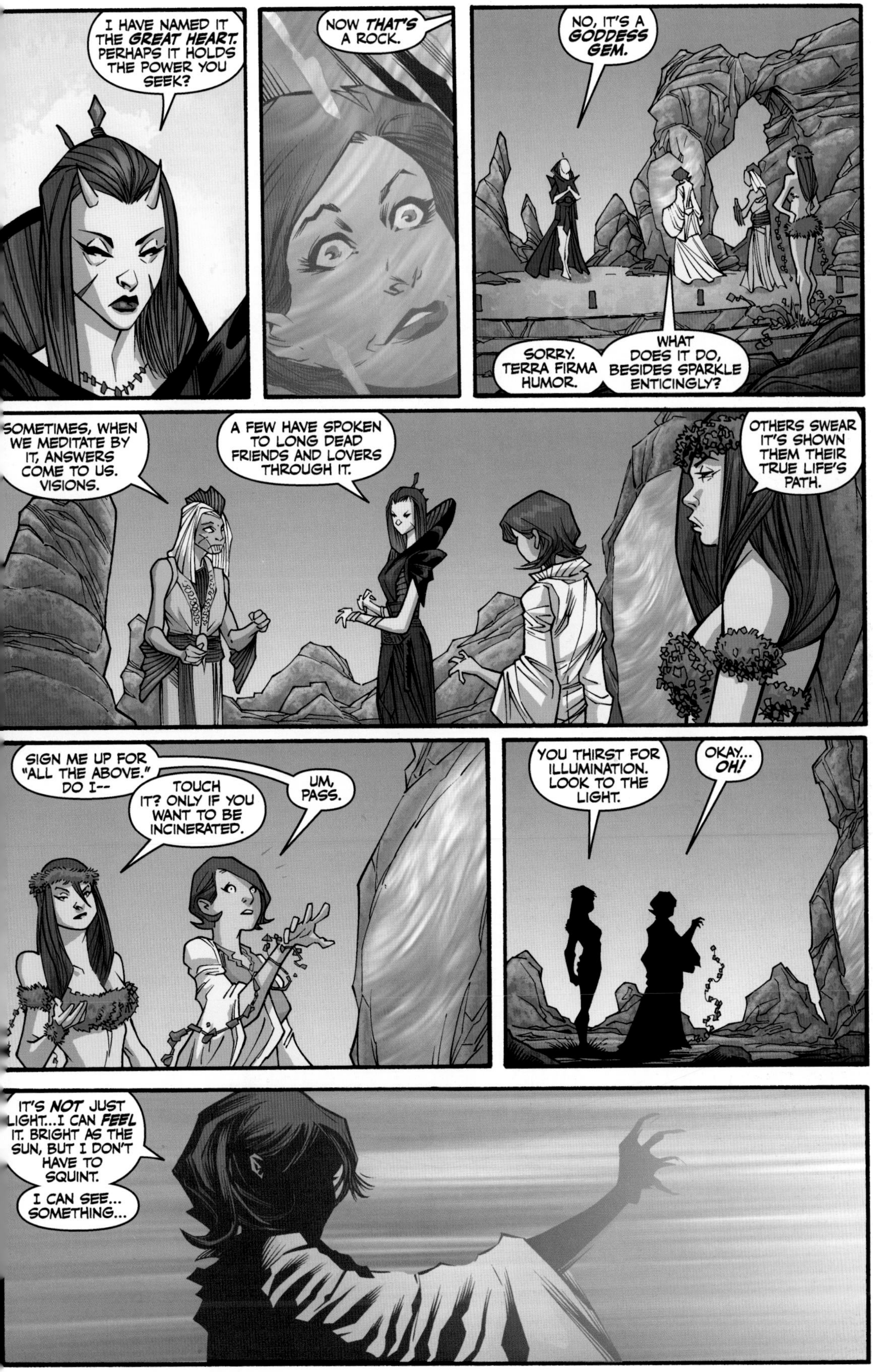

I HAVE NAMED IT THE GREAT HEART. PERHAPS IT HOLDS THE POWER YOU SEEK?
NOW THAT'S A ROCK.
NO, IT'S A GODDESS GEM.
SORRY. TERRA FIRMA HUMOR.
WHAT DOES IT DO, BESIDES SPARKLE ENTICINGLY?
SOMETIMES, WHEN WE MEDITATE BY IT, ANSWERS COME TO US. VISIONS.
A FEW HAVE SPOKEN TO LONG DEAD FRIENDS AND LOVERS THROUGH IT.
OTHERS SWEAR IT'S SHOWN THEM THEIR TRUE LIFE'S PATH.
SIGN ME UP FOR "ALL THE ABOVE." DO I--
TOUCH IT? ONLY IF YOU WANT TO BE INCINERATED.
UM, PASS.
YOU THIRST FOR ILLUMINATION. LOOK TO THE LIGHT.
OKAY... OH!
IT'S NOT JUST LIGHT...I CAN FEEL IT. BRIGHT AS THE SUN, BUT I DON'T HAVE TO SQUINT.
I CAN SEE... SOMETHING...

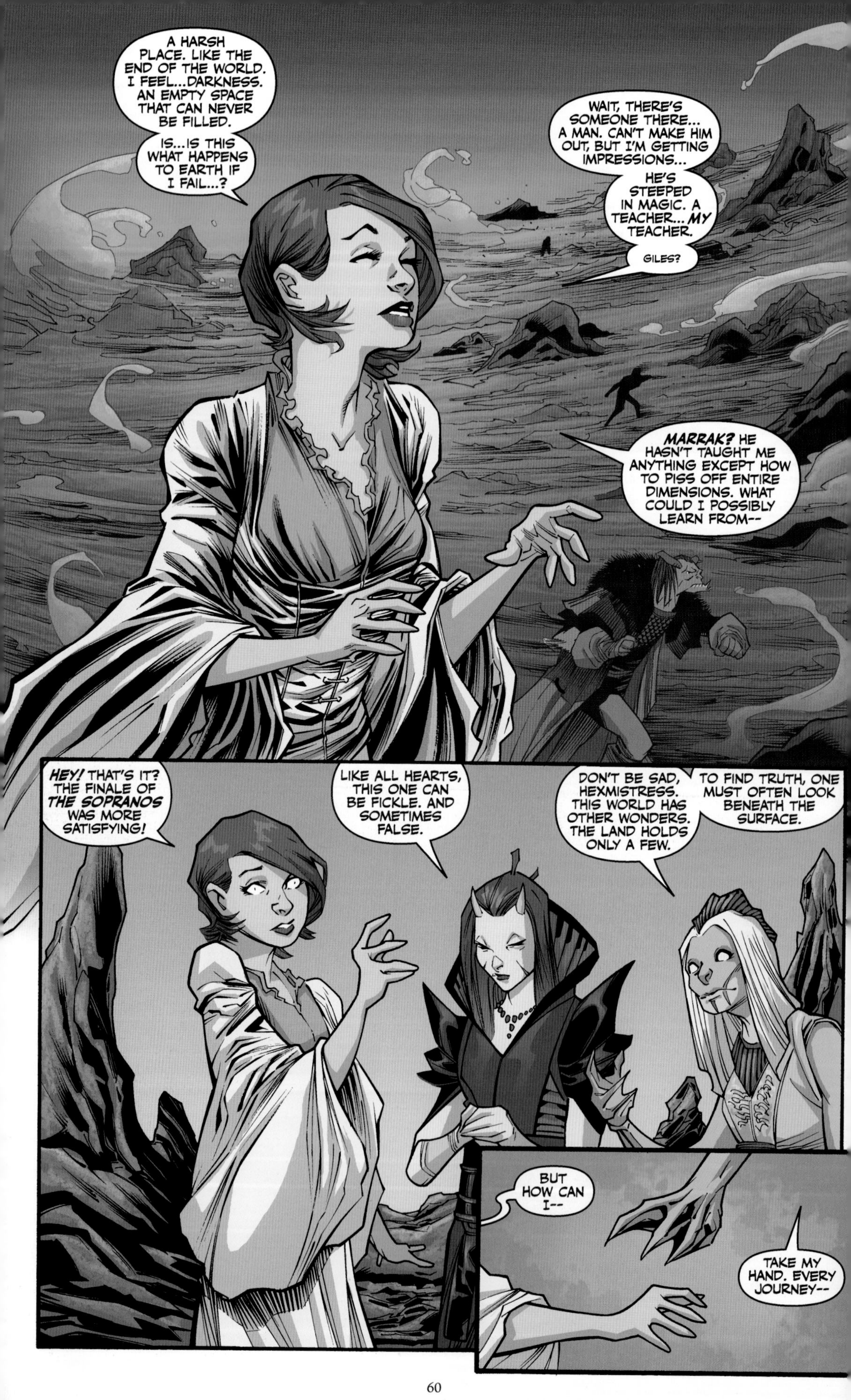

A HARSH PLACE. LIKE THE END OF THE WORLD. I FEEL...DARKNESS. AN EMPTY SPACE THAT CAN NEVER BE FILLED.
IS...IS THIS WHAT HAPPENS TO EARTH IF I FAIL...?
WAIT, THERE'S SOMEONE THERE... A MAN. CAN'T MAKE HIM OUT, BUT I'M GETTING IMPRESSIONS...
HE'S STEEPED IN MAGIC. A TEACHER... MY TEACHER.
GILES?
MARRAK? HE HASN'T TAUGHT ME ANYTHING EXCEPT HOW TO PISS OFF ENTIRE DIMENSIONS. WHAT COULD I POSSIBLY LEARN FROM--
HEY! THAT'S IT? THE FINALE OF THE SOPRANOS WAS MORE SATISFYING!
LIKE ALL HEARTS, THIS ONE CAN BE FICKLE. AND SOMETIMES FALSE.
DON'T BE SAD, HEXMISTRESS. THIS WORLD HAS OTHER WONDERS. THE LAND HOLDS ONLY A FEW.
TO FIND TRUTH, ONE MUST OFTEN LOOK BENEATH THE SURFACE.
BUT HOW CAN I--
TAKE MY HAND. EVERY JOURNEY--

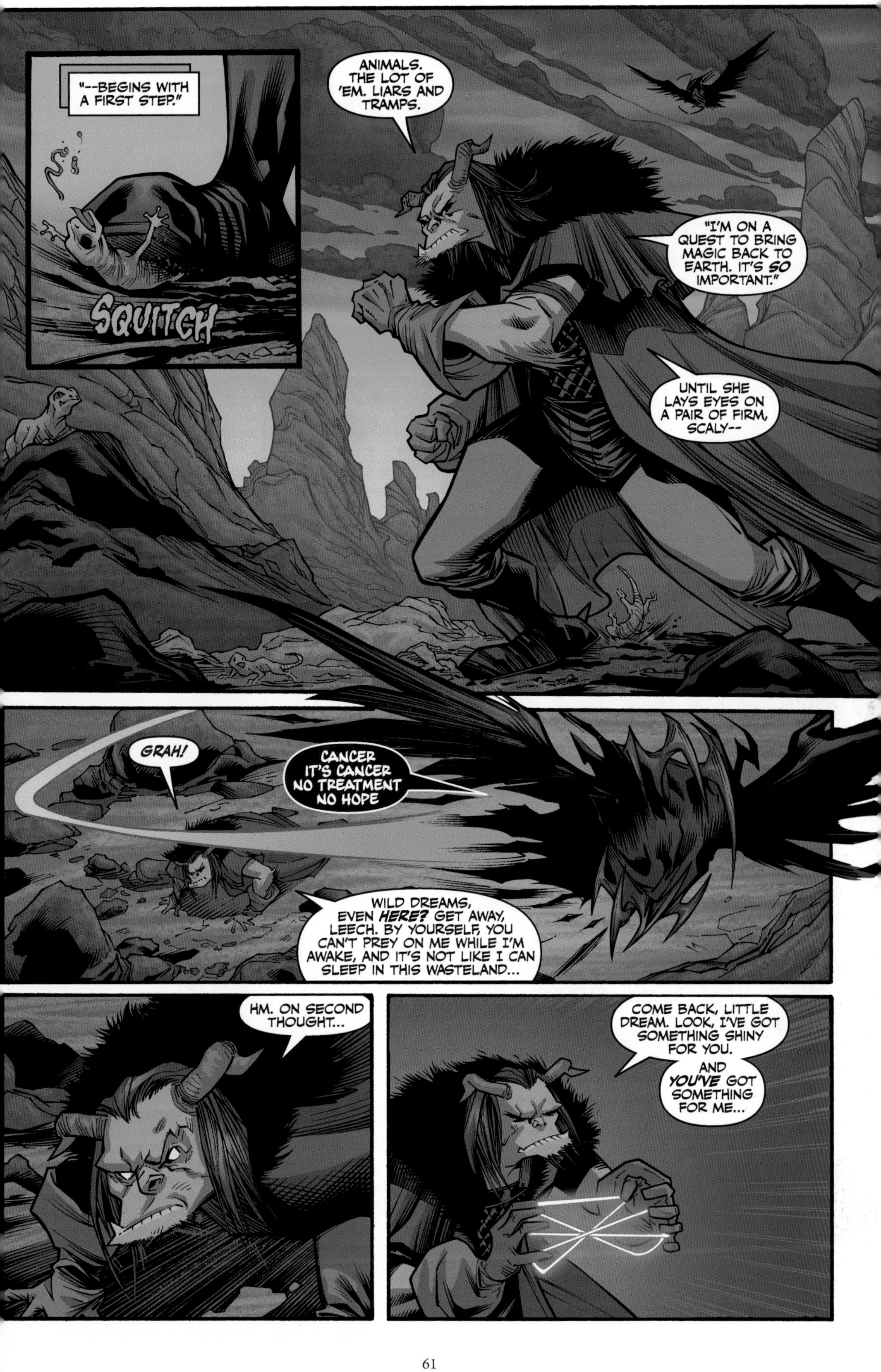
"--BEGINS WITH A FIRST STEP."
SQUITCH
ANIMALS. THE LOT OF 'EM. LIARS AND TRAMPS.
"I'M ON A QUEST TO BRING MAGIC BACK TO EARTH. IT'S SO IMPORTANT."
UNTIL SHE LAYS EYES ON A PAIR OF FIRM, SCALY--
GRAH!
CANCER IT'S CANCER NO TREATMENT NO HOPE
WILD DREAMS, EVEN HERE? GET AWAY, LEECH. BY YOURSELF, YOU CAN'T PREY ON ME WHILE I'M AWAKE, AND IT'S NOT LIKE I CAN SLEEP IN THIS WASTELAND...
HM. ON SECOND THOUGHT...
COME BACK, LITTLE DREAM. LOOK, I'VE GOT SOMETHING SHINY FOR YOU.
AND YOU'VE GOT SOMETHING FOR ME...

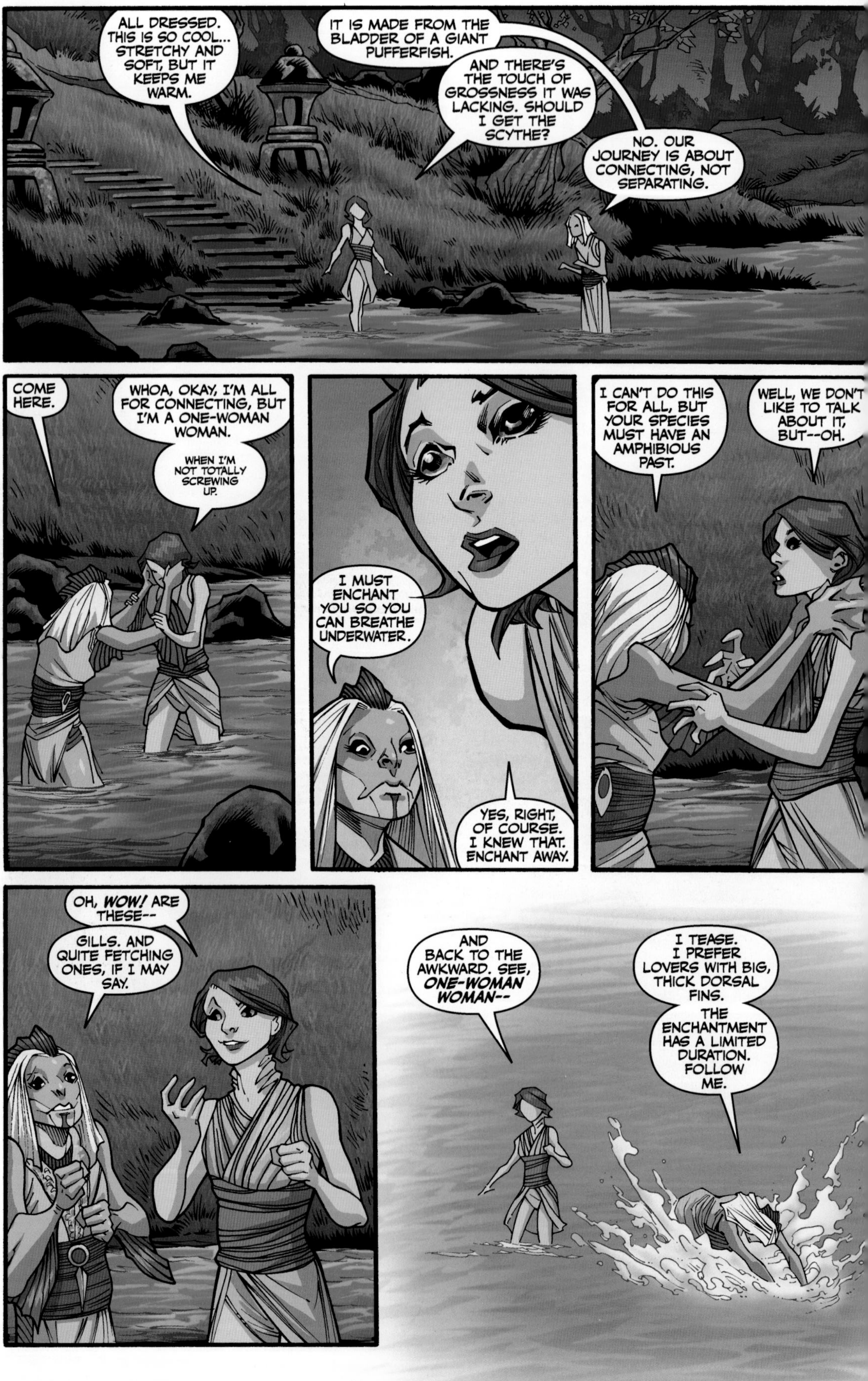
ALL DRESSED. THIS IS SO COOL... STRETCHY AND SOFT, BUT IT KEEPS ME WARM.
IT IS MADE FROM THE BLADDER OF A GIANT PUFFERFISH.
AND THERE'S THE TOUCH OF GROSSNESS IT WAS LACKING. SHOULD I GET THE SCYTHE?
NO. OUR JOURNEY IS ABOUT CONNECTING, NOT SEPARATING.
COME HERE.
WHOA, OKAY, I'M ALL FOR CONNECTING, BUT I'M A ONE-WOMAN WOMAN.
WHEN I'M NOT TOTALLY SCREWING UP.
I MUST ENCHANT YOU SO YOU CAN BREATHE UNDERWATER.
YES, RIGHT, OF COURSE. I KNEW THAT. ENCHANT AWAY.
I CAN'T DO THIS FOR ALL, BUT YOUR SPECIES MUST HAVE AN AMPHIBIOUS PAST.
WELL, WE DON'T LIKE TO TALK ABOUT IT, BUT--OH.
OH, WOW! ARE THESE--
GILLS. AND QUITE FETCHING ONES, IF I MAY SAY.
AND BACK TO THE AWKWARD. SEE, ONE-WOMAN WOMAN--
I TEASE. I PREFER LOVERS WITH BIG, THICK DORSAL FINS.
THE ENCHANTMENT HAS A LIMITED DURATION. FOLLOW ME.

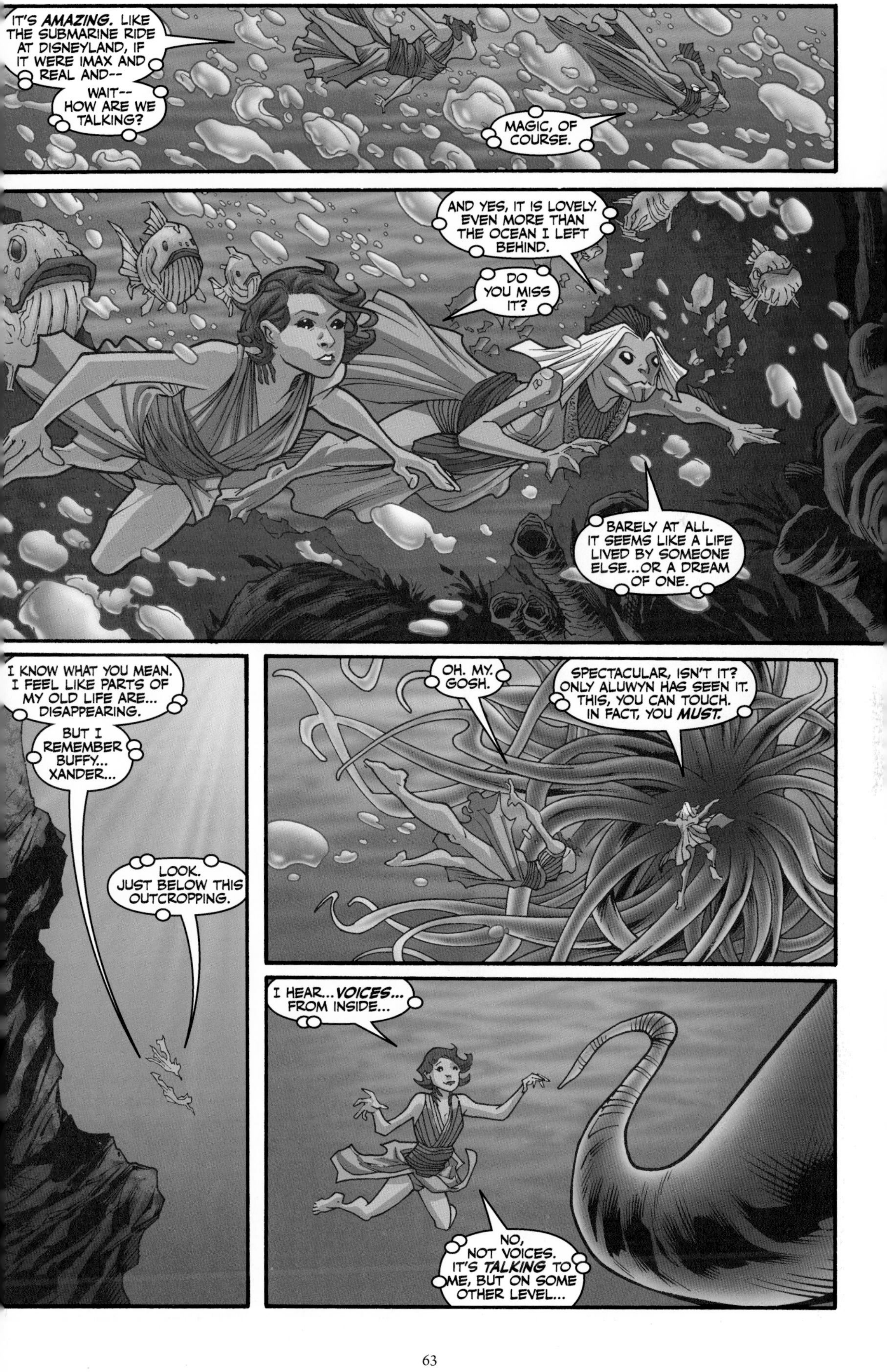

IT'S AMAZING. LIKE THE SUBMARINE RIDE AT DISNEYLAND, IF IT WERE IMAX AND REAL AND--
WAIT-- HOW ARE WE TALKING?
MAGIC, OF COURSE.
AND YES, IT IS LOVELY. EVEN MORE THAN THE OCEAN I LEFT BEHIND.
DO YOU MISS IT?
BARELY AT ALL. IT SEEMS LIKE A LIFE LIVED BY SOMEONE ELSE...OR A DREAM OF ONE.
I KNOW WHAT YOU MEAN. I FEEL LIKE PARTS OF MY OLD LIFE ARE... DISAPPEARING.
BUT I REMEMBER BUFFY... XANDER...
LOOK. JUST BELOW THIS OUTCROPPING.
OH. MY. GOSH.
SPECTACULAR, ISN'T IT? ONLY ALUWYN HAS SEEN IT. THIS, YOU CAN TOUCH. IN FACT, YOU MUST.
I HEAR...VOICES... FROM INSIDE...
NO, NOT VOICES. IT'S TALKING TO ME, BUT ON SOME OTHER LEVEL...

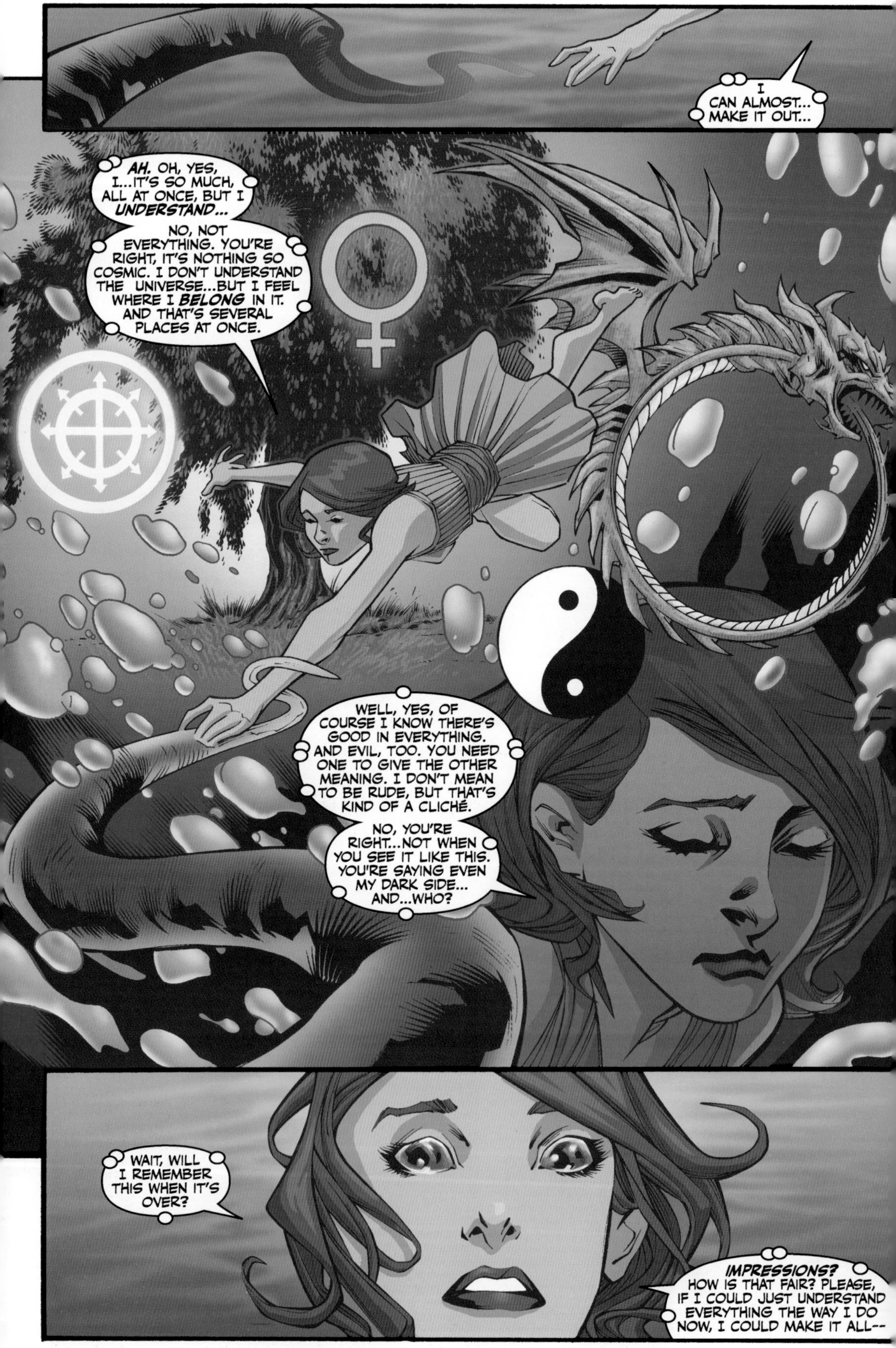
I CAN ALMOST... MAKE IT OUT...
AH. OH, YES, I...IT'S SO MUCH, ALL AT ONCE, BUT I UNDERSTAND...
NO, NOT EVERYTHING. YOU'RE RIGHT, IT'S NOTHING SO COSMIC. I DON'T UNDERSTAND THE UNIVERSE...BUT I FEEL WHERE I BELONG IN IT. AND THAT'S SEVERAL PLACES AT ONCE.
WELL, YES, OF COURSE I KNOW THERE'S GOOD IN EVERYTHING. AND EVIL, TOO. YOU NEED ONE TO GIVE THE OTHER MEANING. I DON'T MEAN TO BE RUDE, BUT THAT'S KIND OF A CLICHÉ.
NO, YOU'RE RIGHT...NOT WHEN YOU SEE IT LIKE THIS. YOU'RE SAYING EVEN MY DARK SIDE... AND...WHO?
WAIT, WILL I REMEMBER THIS WHEN IT'S OVER?
IMPRESSIONS? HOW IS THAT FAIR? PLEASE, IF I COULD JUST UNDERSTAND EVERYTHING THE WAY I DO NOW, I COULD MAKE IT ALL--

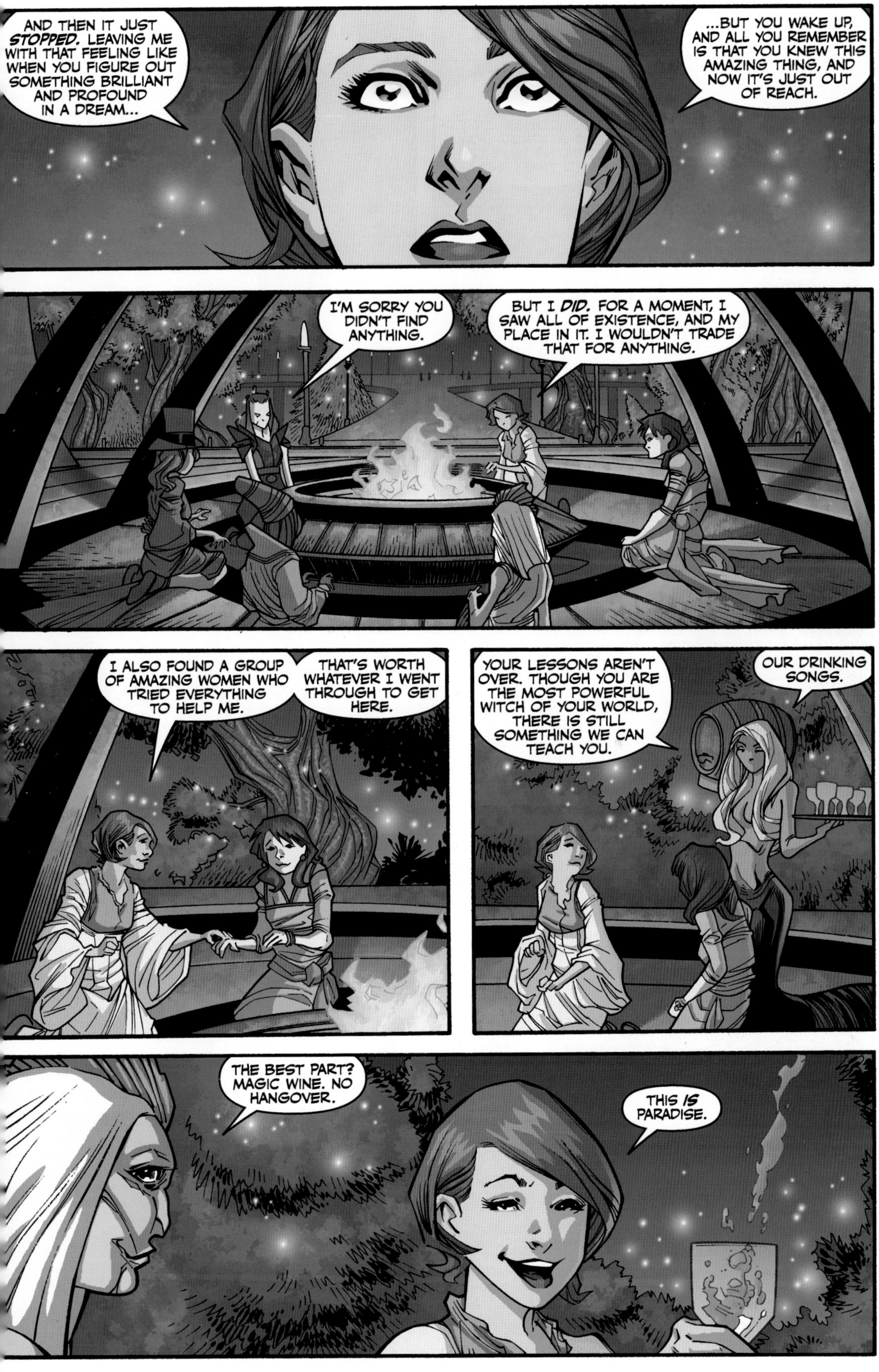
AND THEN IT JUST *STOPPED.* LEAVING ME WITH THAT FEELING LIKE WHEN YOU FIGURE OUT SOMETHING BRILLIANT AND PROFOUND IN A DREAM...
...BUT YOU WAKE UP, AND ALL YOU REMEMBER IS THAT YOU KNEW THIS AMAZING THING, AND NOW IT'S JUST OUT OF REACH.
I'M SORRY YOU DIDN'T FIND ANYTHING.
BUT I *DID.* FOR A MOMENT, I SAW ALL OF EXISTENCE, AND MY PLACE IN IT. I WOULDN'T TRADE THAT FOR ANYTHING.
I ALSO FOUND A GROUP OF AMAZING WOMEN WHO TRIED EVERYTHING TO HELP ME.
THAT'S WORTH WHATEVER I WENT THROUGH TO GET HERE.
YOUR LESSONS AREN'T OVER. THOUGH YOU ARE THE MOST POWERFUL WITCH OF YOUR WORLD, THERE IS STILL SOMETHING WE CAN TEACH YOU.
OUR DRINKING SONGS.
THE BEST PART? MAGIC WINE. NO HANGOVER.
THIS *IS* PARADISE.

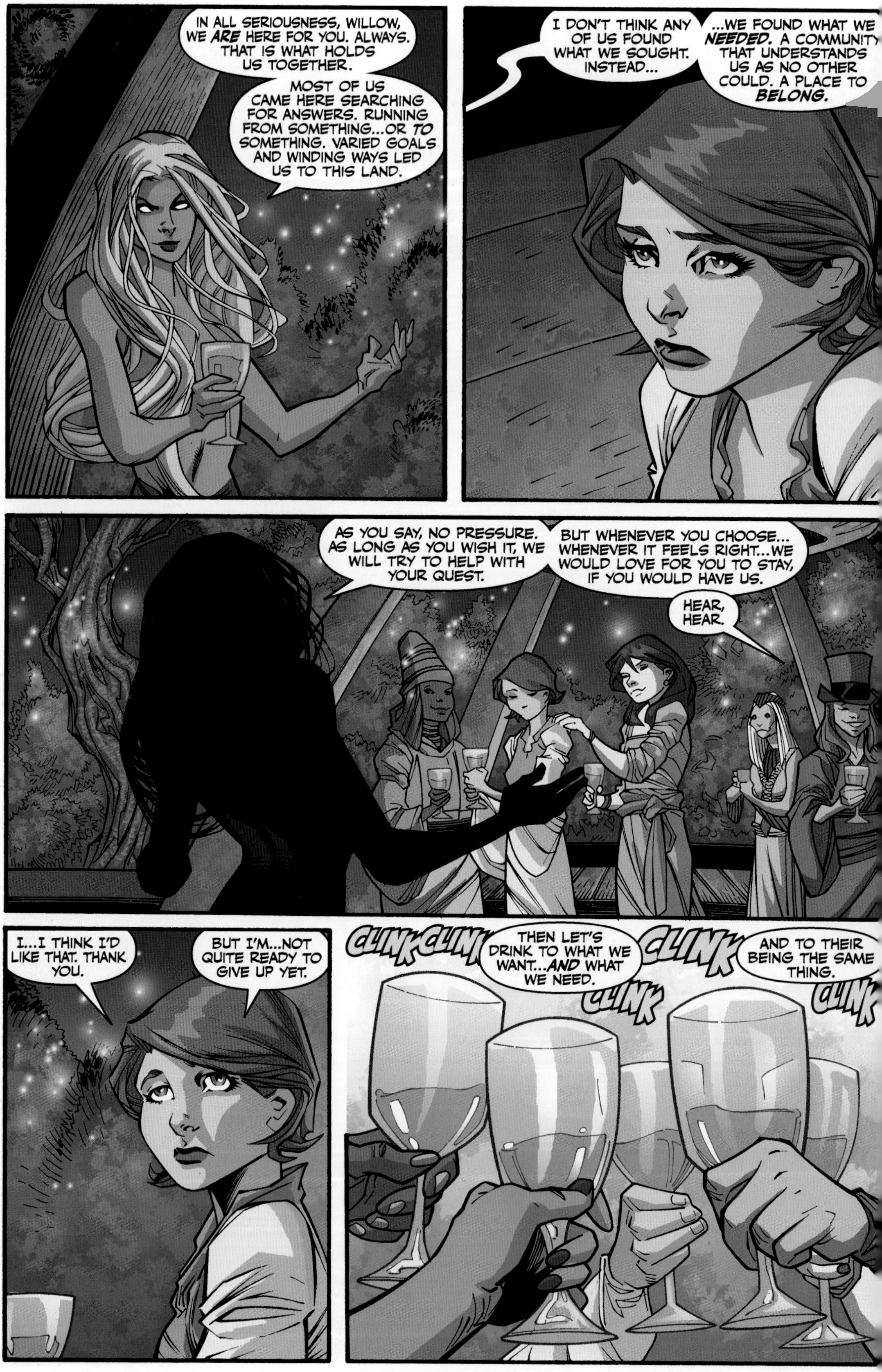
IN ALL SERIOUSNESS, WILLOW, WE ARE HERE FOR YOU. ALWAYS. THAT IS WHAT HOLDS US TOGETHER.
MOST OF US CAME HERE SEARCHING FOR ANSWERS. RUNNING FROM SOMETHING...OR TO SOMETHING. VARIED GOALS AND WINDING WAYS LED US TO THIS LAND.
I DON'T THINK ANY OF US FOUND WHAT WE SOUGHT. INSTEAD...
...WE FOUND WHAT WE NEEDED. A COMMUNITY THAT UNDERSTANDS US AS NO OTHER COULD. A PLACE TO BELONG.
AS YOU SAY, NO PRESSURE. AS LONG AS YOU WISH IT, WE WILL TRY TO HELP WITH YOUR QUEST.
BUT WHENEVER YOU CHOOSE... WHENEVER IT FEELS RIGHT...WE WOULD LOVE FOR YOU TO STAY, IF YOU WOULD HAVE US.
HEAR, HEAR.
I...I THINK I'D LIKE THAT. THANK YOU.
BUT I'M...NOT QUITE READY TO GIVE UP YET.
CLINK CLINK
THEN LET'S DRINK TO WHAT WE WANT...AND WHAT WE NEED.
CLINK
CLINK
AND TO THEIR BEING THE SAME THING.
CLINK

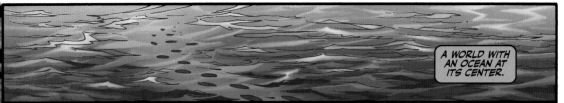

A WORLD WITH AN OCEAN AT ITS CENTER.

A DEEP CORE OF MYSTERY, WONDER, AND REVELATION.

I'M SURE THERE'S A GRAND METAPHOR I COULD MAKE ABOUT MAGIC, OR WOMANHOOD, OR SOMETHING EQUALLY POETIC.

BUT RIGHT NOW ALL I CAN THINK ABOUT IS--

--THAT ADORABLE LITTLE FLYING OCTOPUS!

WANT WANT WANT!

OMIGOSH, I JUST THOUGHT OF THE BEST NAME FOR YOU. MR. OCTOPUS FANTASTICUS!

HEY, CUTENESS! COME BACK! DON'T BE SCARED!

THERE'S NOTHING HERE THAT'S GOING TO HURT YOU!

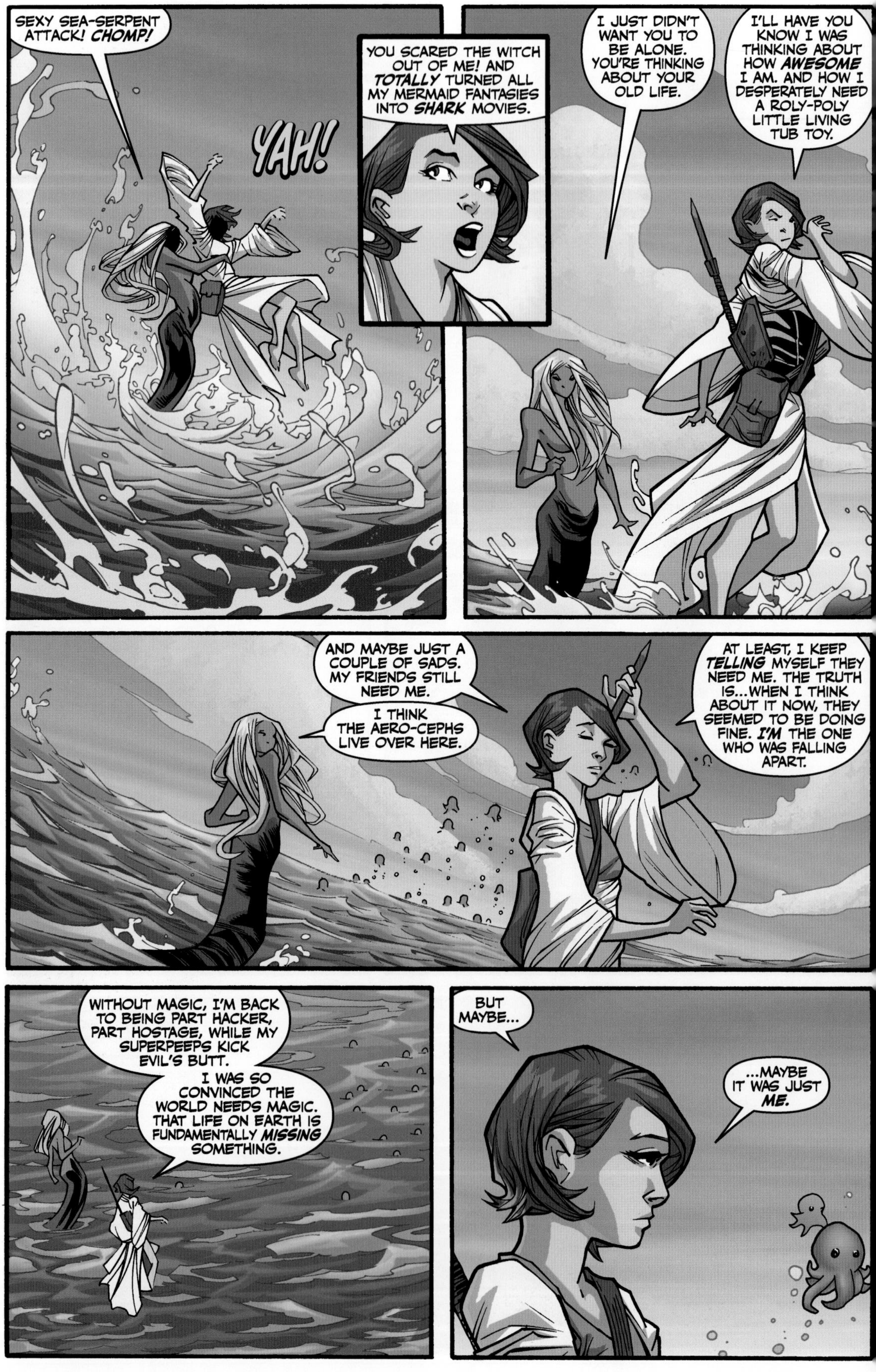
SEXY SEA-SERPENT ATTACK! CHOMP!
YAH!
YOU SCARED THE WITCH OUT OF ME! AND TOTALLY TURNED ALL MY MERMAID FANTASIES INTO SHARK MOVIES.
I JUST DIDN'T WANT YOU TO BE ALONE. YOU'RE THINKING ABOUT YOUR OLD LIFE.
I'LL HAVE YOU KNOW I WAS THINKING ABOUT HOW AWESOME I AM. AND HOW I DESPERATELY NEED A ROLY-POLY LITTLE LIVING TUB TOY.
AND MAYBE JUST A COUPLE OF SADS. MY FRIENDS STILL NEED ME.
I THINK THE AERO-CEPHS LIVE OVER HERE.
AT LEAST, I KEEP TELLING MYSELF THEY NEED ME. THE TRUTH IS...WHEN I THINK ABOUT IT NOW, THEY SEEMED TO BE DOING FINE. I'M THE ONE WHO WAS FALLING APART.
WITHOUT MAGIC, I'M BACK TO BEING PART HACKER, PART HOSTAGE, WHILE MY SUPERPEEPS KICK EVIL'S BUTT.
I WAS SO CONVINCED THE WORLD NEEDS MAGIC. THAT LIFE ON EARTH IS FUNDAMENTALLY MISSING SOMETHING.
BUT MAYBE...
...MAYBE IT WAS JUST ME.

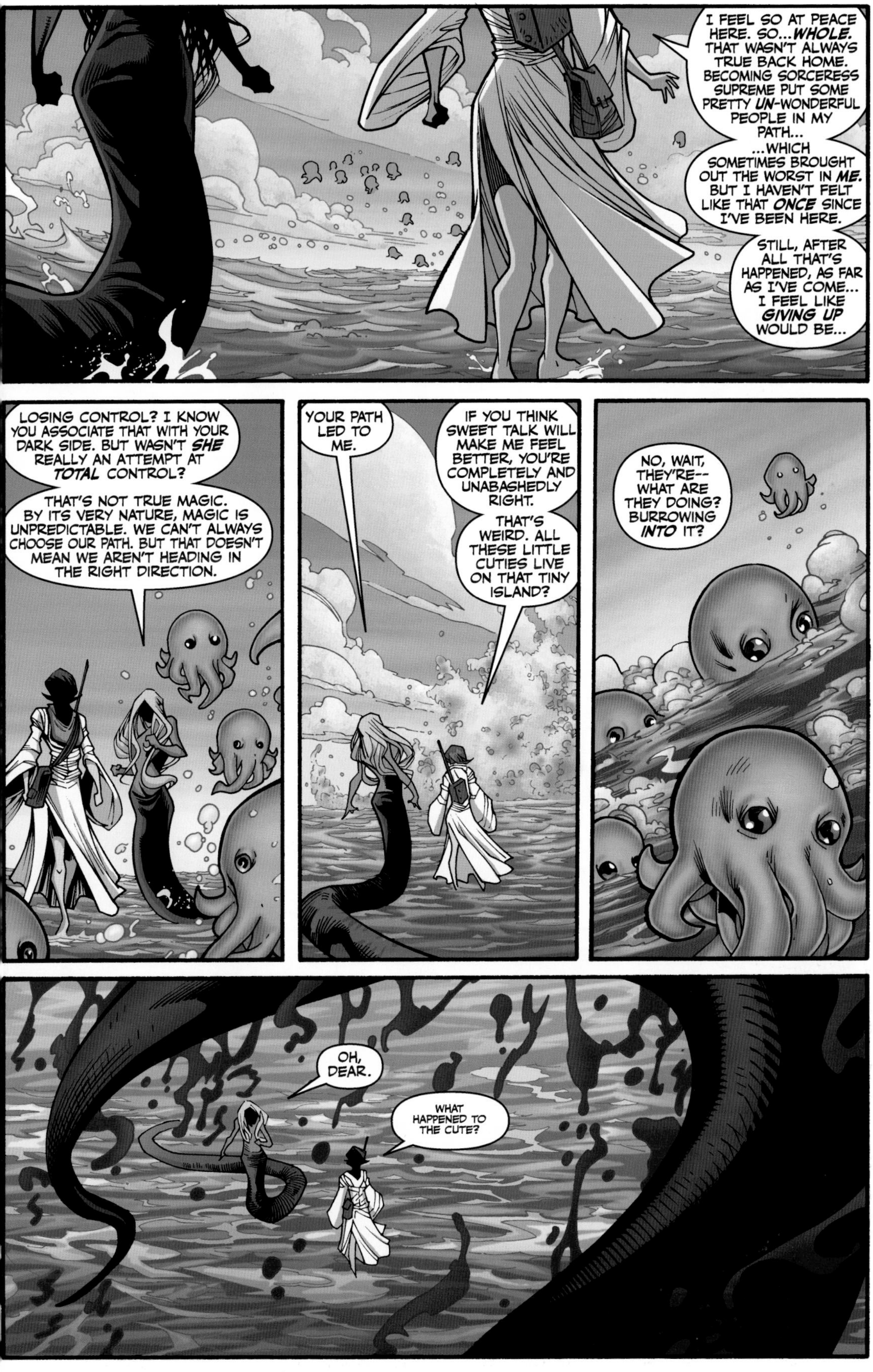
I FEEL SO AT PEACE HERE. SO...WHOLE. THAT WASN'T ALWAYS TRUE BACK HOME. BECOMING SORCERESS SUPREME PUT SOME PRETTY UN-WONDERFUL PEOPLE IN MY PATH...
...WHICH SOMETIMES BROUGHT OUT THE WORST IN ME. BUT I HAVEN'T FELT LIKE THAT ONCE SINCE I'VE BEEN HERE.
STILL, AFTER ALL THAT'S HAPPENED, AS FAR AS I'VE COME... I FEEL LIKE GIVING UP WOULD BE...
LOSING CONTROL? I KNOW YOU ASSOCIATE THAT WITH YOUR DARK SIDE. BUT WASN'T SHE REALLY AN ATTEMPT AT TOTAL CONTROL?
THAT'S NOT TRUE MAGIC. BY ITS VERY NATURE, MAGIC IS UNPREDICTABLE. WE CAN'T ALWAYS CHOOSE OUR PATH. BUT THAT DOESN'T MEAN WE AREN'T HEADING IN THE RIGHT DIRECTION.
YOUR PATH LED TO ME.
IF YOU THINK SWEET TALK WILL MAKE ME FEEL BETTER, YOU'RE COMPLETELY AND UNABASHEDLY RIGHT.
THAT'S WEIRD. ALL THESE LITTLE CUTIES LIVE ON THAT TINY ISLAND?
NO, WAIT, THEY'RE-- WHAT ARE THEY DOING? BURROWING INTO IT?
OH, DEAR.
WHAT HAPPENED TO THE CUTE?

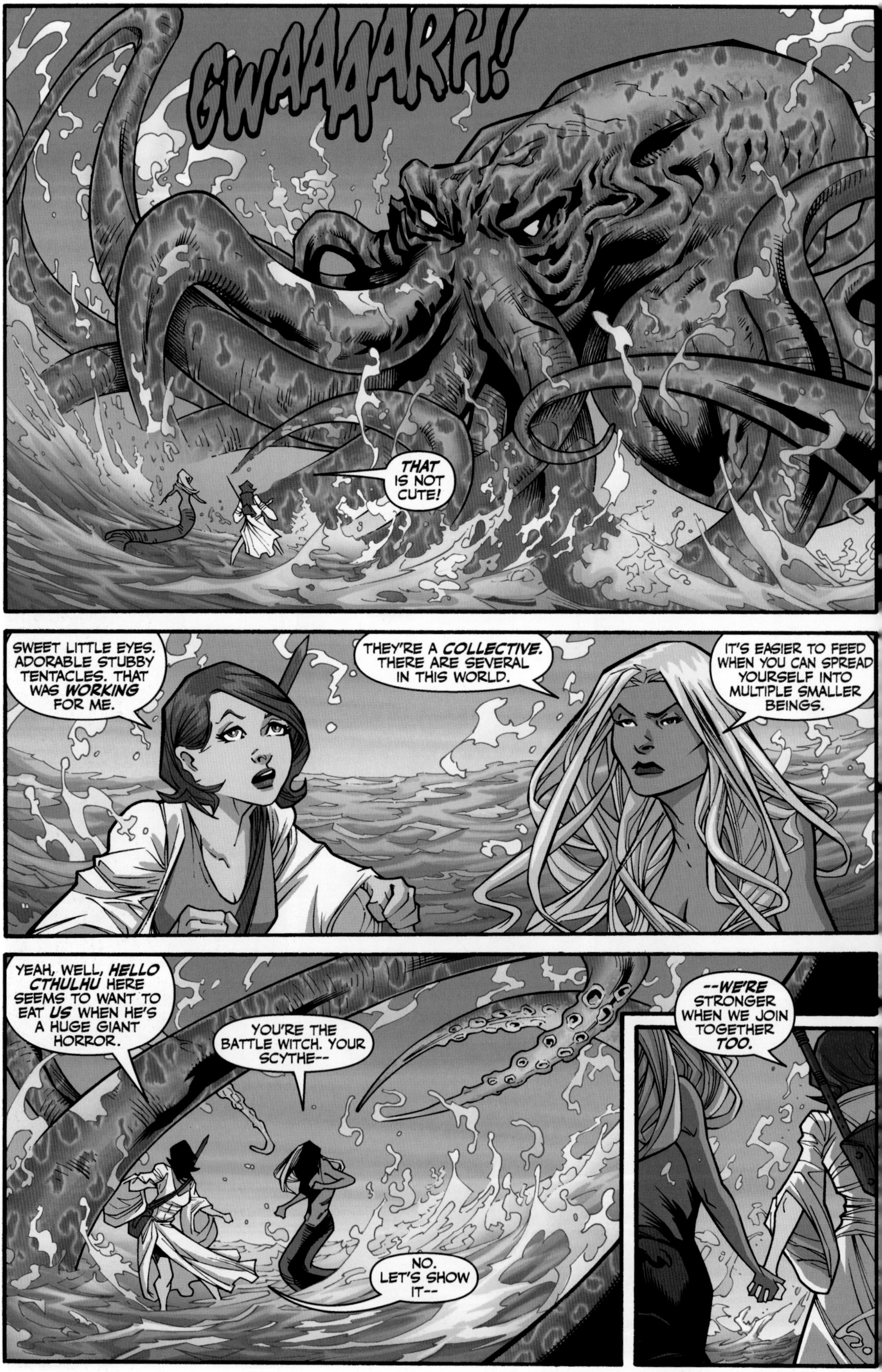
GWAAAARH!
THAT IS NOT CUTE!
SWEET LITTLE EYES. ADORABLE STUBBY TENTACLES. THAT WAS WORKING FOR ME.
THEY'RE A COLLECTIVE. THERE ARE SEVERAL IN THIS WORLD.
IT'S EASIER TO FEED WHEN YOU CAN SPREAD YOURSELF INTO MULTIPLE SMALLER BEINGS.
YEAH, WELL, HELLO CTHULHU HERE SEEMS TO WANT TO EAT US WHEN HE'S A HUGE GIANT HORROR.
YOU'RE THE BATTLE WITCH. YOUR SCYTHE--
NO. LET'S SHOW IT--
--WE'RE STRONGER WHEN WE JOIN TOGETHER TOO.

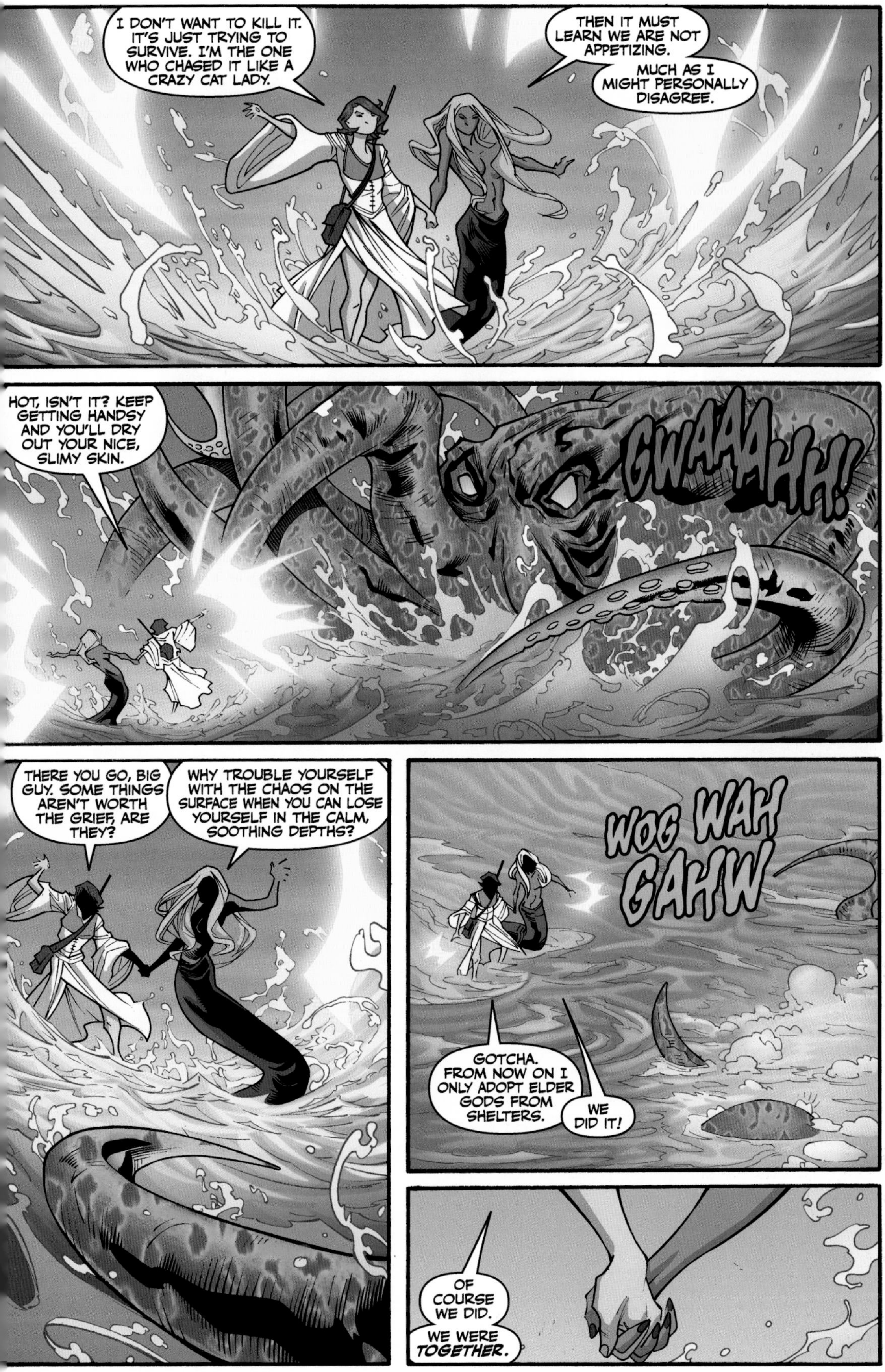
I DON'T WANT TO KILL IT. IT'S JUST TRYING TO SURVIVE. I'M THE ONE WHO CHASED IT LIKE A CRAZY CAT LADY.
THEN IT MUST LEARN WE ARE NOT APPETIZING.
MUCH AS I MIGHT PERSONALLY DISAGREE.
HOT, ISN'T IT? KEEP GETTING HANDSY AND YOU'LL DRY OUT YOUR NICE, SLIMY SKIN.
GWAAAAHH!
THERE YOU GO, BIG GUY. SOME THINGS AREN'T WORTH THE GRIEF, ARE THEY?
WHY TROUBLE YOURSELF WITH THE CHAOS ON THE SURFACE WHEN YOU CAN LOSE YOURSELF IN THE CALM, SOOTHING DEPTHS?
WOG WAH GAHW
GOTCHA. FROM NOW ON I ONLY ADOPT ELDER GODS FROM SHELTERS.
WE DID IT!
OF COURSE WE DID.
WE WERE *TOGETHER*.

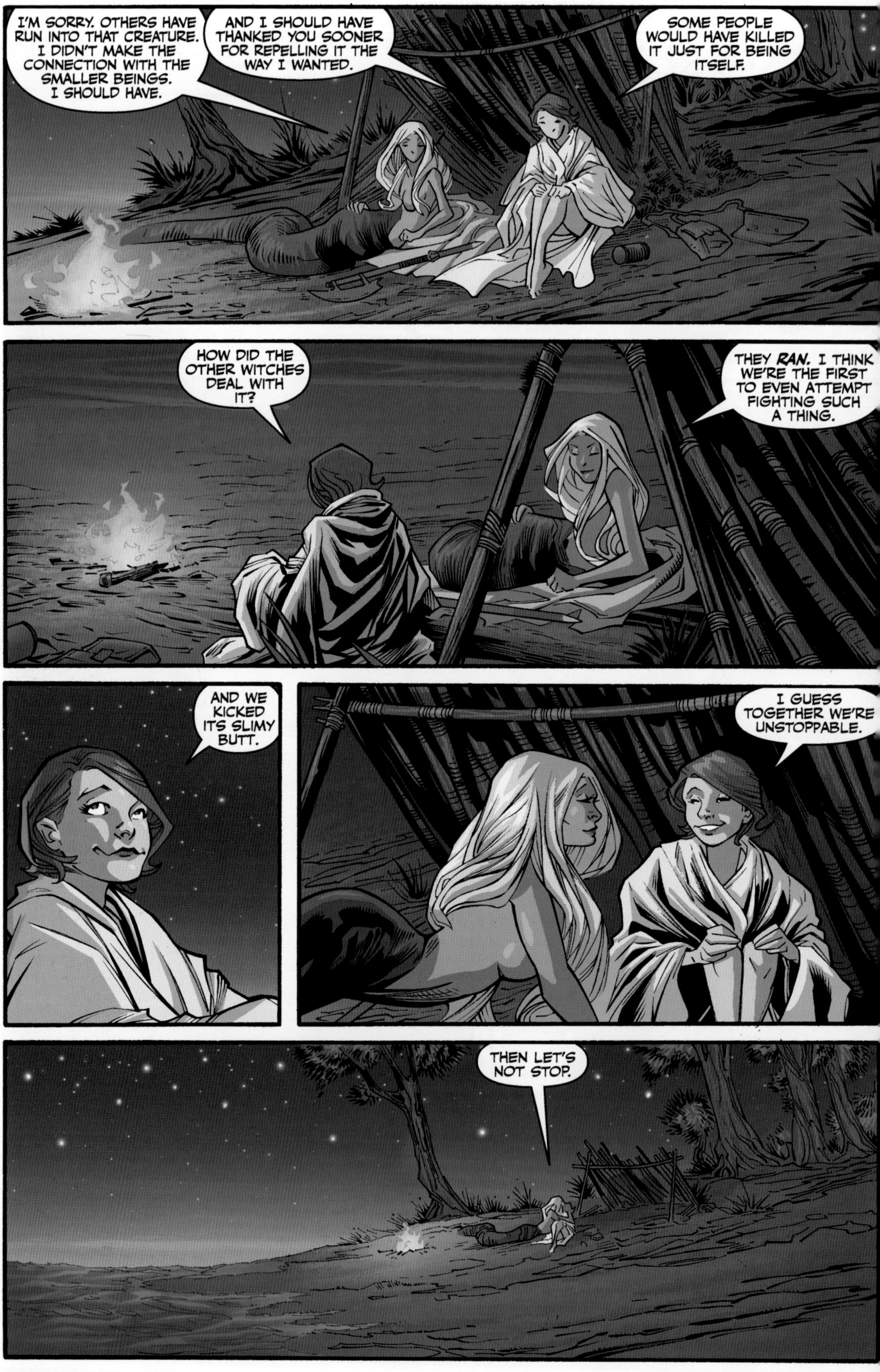
I'M SORRY. OTHERS HAVE RUN INTO THAT CREATURE. I DIDN'T MAKE THE CONNECTION WITH THE SMALLER BEINGS. I SHOULD HAVE.
AND I SHOULD HAVE THANKED YOU SOONER FOR REPELLING IT THE WAY I WANTED.
SOME PEOPLE WOULD HAVE KILLED IT JUST FOR BEING ITSELF.
HOW DID THE OTHER WITCHES DEAL WITH IT?
THEY *RAN*. I THINK WE'RE THE FIRST TO EVEN ATTEMPT FIGHTING SUCH A THING.
AND WE KICKED ITS SLIMY BUTT.
I GUESS TOGETHER WE'RE UNSTOPPABLE.
THEN LET'S NOT STOP.

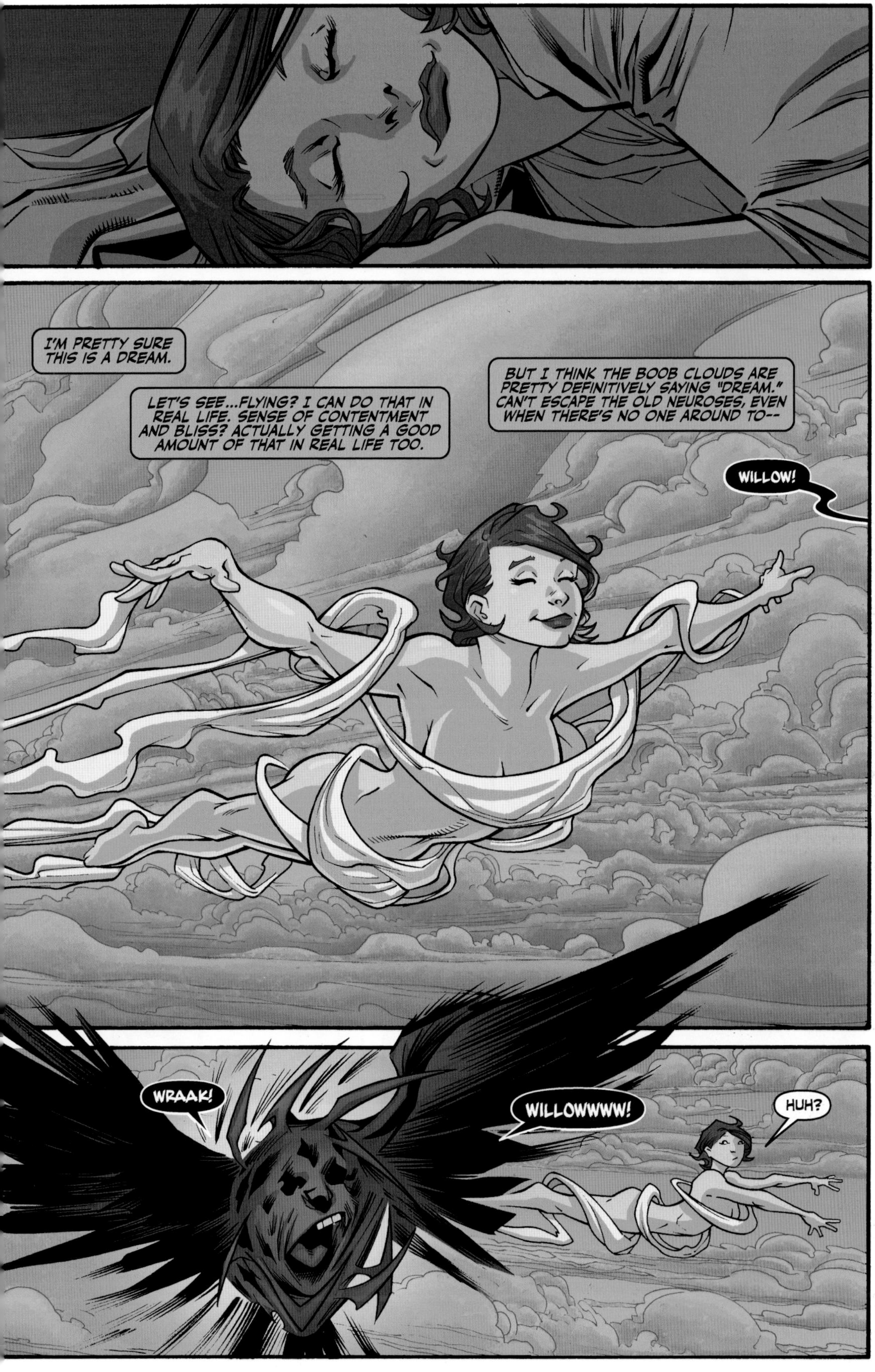

I'M PRETTY SURE THIS IS A DREAM.
LET'S SEE...FLYING? I CAN DO THAT IN REAL LIFE. SENSE OF CONTENTMENT AND BLISS? ACTUALLY GETTING A GOOD AMOUNT OF THAT IN REAL LIFE TOO.
BUT I THINK THE BOOB CLOUDS ARE PRETTY DEFINITIVELY SAYING "DREAM." CAN'T ESCAPE THE OLD NEUROSES, EVEN WHEN THERE'S NO ONE AROUND TO--
WILLOW!
WRAAK!
WILLOWWWW!
HUH?

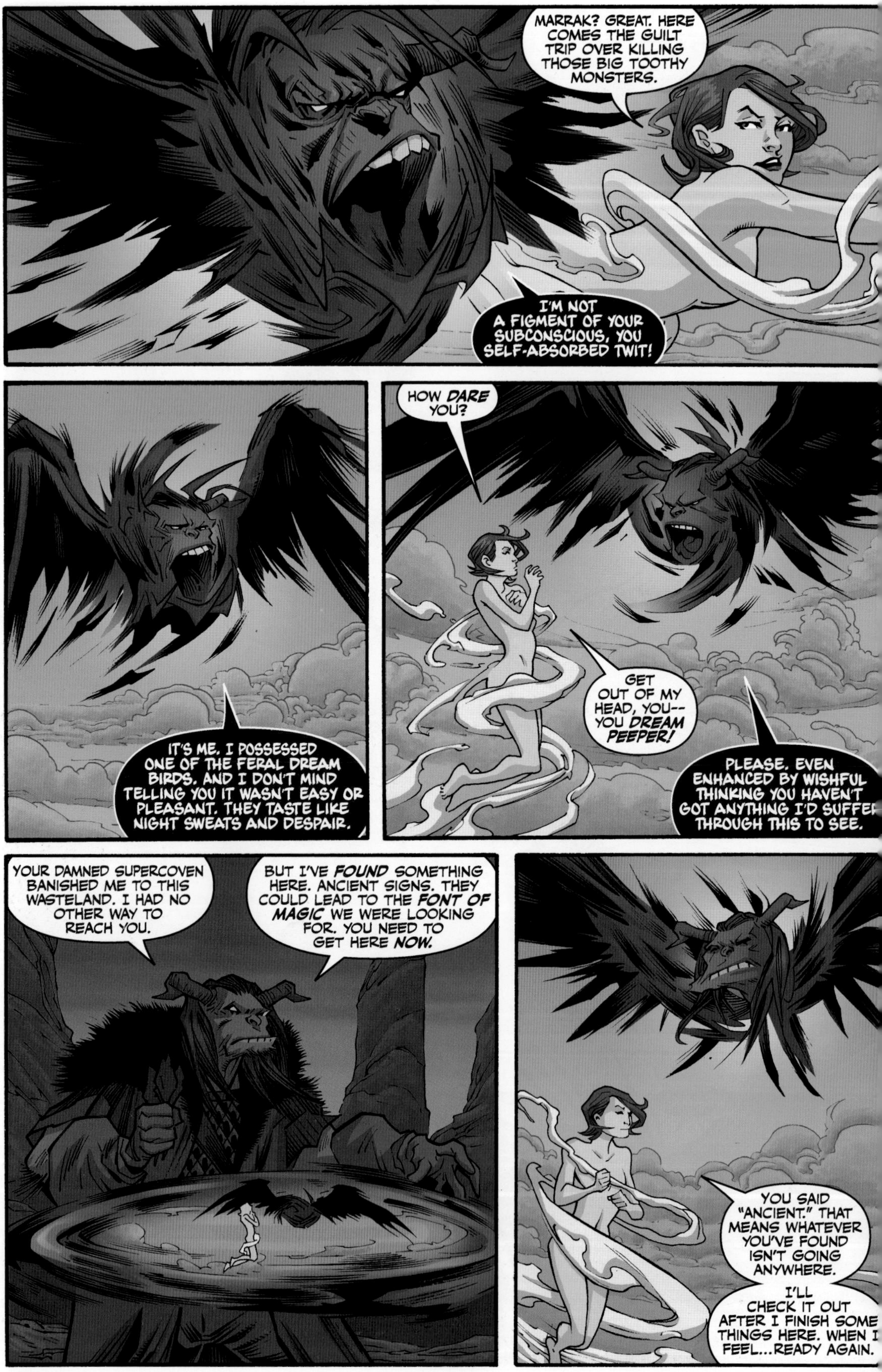
MARRAK? GREAT. HERE COMES THE GUILT TRIP OVER KILLING THOSE BIG TOOTHY MONSTERS.
I'M NOT A FIGMENT OF YOUR SUBCONSCIOUS, YOU SELF-ABSORBED TWIT!
IT'S ME. I POSSESSED ONE OF THE FERAL DREAM BIRDS. AND I DON'T MIND TELLING YOU IT WASN'T EASY OR PLEASANT. THEY TASTE LIKE NIGHT SWEATS AND DESPAIR.
HOW DARE YOU?
GET OUT OF MY HEAD, YOU-- YOU DREAM PEEPER!
PLEASE. EVEN ENHANCED BY WISHFUL THINKING YOU HAVEN'T GOT ANYTHING I'D SUFFER THROUGH THIS TO SEE.
YOUR DAMNED SUPERCOVEN BANISHED ME TO THIS WASTELAND. I HAD NO OTHER WAY TO REACH YOU.
BUT I'VE FOUND SOMETHING HERE. ANCIENT SIGNS. THEY COULD LEAD TO THE FONT OF MAGIC WE WERE LOOKING FOR. YOU NEED TO GET HERE NOW.
YOU SAID "ANCIENT." THAT MEANS WHATEVER YOU'VE FOUND ISN'T GOING ANYWHERE.
I'LL CHECK IT OUT AFTER I FINISH SOME THINGS HERE. WHEN I FEEL...READY AGAIN.

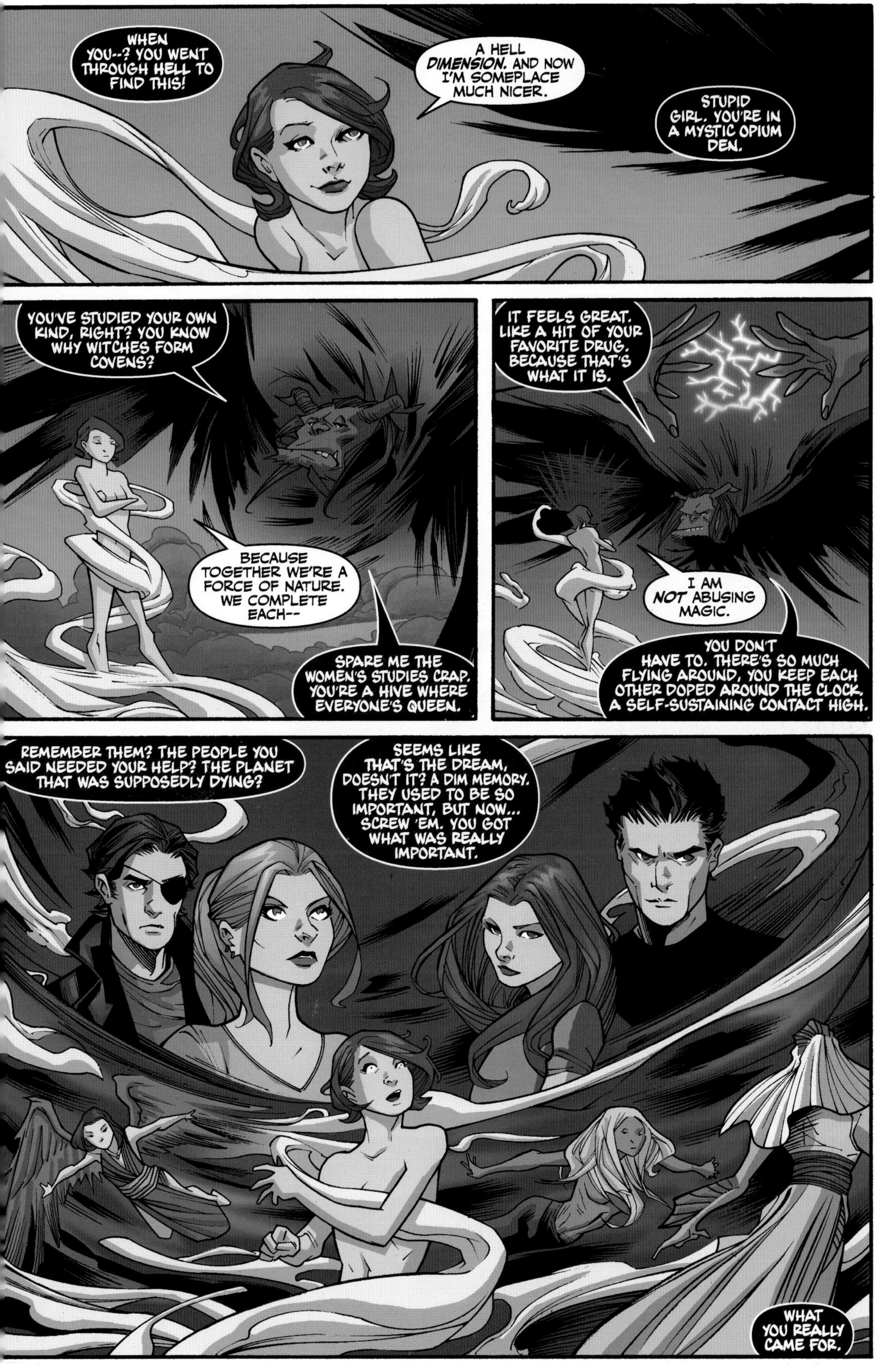

WHEN YOU--? YOU WENT THROUGH HELL TO FIND THIS!
A HELL DIMENSION. AND NOW I'M SOMEPLACE MUCH NICER.
STUPID GIRL. YOU'RE IN A MYSTIC OPIUM DEN.
YOU'VE STUDIED YOUR OWN KIND, RIGHT? YOU KNOW WHY WITCHES FORM COVENS?
BECAUSE TOGETHER WE'RE A FORCE OF NATURE. WE COMPLETE EACH--
SPARE ME THE WOMEN'S STUDIES CRAP. YOU'RE A HIVE WHERE EVERYONE'S QUEEN.
IT FEELS GREAT. LIKE A HIT OF YOUR FAVORITE DRUG. BECAUSE THAT'S WHAT IT IS.
I AM NOT ABUSING MAGIC.
YOU DON'T HAVE TO. THERE'S SO MUCH FLYING AROUND, YOU KEEP EACH OTHER DOPED AROUND THE CLOCK. A SELF-SUSTAINING CONTACT HIGH.
REMEMBER THEM? THE PEOPLE YOU SAID NEEDED YOUR HELP? THE PLANET THAT WAS SUPPOSEDLY DYING?
SEEMS LIKE THAT'S THE DREAM, DOESN'T IT? A DIM MEMORY. THEY USED TO BE SO IMPORTANT, BUT NOW... SCREW 'EM. YOU GOT WHAT WAS REALLY IMPORTANT.
WHAT YOU REALLY CAME FOR.

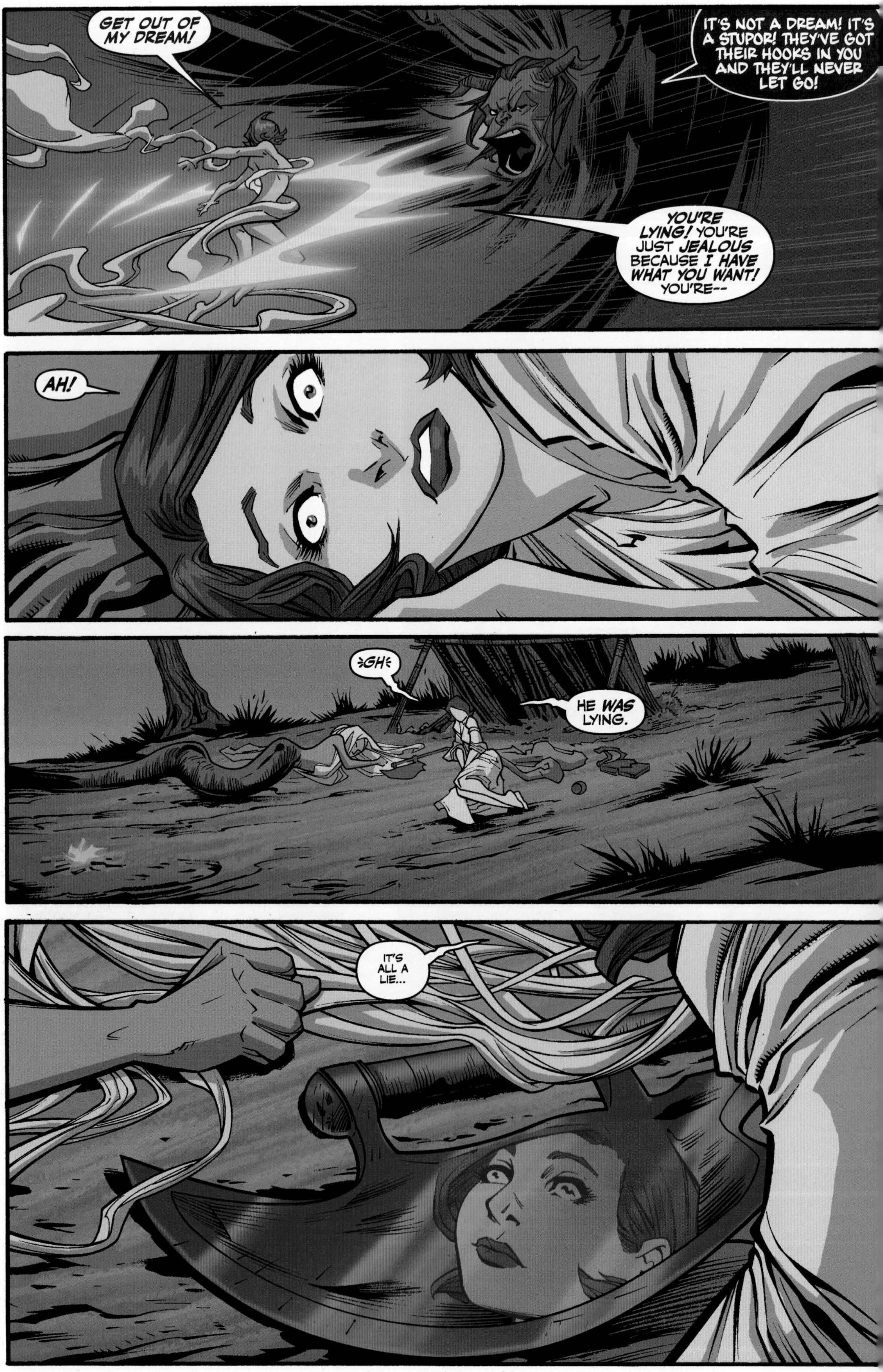
GET OUT OF MY DREAM!
IT'S NOT A DREAM! IT'S A STUPOR! THEY'VE GOT THEIR HOOKS IN YOU AND THEY'LL NEVER LET GO!
YOU'RE LYING! YOU'RE JUST JEALOUS BECAUSE I HAVE WHAT YOU WANT! YOU'RE--
AH!
GH
HE WAS LYING.
IT'S ALL A LIE...

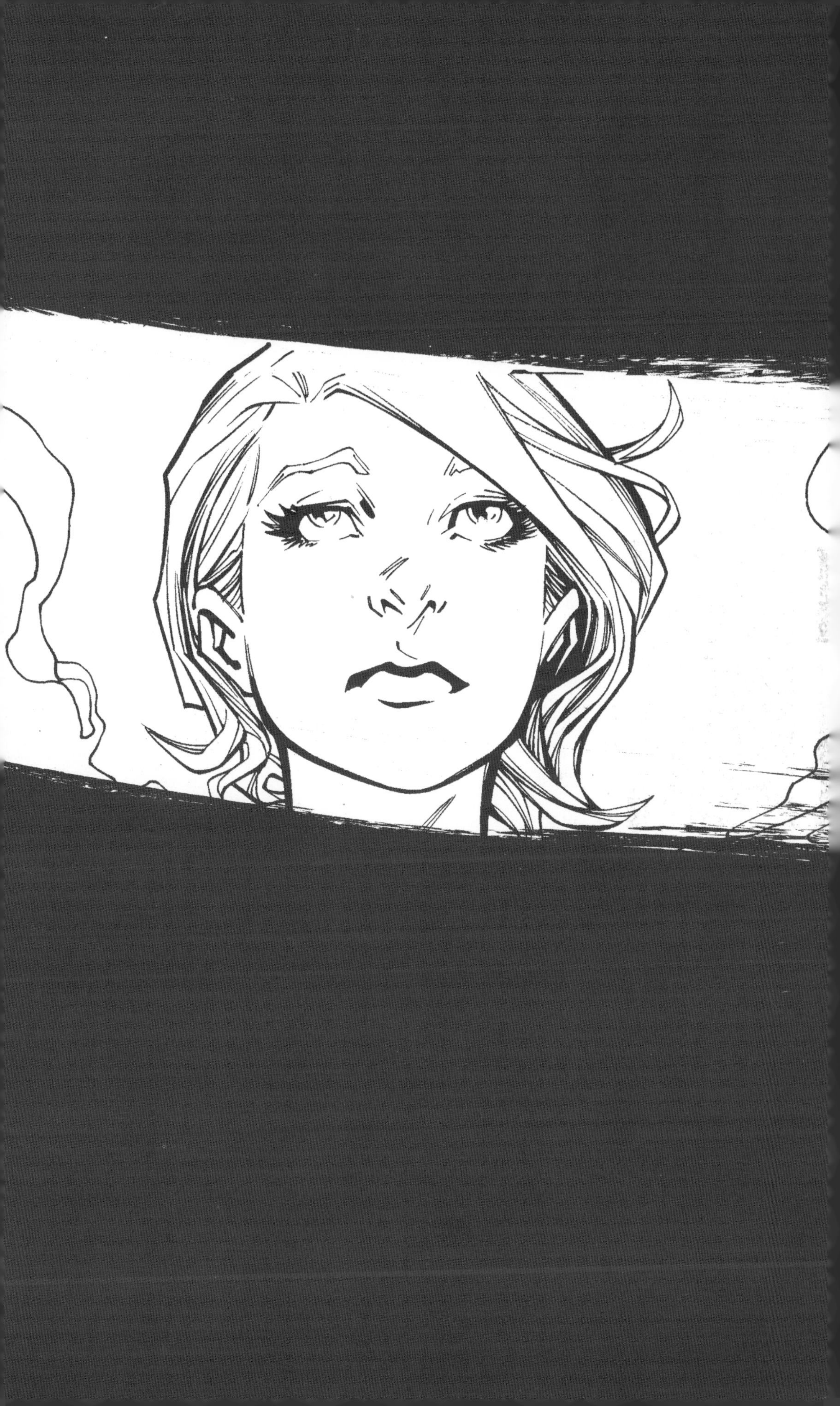

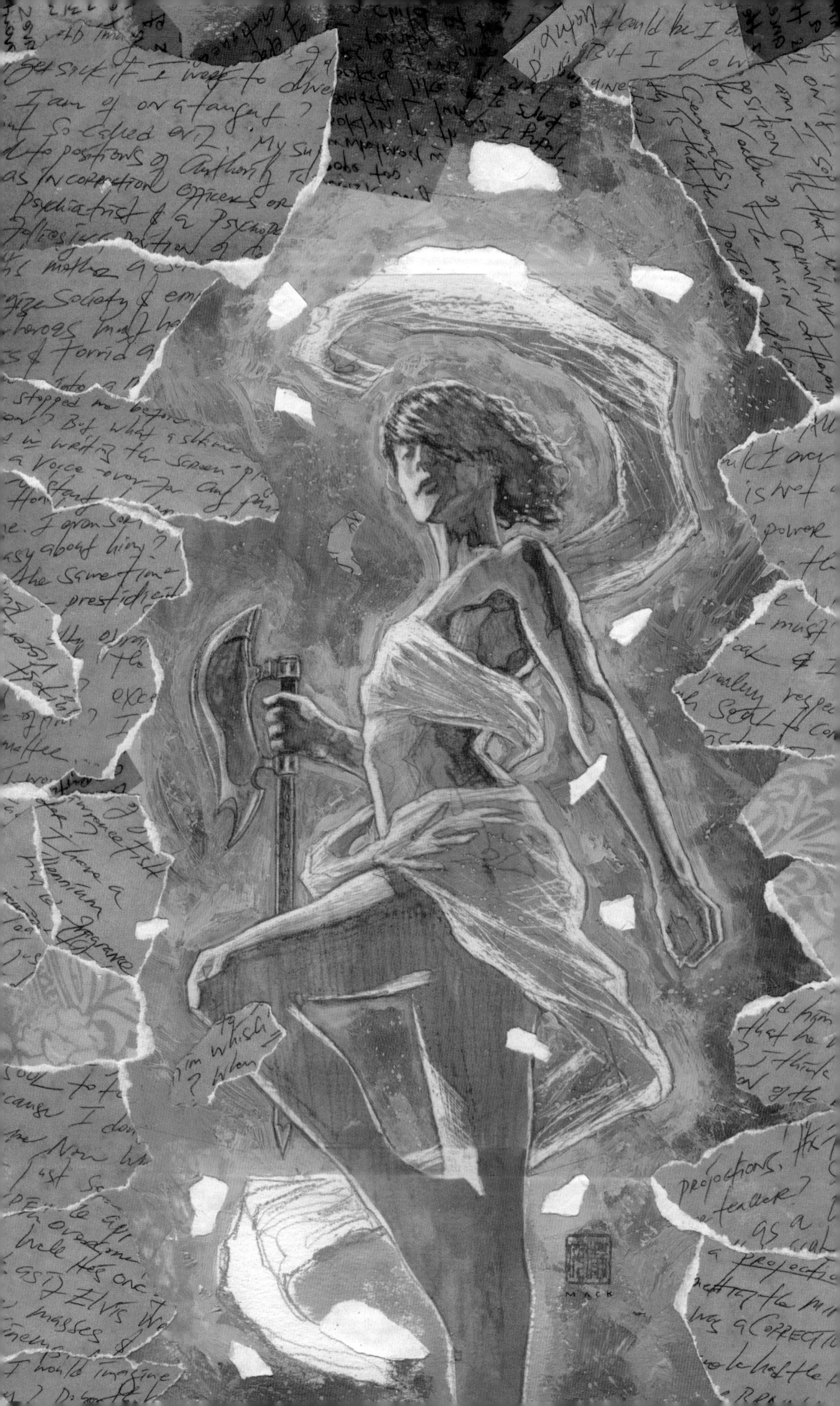

I am of or a tangent?
So called evil. My su
to positions of authority
as in correction officers or
psychiatrist & a psychop
stopped me before
But what a shame
in writing the screen-
a voice-over for any
Should it be I
But I
projections.
teacher?
as a
a projection
was a correctio
MACK

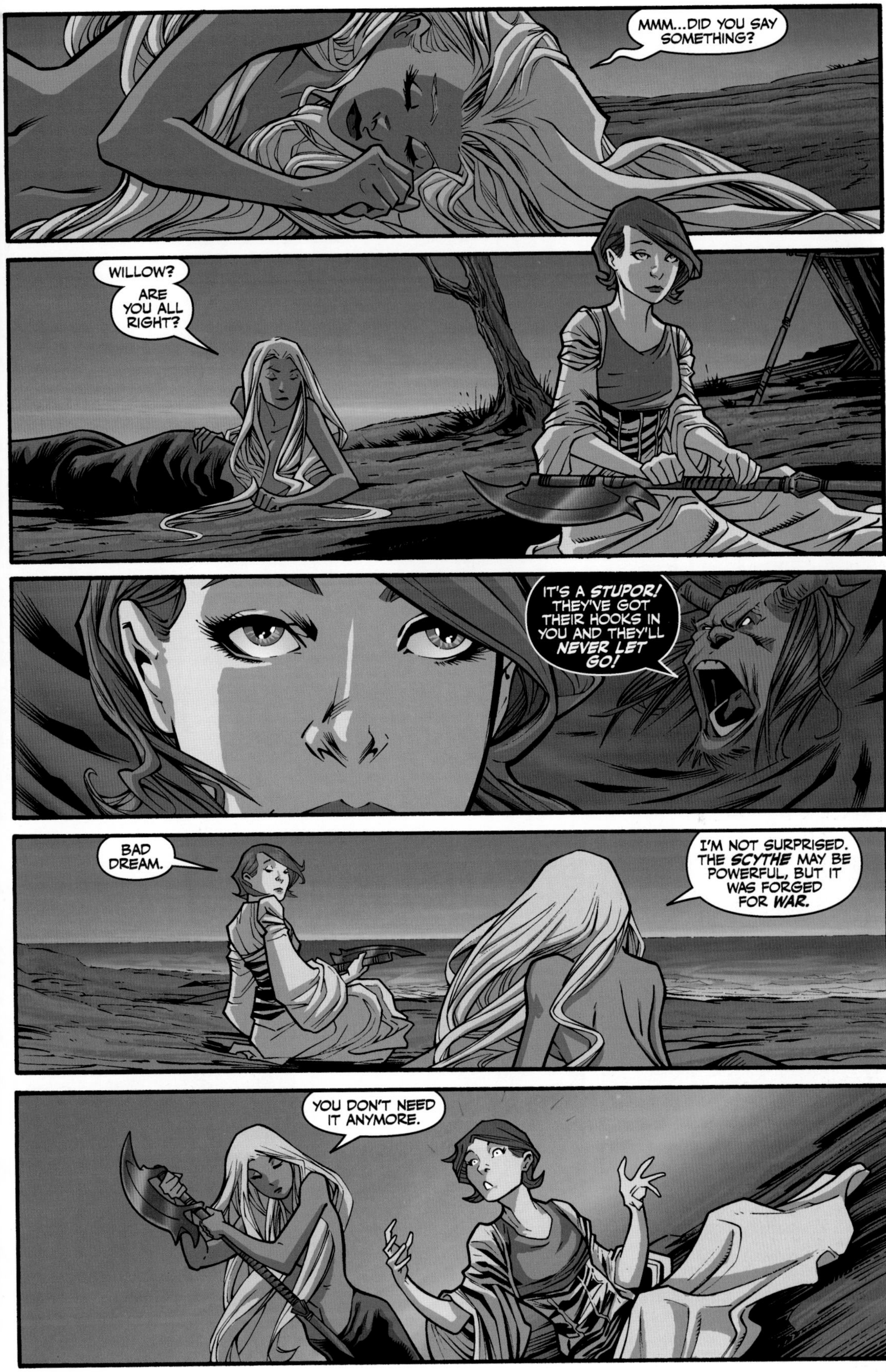
MMM...DID YOU SAY SOMETHING?
WILLOW? ARE YOU ALL RIGHT?
IT'S A STUPOR! THEY'VE GOT THEIR HOOKS IN YOU AND THEY'LL NEVER LET GO!
BAD DREAM.
I'M NOT SURPRISED. THE SCYTHE MAY BE POWERFUL, BUT IT WAS FORGED FOR WAR.
YOU DON'T NEED IT ANYMORE.

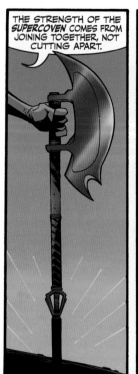

THE STRENGTH OF THE *SUPERCOVEN* COMES FROM JOINING TOGETHER, NOT CUTTING APART.

THAT'S THE SOURCE OF OUR POWER.

WE ARE AS ONE. WE SHARE TOGETHER. WE MAKE EACH OTHER *BETTER...*

WONDERLAND
Part Four

WILLOW, ARE YOU WELL...?

OH...MY...GODDESS.

JUST... STILL PARTLY CLOUDY.

I THINK I NEED WATER.

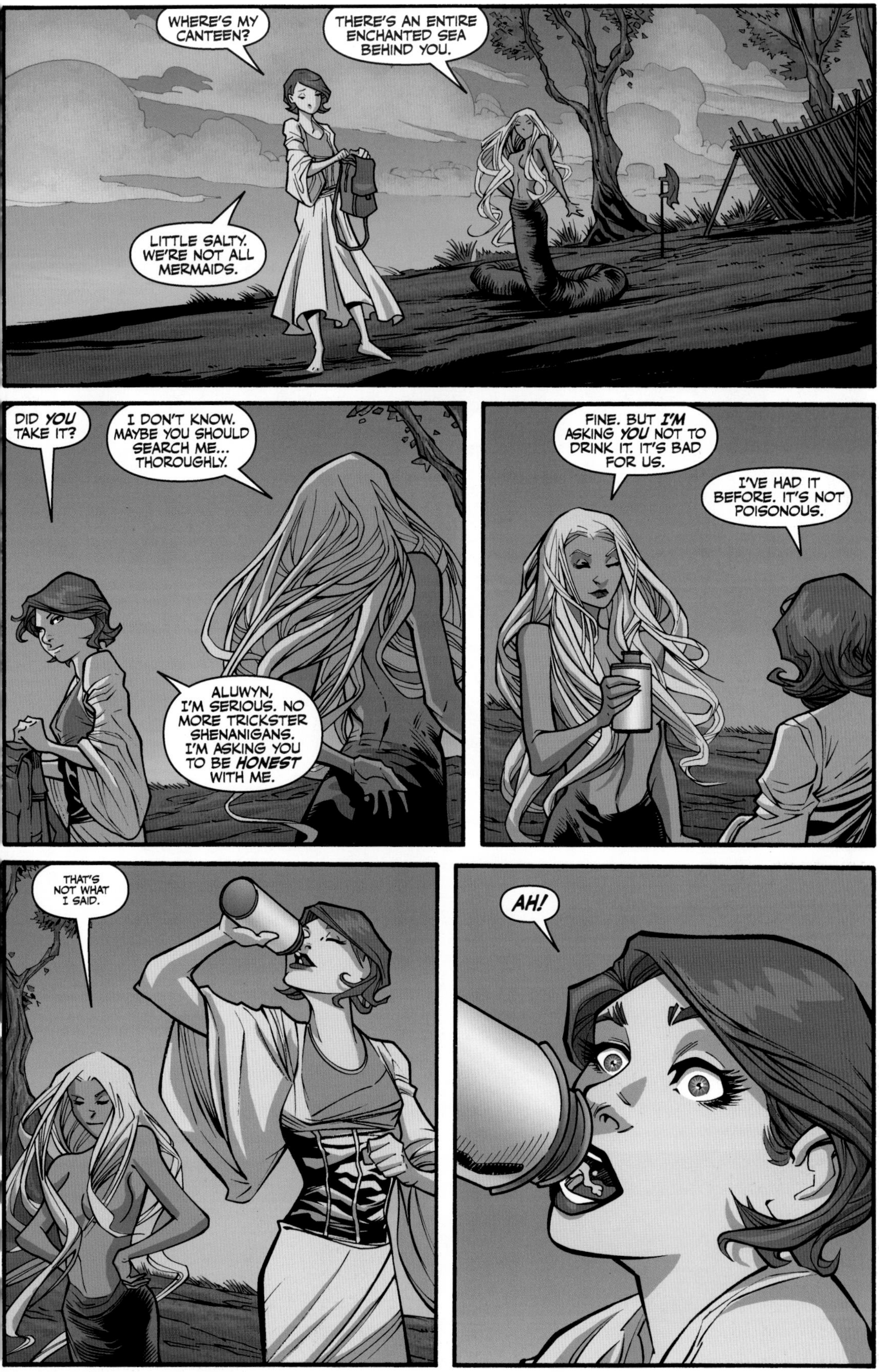
WHERE'S MY CANTEEN?
THERE'S AN ENTIRE ENCHANTED SEA BEHIND YOU.
LITTLE SALTY. WE'RE NOT ALL MERMAIDS.
DID YOU TAKE IT?
I DON'T KNOW. MAYBE YOU SHOULD SEARCH ME... THOROUGHLY.
ALUWYN, I'M SERIOUS. NO MORE TRICKSTER SHENANIGANS. I'M ASKING YOU TO BE HONEST WITH ME.
FINE. BUT I'M ASKING YOU NOT TO DRINK IT. IT'S BAD FOR US.
I'VE HAD IT BEFORE. IT'S NOT POISONOUS.
THAT'S NOT WHAT I SAID.
AH!

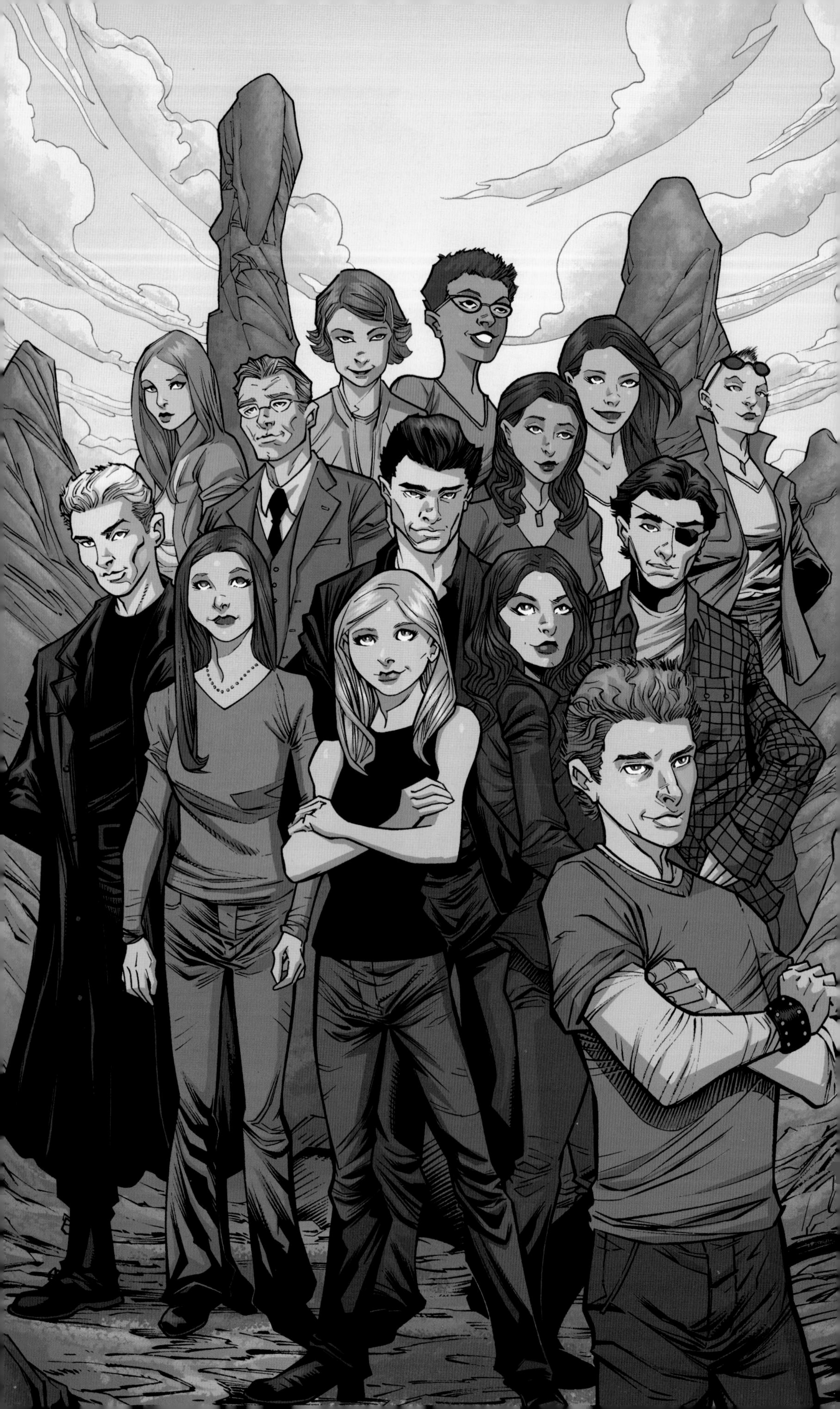

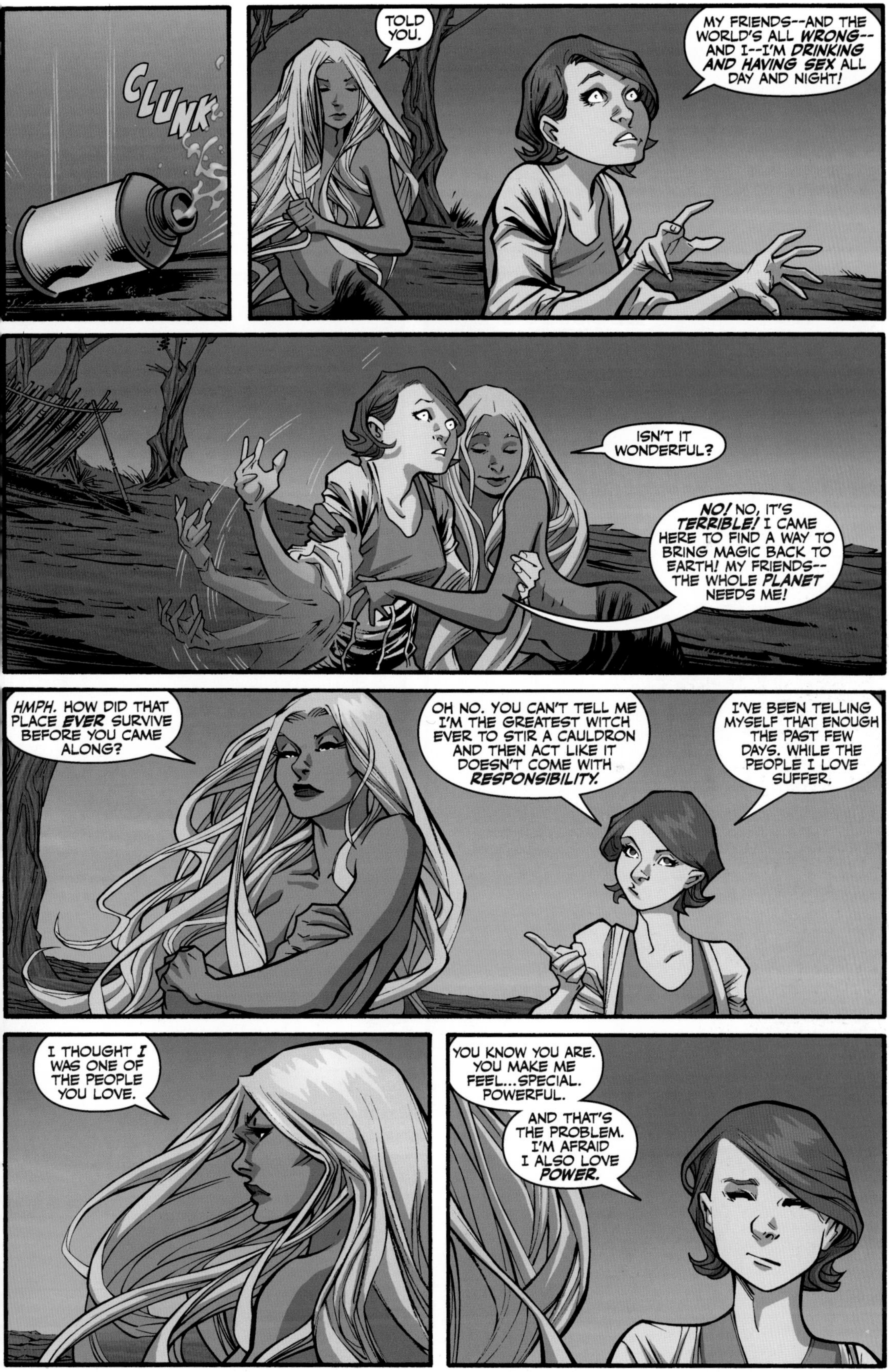
CLUNK
TOLD YOU.
MY FRIENDS--AND THE WORLD'S ALL WRONG--AND I--I'M DRINKING AND HAVING SEX ALL DAY AND NIGHT!
ISN'T IT WONDERFUL?
NO! NO, IT'S TERRIBLE! I CAME HERE TO FIND A WAY TO BRING MAGIC BACK TO EARTH! MY FRIENDS--THE WHOLE PLANET NEEDS ME!
HMPH. HOW DID THAT PLACE EVER SURVIVE BEFORE YOU CAME ALONG?
OH NO. YOU CAN'T TELL ME I'M THE GREATEST WITCH EVER TO STIR A CAULDRON AND THEN ACT LIKE IT DOESN'T COME WITH RESPONSIBILITY.
I'VE BEEN TELLING MYSELF THAT ENOUGH THE PAST FEW DAYS. WHILE THE PEOPLE I LOVE SUFFER.
I THOUGHT I WAS ONE OF THE PEOPLE YOU LOVE.
YOU KNOW YOU ARE. YOU MAKE ME FEEL...SPECIAL. POWERFUL.
AND THAT'S THE PROBLEM. I'M AFRAID I ALSO LOVE POWER.

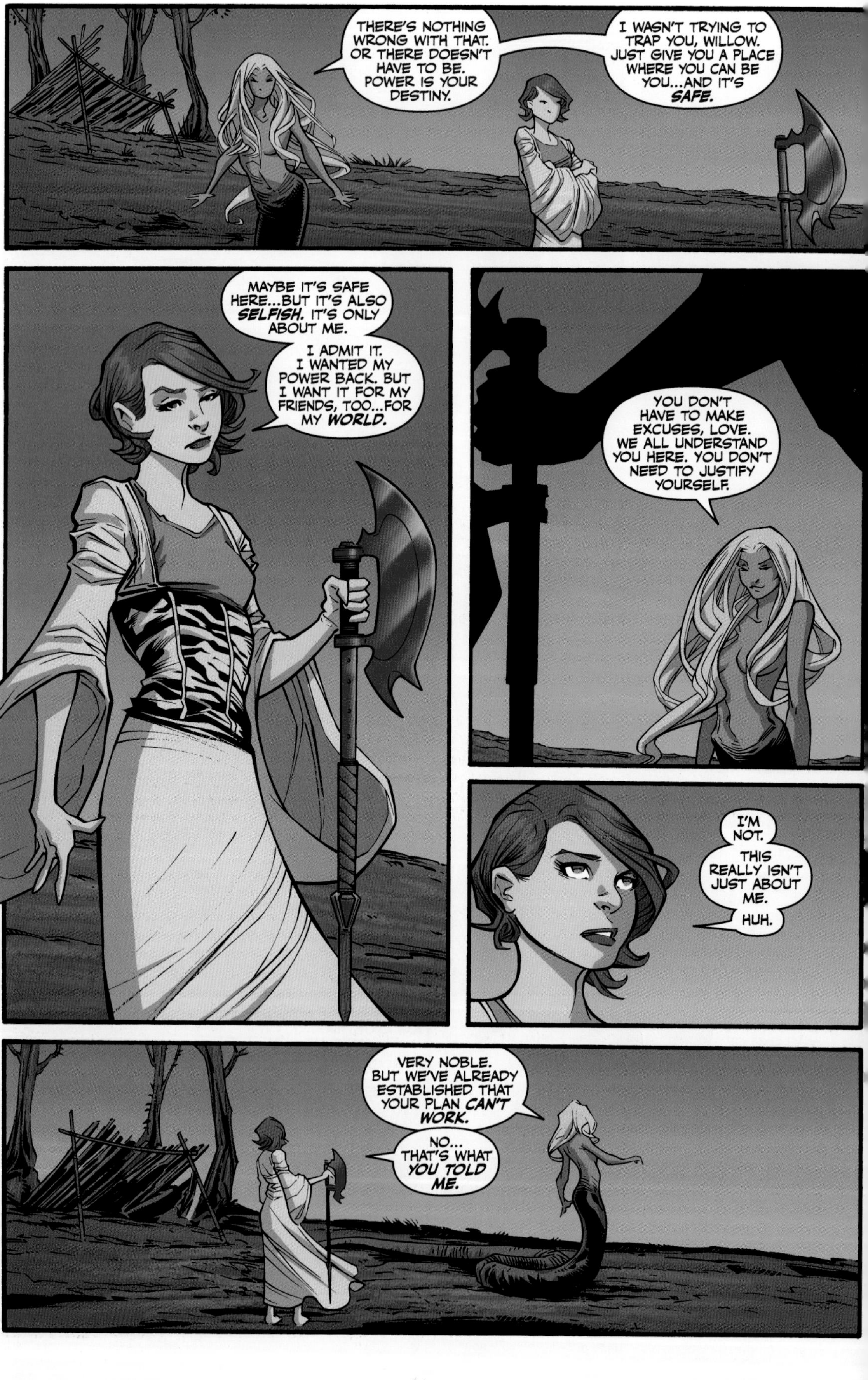
THERE'S NOTHING WRONG WITH THAT. OR THERE DOESN'T HAVE TO BE. POWER IS YOUR DESTINY.
I WASN'T TRYING TO TRAP YOU, WILLOW. JUST GIVE YOU A PLACE WHERE YOU CAN BE YOU...AND IT'S SAFE.
MAYBE IT'S SAFE HERE...BUT IT'S ALSO SELFISH. IT'S ONLY ABOUT ME.
I ADMIT IT. I WANTED MY POWER BACK. BUT I WANT IT FOR MY FRIENDS, TOO...FOR MY WORLD.
YOU DON'T HAVE TO MAKE EXCUSES, LOVE. WE ALL UNDERSTAND YOU HERE. YOU DON'T NEED TO JUSTIFY YOURSELF.
I'M NOT.
THIS REALLY ISN'T JUST ABOUT ME.
HUH.
VERY NOBLE. BUT WE'VE ALREADY ESTABLISHED THAT YOUR PLAN CAN'T WORK.
NO... THAT'S WHAT YOU TOLD ME.

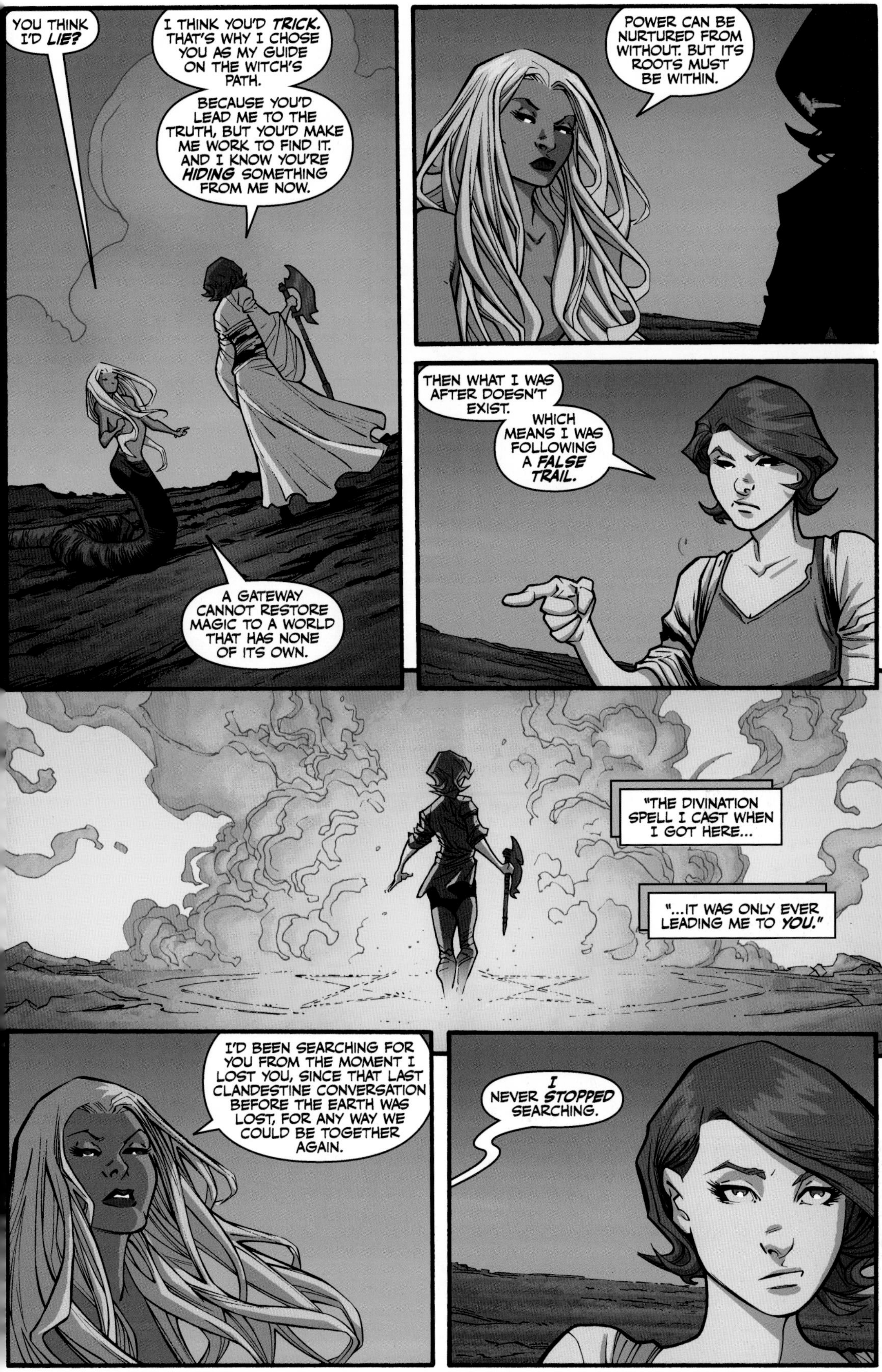
YOU THINK I'D *LIE?*
I THINK YOU'D *TRICK.* THAT'S WHY I CHOSE YOU AS MY GUIDE ON THE WITCH'S PATH.
BECAUSE YOU'D LEAD ME TO THE TRUTH, BUT YOU'D MAKE ME WORK TO FIND IT. AND I KNOW YOU'RE *HIDING* SOMETHING FROM ME NOW.
A GATEWAY CANNOT RESTORE MAGIC TO A WORLD THAT HAS NONE OF ITS OWN.
POWER CAN BE NURTURED FROM WITHOUT. BUT ITS ROOTS MUST BE WITHIN.
THEN WHAT I WAS AFTER DOESN'T EXIST.
WHICH MEANS I WAS FOLLOWING A *FALSE TRAIL.*
"THE DIVINATION SPELL I CAST WHEN I GOT HERE...
"...IT WAS ONLY EVER LEADING ME TO *YOU.*"
I'D BEEN SEARCHING FOR YOU FROM THE MOMENT I LOST YOU, SINCE THAT LAST CLANDESTINE CONVERSATION BEFORE THE EARTH WAS LOST, FOR ANY WAY WE COULD BE TOGETHER AGAIN.
I NEVER *STOPPED* SEARCHING.

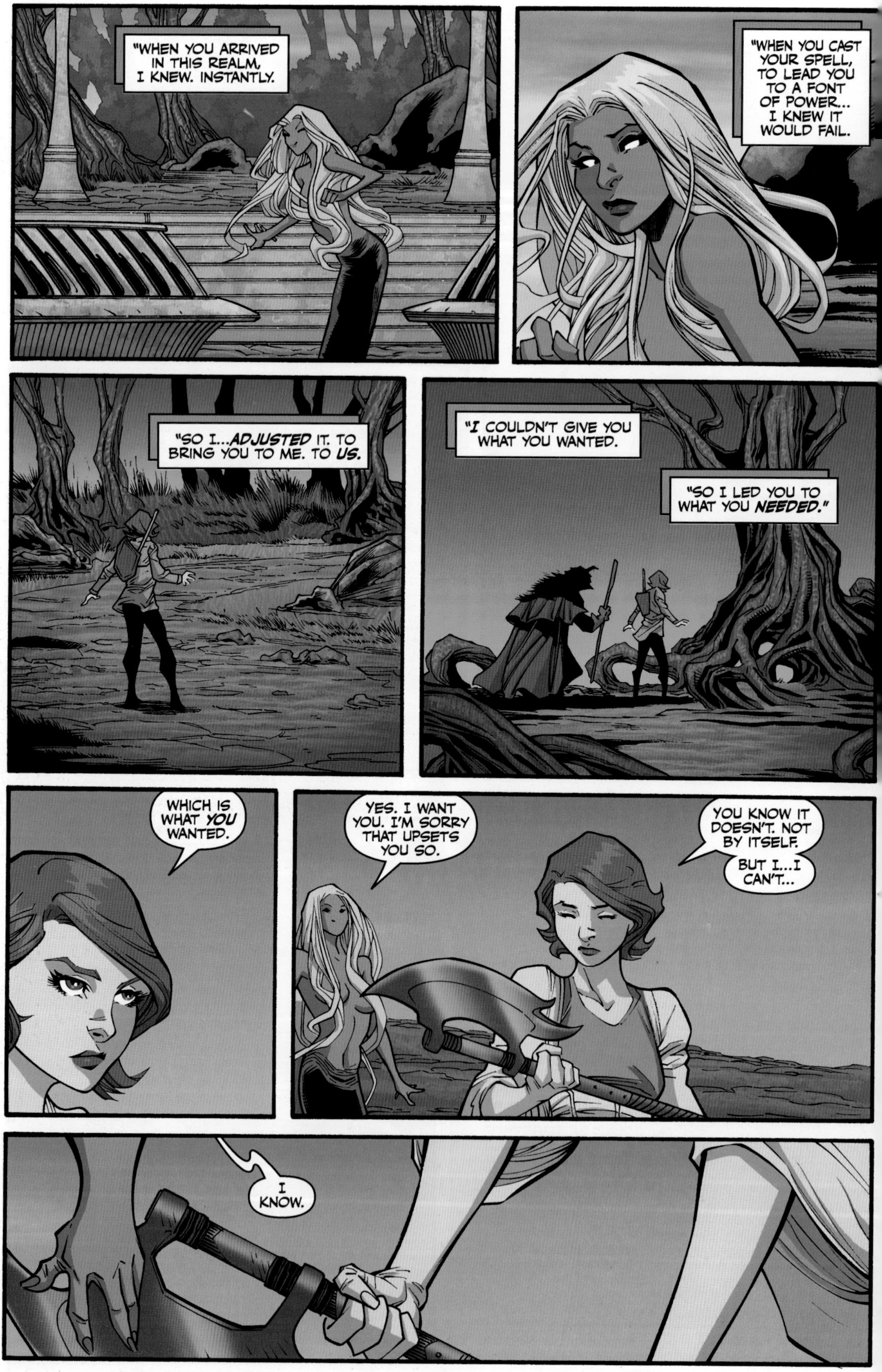
"WHEN YOU ARRIVED IN THIS REALM, I KNEW. INSTANTLY.
"WHEN YOU CAST YOUR SPELL, TO LEAD YOU TO A FONT OF POWER... I KNEW IT WOULD FAIL.
"SO I...ADJUSTED IT. TO BRING YOU TO ME. TO US.
"I COULDN'T GIVE YOU WHAT YOU WANTED.
"SO I LED YOU TO WHAT YOU NEEDED."
WHICH IS WHAT YOU WANTED.
YES. I WANT YOU. I'M SORRY THAT UPSETS YOU SO.
YOU KNOW IT DOESN'T. NOT BY ITSELF.
BUT I...I CAN'T...
I KNOW.

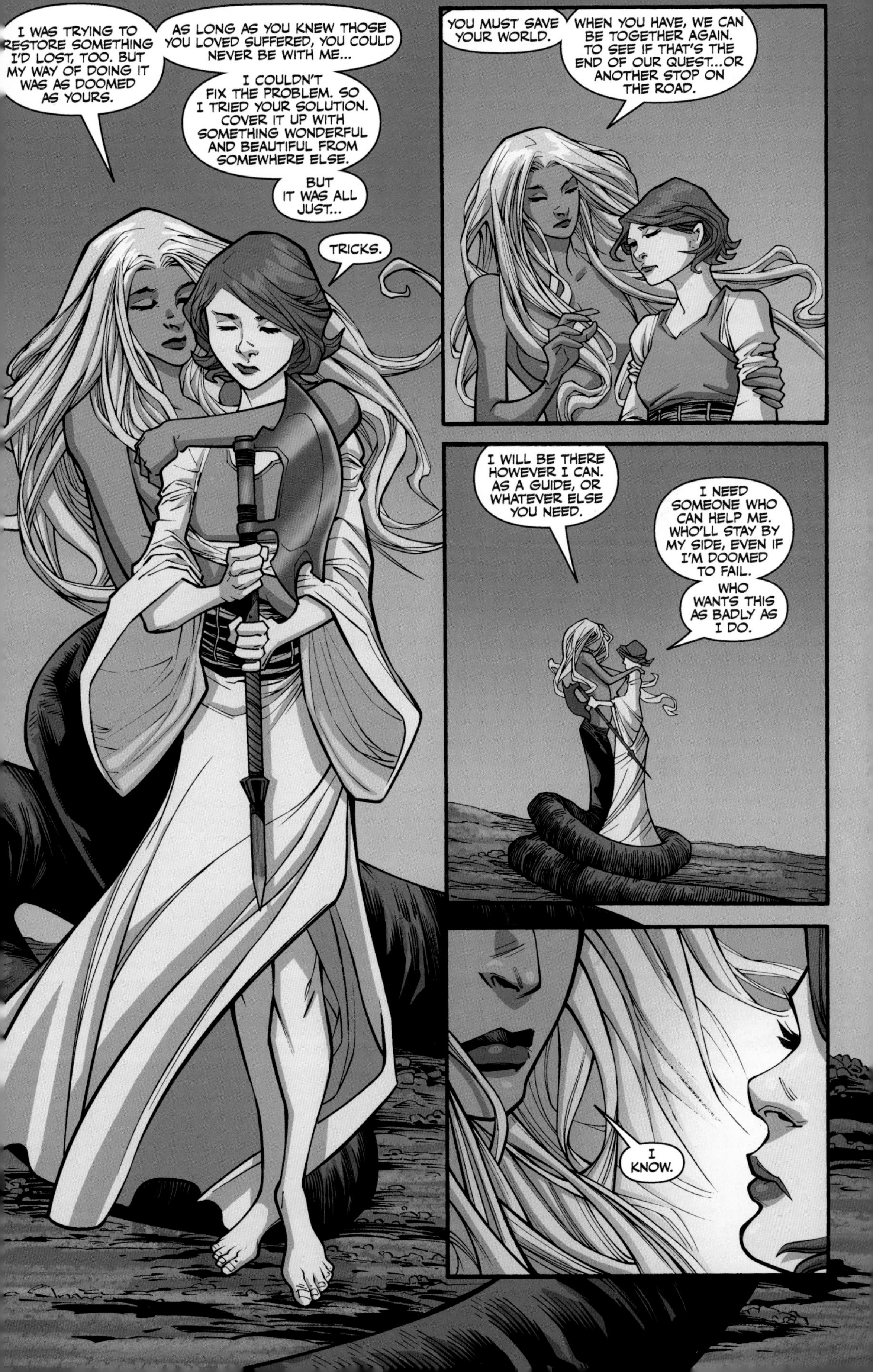
I WAS TRYING TO RESTORE SOMETHING I'D LOST, TOO. BUT MY WAY OF DOING IT WAS AS DOOMED AS YOURS.
AS LONG AS YOU KNEW THOSE YOU LOVED SUFFERED, YOU COULD NEVER BE WITH ME...
I COULDN'T FIX THE PROBLEM. SO I TRIED YOUR SOLUTION. COVER IT UP WITH SOMETHING WONDERFUL AND BEAUTIFUL FROM SOMEWHERE ELSE.
BUT IT WAS ALL JUST...
TRICKS.
YOU MUST SAVE YOUR WORLD.
WHEN YOU HAVE, WE CAN BE TOGETHER AGAIN. TO SEE IF THAT'S THE END OF OUR QUEST...OR ANOTHER STOP ON THE ROAD.
I WILL BE THERE HOWEVER I CAN. AS A GUIDE, OR WHATEVER ELSE YOU NEED.
I NEED SOMEONE WHO CAN HELP ME. WHO'LL STAY BY MY SIDE, EVEN IF I'M DOOMED TO FAIL.
WHO WANTS THIS AS BADLY AS I DO.
I KNOW.

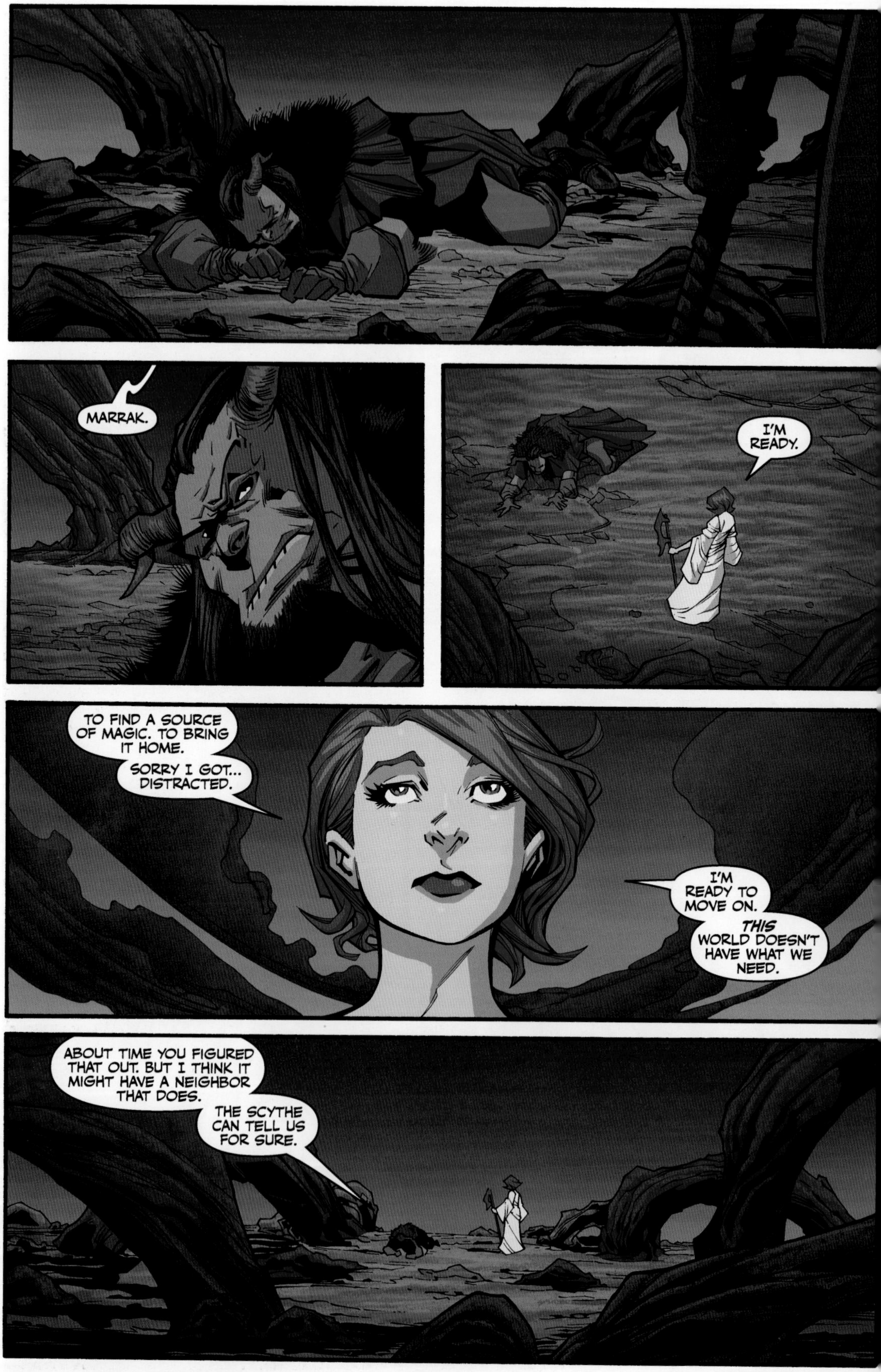
MARRAK.
I'M READY.
TO FIND A SOURCE OF MAGIC. TO BRING IT HOME.
SORRY I GOT... DISTRACTED.
I'M READY TO MOVE ON.
THIS WORLD DOESN'T HAVE WHAT WE NEED.
ABOUT TIME YOU FIGURED THAT OUT. BUT I THINK IT MIGHT HAVE A NEIGHBOR THAT DOES.
THE SCYTHE CAN TELL US FOR SURE.

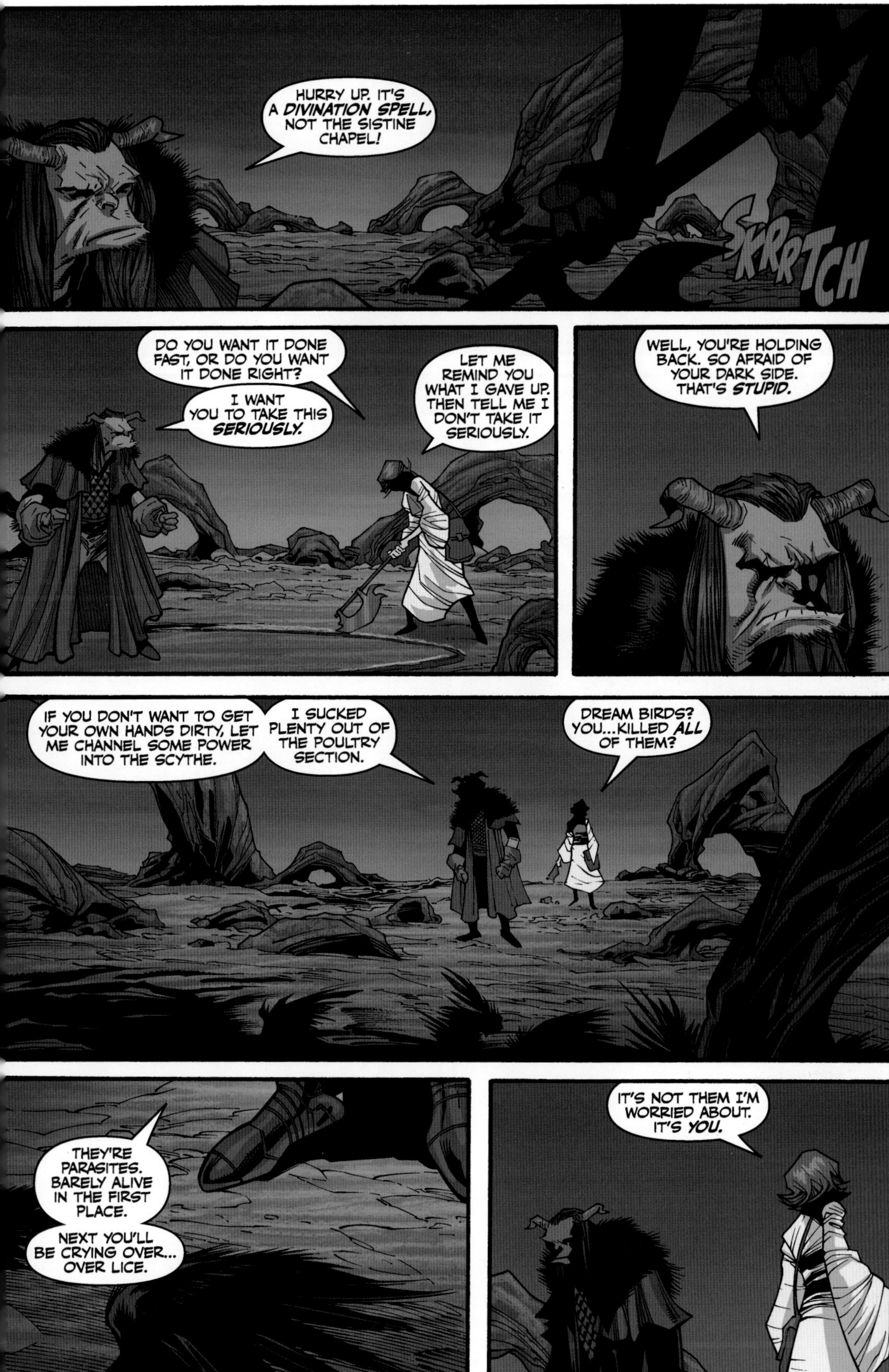
HURRY UP. IT'S A *DIVINATION SPELL*, NOT THE SISTINE CHAPEL!
SKRRTCH
DO YOU WANT IT DONE FAST, OR DO YOU WANT IT DONE RIGHT?
I WANT YOU TO TAKE THIS *SERIOUSLY*.
LET ME REMIND YOU WHAT I GAVE UP. THEN TELL ME I DON'T TAKE IT SERIOUSLY.
WELL, YOU'RE HOLDING BACK. SO AFRAID OF YOUR DARK SIDE. THAT'S *STUPID*.
IF YOU DON'T WANT TO GET YOUR OWN HANDS DIRTY, LET ME CHANNEL SOME POWER INTO THE SCYTHE.
I SUCKED PLENTY OUT OF THE POULTRY SECTION.
DREAM BIRDS? YOU...KILLED *ALL* OF THEM?
THEY'RE PARASITES. BARELY ALIVE IN THE FIRST PLACE.
NEXT YOU'LL BE CRYING OVER... OVER LICE.
IT'S NOT THEM I'M WORRIED ABOUT. IT'S *YOU*.

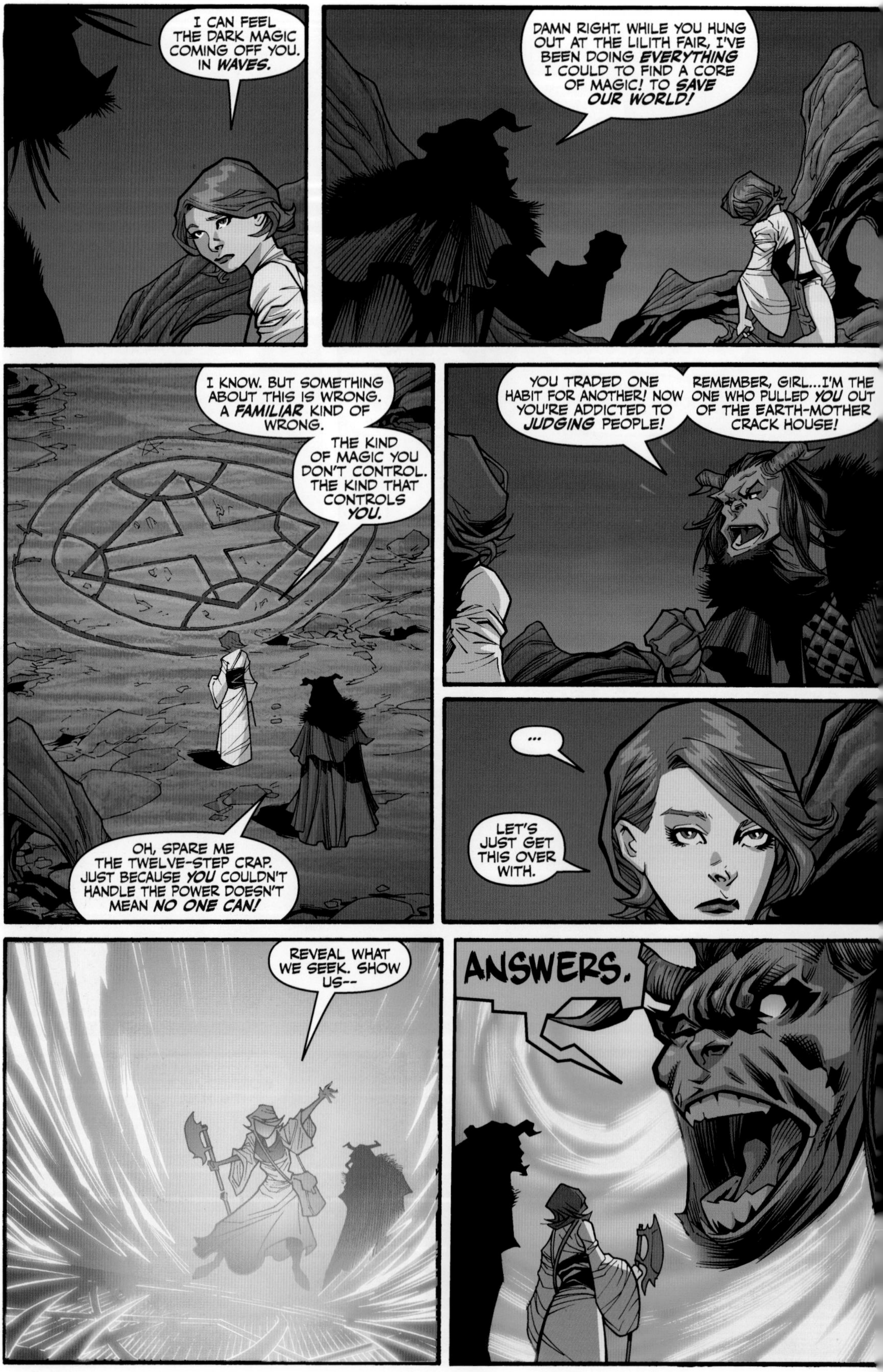

I CAN FEEL THE DARK MAGIC COMING OFF YOU. IN *WAVES.*
DAMN RIGHT. WHILE YOU HUNG OUT AT THE LILITH FAIR, I'VE BEEN DOING *EVERYTHING* I COULD TO FIND A CORE OF MAGIC! TO *SAVE OUR WORLD!*
I KNOW. BUT SOMETHING ABOUT THIS IS WRONG. A *FAMILIAR* KIND OF WRONG.
THE KIND OF MAGIC YOU DON'T CONTROL. THE KIND THAT CONTROLS *YOU.*
OH, SPARE ME THE TWELVE-STEP CRAP. JUST BECAUSE *YOU* COULDN'T HANDLE THE POWER DOESN'T MEAN *NO ONE CAN!*
YOU TRADED ONE HABIT FOR ANOTHER! NOW YOU'RE ADDICTED TO *JUDGING* PEOPLE!
REMEMBER, GIRL...I'M THE ONE WHO PULLED *YOU* OUT OF THE EARTH-MOTHER CRACK HOUSE!
...
LET'S JUST GET THIS OVER WITH.
REVEAL WHAT WE SEEK. SHOW US--
ANSWERS.

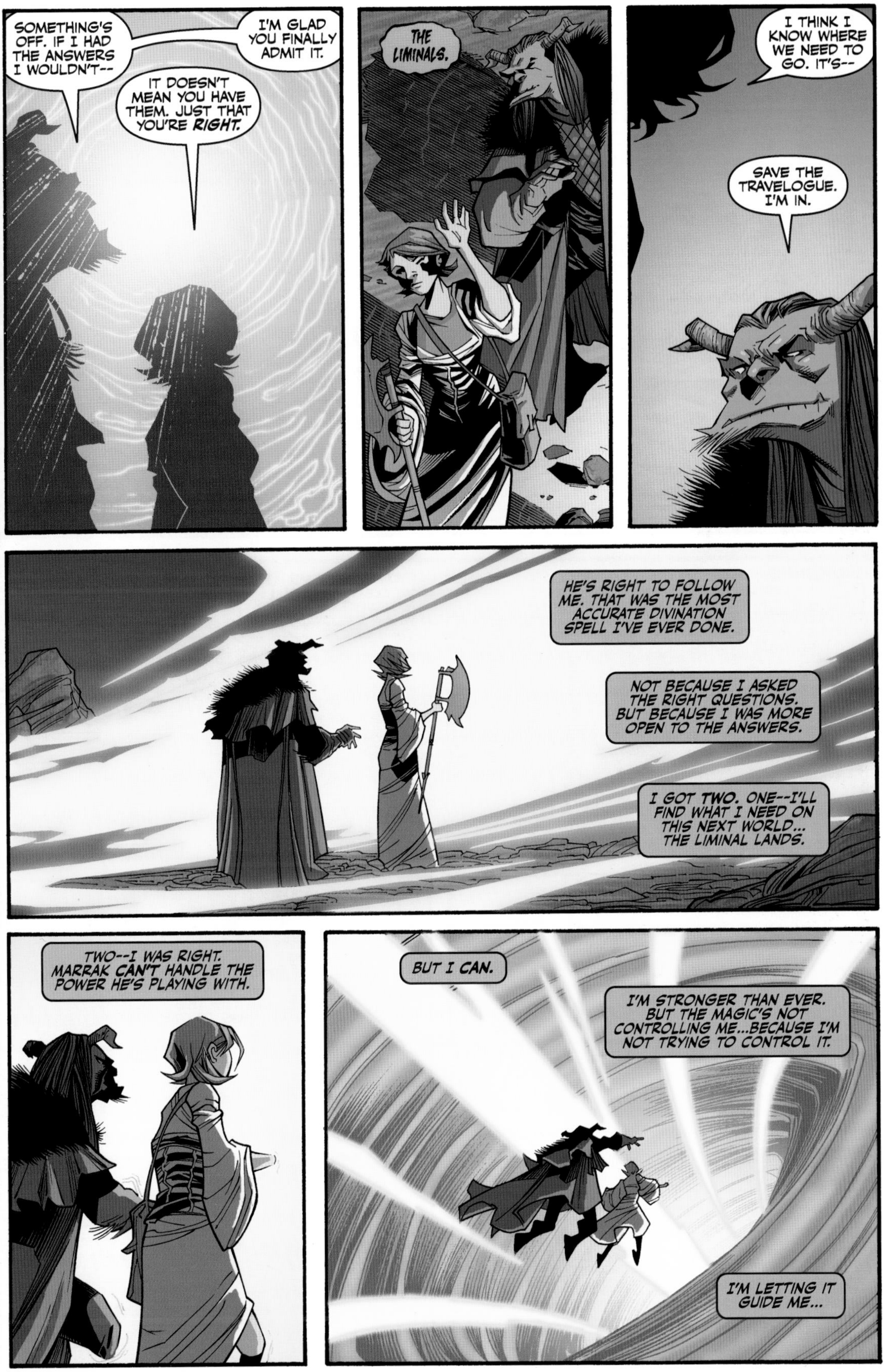
SOMETHING'S OFF. IF I HAD THE ANSWERS I WOULDN'T--
I'M GLAD YOU FINALLY ADMIT IT.
IT DOESN'T MEAN YOU HAVE THEM. JUST THAT YOU'RE RIGHT.
THE LIMINALS.
I THINK I KNOW WHERE WE NEED TO GO. IT'S--
SAVE THE TRAVELOGUE. I'M IN.
HE'S RIGHT TO FOLLOW ME. THAT WAS THE MOST ACCURATE DIVINATION SPELL I'VE EVER DONE.
NOT BECAUSE I ASKED THE RIGHT QUESTIONS. BUT BECAUSE I WAS MORE OPEN TO THE ANSWERS.
I GOT TWO. ONE--I'LL FIND WHAT I NEED ON THIS NEXT WORLD... THE LIMINAL LANDS.
TWO--I WAS RIGHT. MARRAK CAN'T HANDLE THE POWER HE'S PLAYING WITH.
BUT I CAN.
I'M STRONGER THAN EVER. BUT THE MAGIC'S NOT CONTROLLING ME...BECAUSE I'M NOT TRYING TO CONTROL IT.
I'M LETTING IT GUIDE ME...

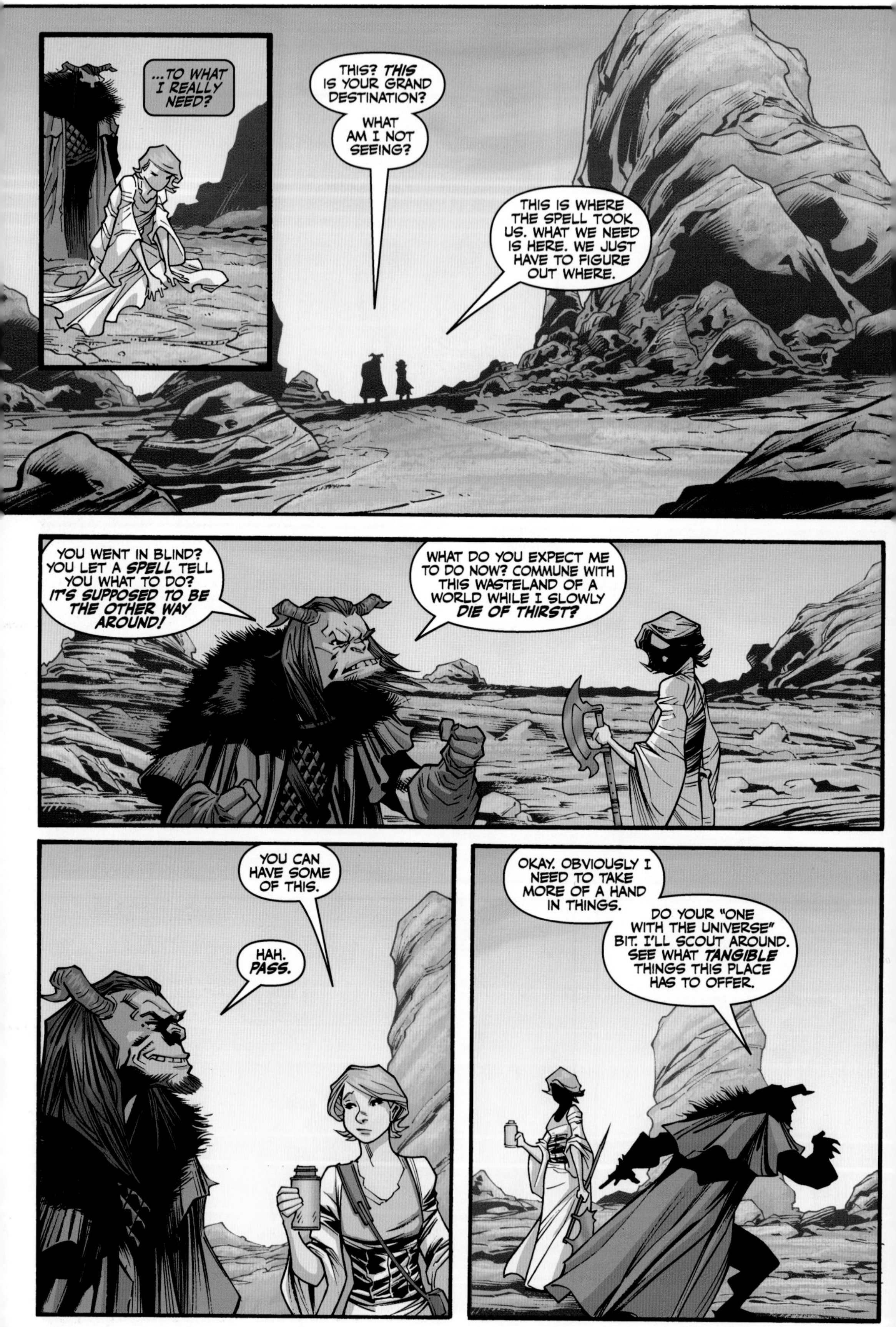

...TO WHAT I REALLY NEED?
THIS? *THIS* IS YOUR GRAND DESTINATION?
WHAT AM I NOT SEEING?
THIS IS WHERE THE SPELL TOOK US. WHAT WE NEED IS HERE. WE JUST HAVE TO FIGURE OUT WHERE.
YOU WENT IN BLIND? YOU LET A *SPELL* TELL YOU WHAT TO DO? *IT'S SUPPOSED TO BE THE OTHER WAY AROUND!*
WHAT DO YOU EXPECT ME TO DO NOW? COMMUNE WITH THIS WASTELAND OF A WORLD WHILE I SLOWLY *DIE OF THIRST?*
YOU CAN HAVE SOME OF THIS.
HAH. *PASS.*
OKAY. OBVIOUSLY I NEED TO TAKE MORE OF A HAND IN THINGS.
DO YOUR "ONE WITH THE UNIVERSE" BIT. I'LL SCOUT AROUND. SEE WHAT *TANGIBLE* THINGS THIS PLACE HAS TO OFFER.

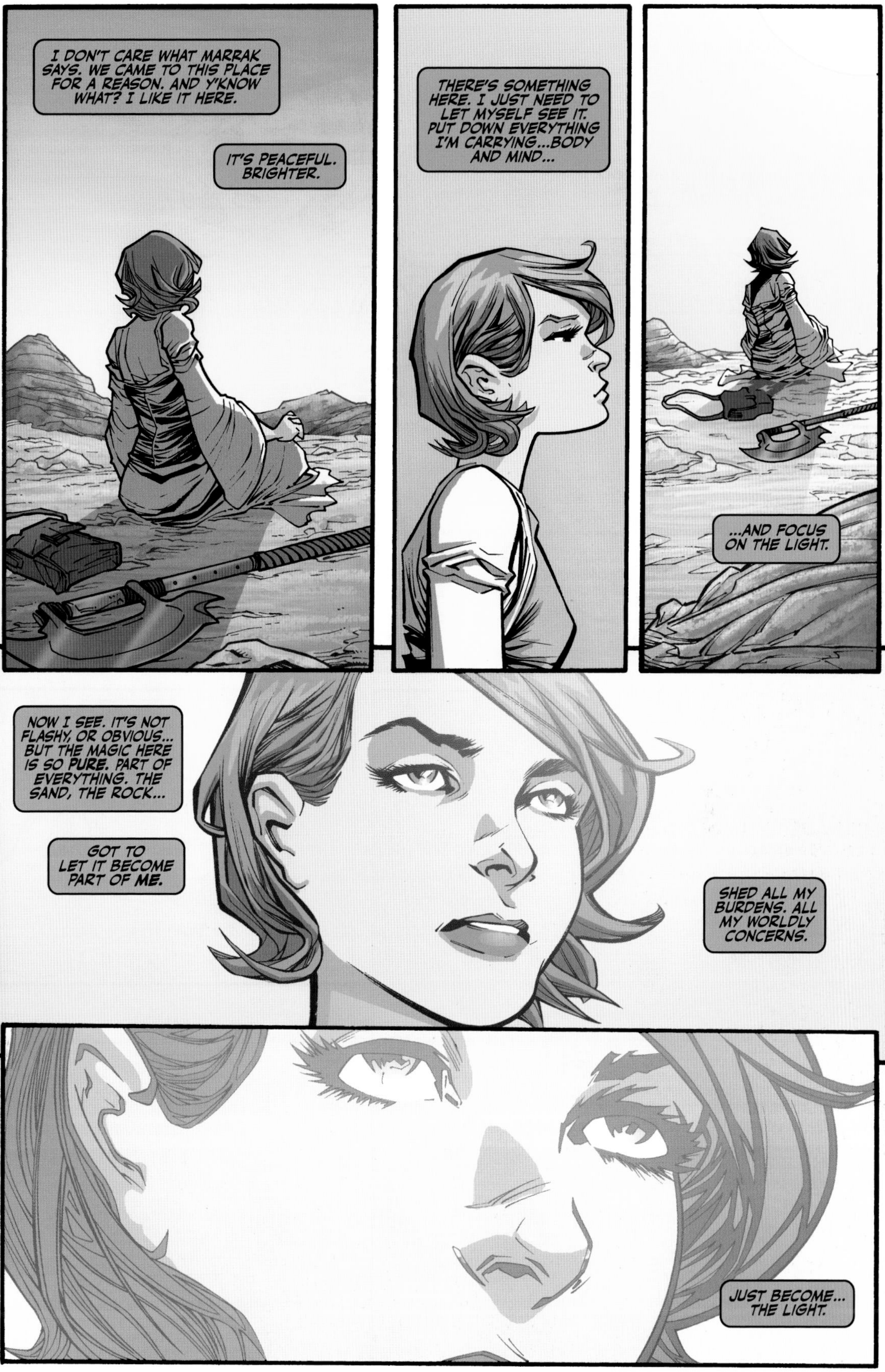
I DON'T CARE WHAT MARRAK SAYS. WE CAME TO THIS PLACE FOR A REASON. AND Y'KNOW WHAT? I LIKE IT HERE.
IT'S PEACEFUL. BRIGHTER.
THERE'S SOMETHING HERE. I JUST NEED TO LET MYSELF SEE IT. PUT DOWN EVERYTHING I'M CARRYING...BODY AND MIND...
...AND FOCUS ON THE LIGHT.
NOW I SEE. IT'S NOT FLASHY, OR OBVIOUS... BUT THE MAGIC HERE IS SO **PURE**. PART OF EVERYTHING. THE SAND, THE ROCK...
GOT TO LET IT BECOME PART OF **ME**.
SHED ALL MY BURDENS. ALL MY WORLDLY CONCERNS.
JUST BECOME... THE LIGHT.

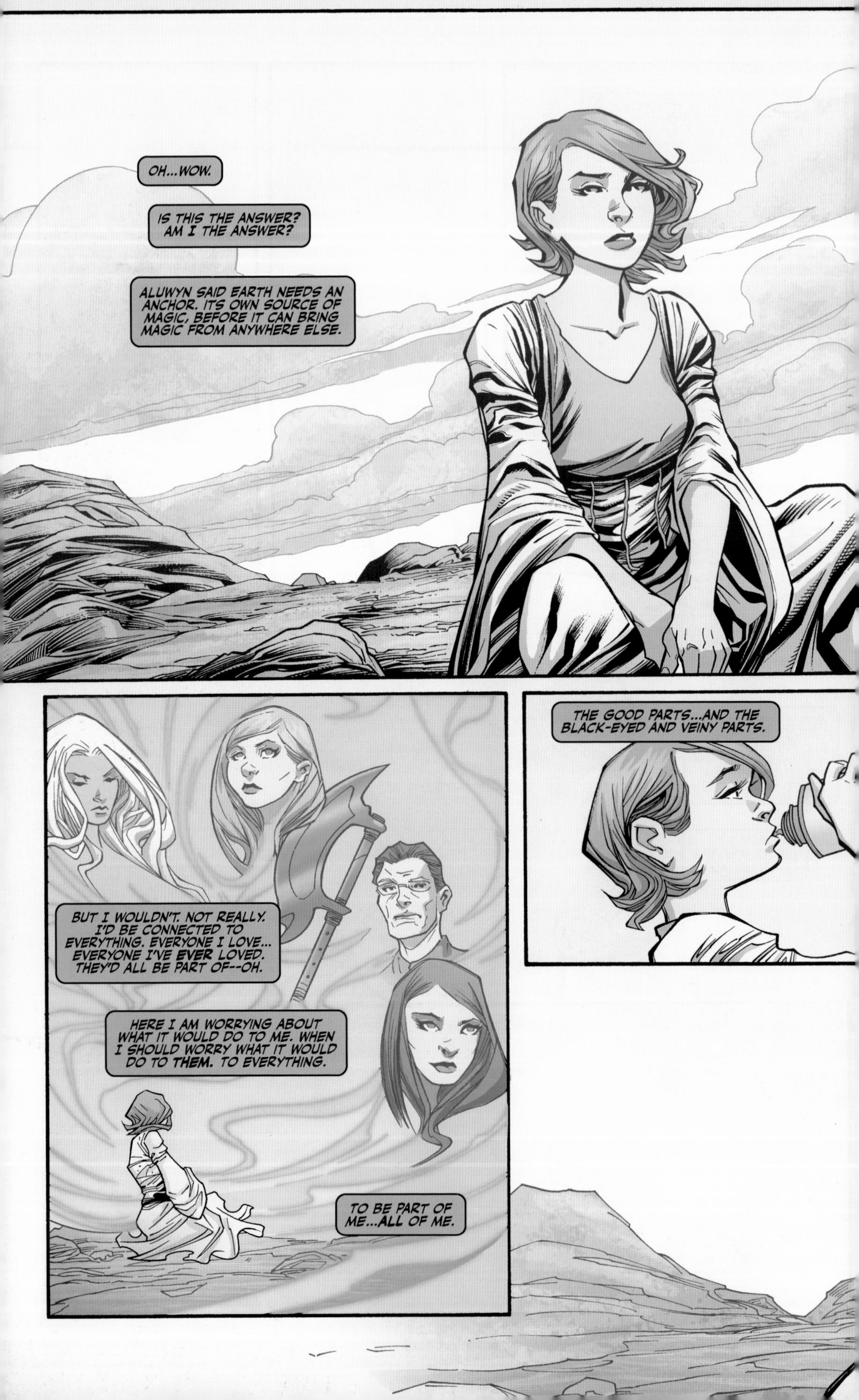
OH...WOW.
IS THIS THE ANSWER? AM I THE ANSWER?
ALUWYN SAID EARTH NEEDS AN ANCHOR. ITS OWN SOURCE OF MAGIC, BEFORE IT CAN BRING MAGIC FROM ANYWHERE ELSE.
BUT I WOULDN'T. NOT REALLY. I'D BE CONNECTED TO EVERYTHING. EVERYONE I LOVE... EVERYONE I'VE EVER LOVED. THEY'D ALL BE PART OF--OH.
HERE I AM WORRYING ABOUT WHAT IT WOULD DO TO ME. WHEN I SHOULD WORRY WHAT IT WOULD DO TO THEM. TO EVERYTHING.
TO BE PART OF ME...ALL OF ME.
THE GOOD PARTS...AND THE BLACK-EYED AND VEINY PARTS.

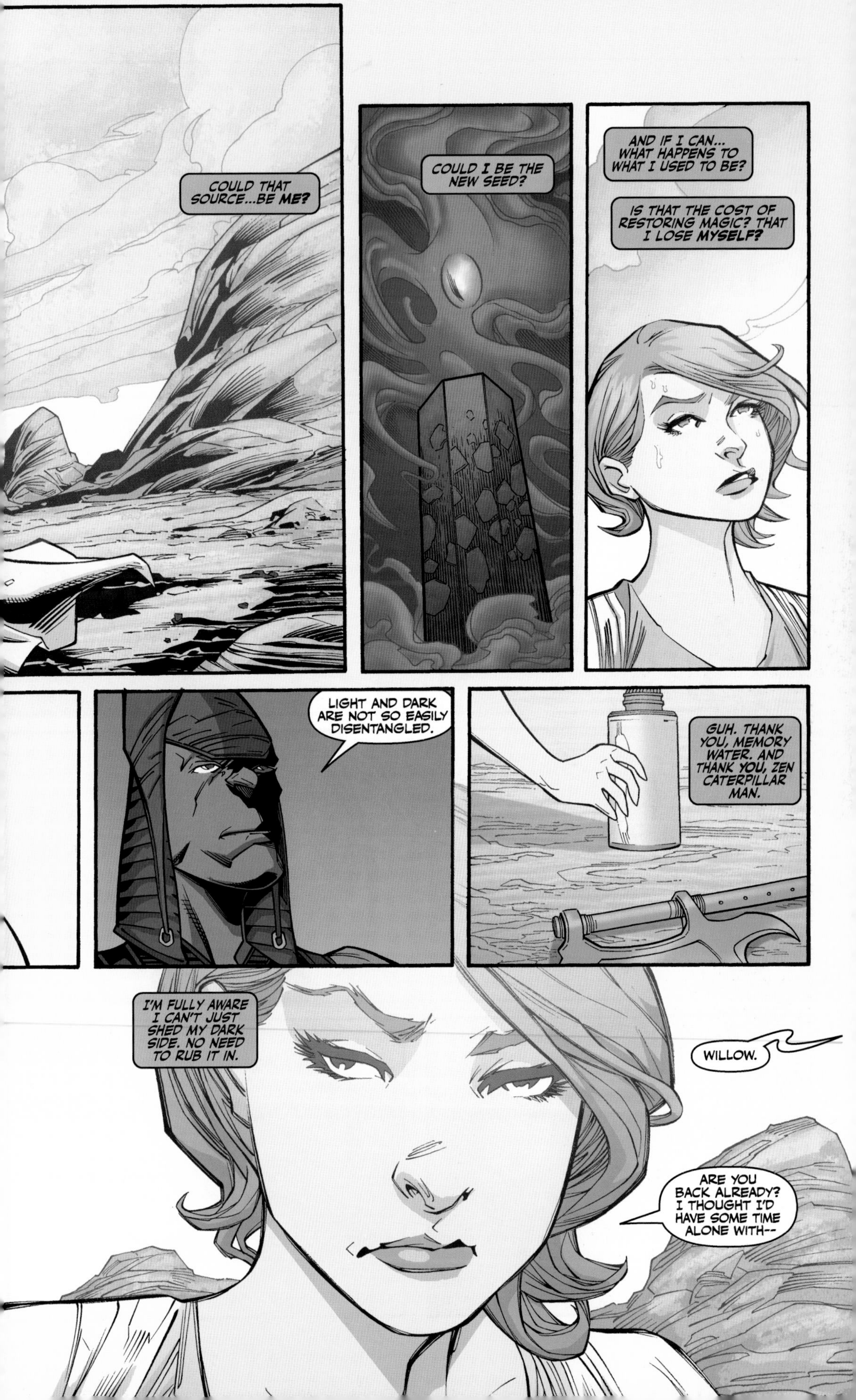

COULD THAT SOURCE...BE ME?
COULD I BE THE NEW SEED?
AND IF I CAN... WHAT HAPPENS TO WHAT I USED TO BE?
IS THAT THE COST OF RESTORING MAGIC? THAT I LOSE MYSELF?
LIGHT AND DARK ARE NOT SO EASILY DISENTANGLED.
GUH. THANK YOU, MEMORY WATER. AND THANK YOU, ZEN CATERPILLAR MAN.
I'M FULLY AWARE I CAN'T JUST SHED MY DARK SIDE. NO NEED TO RUB IT IN.
WILLOW.
ARE YOU BACK ALREADY? I THOUGHT I'D HAVE SOME TIME ALONE WITH--

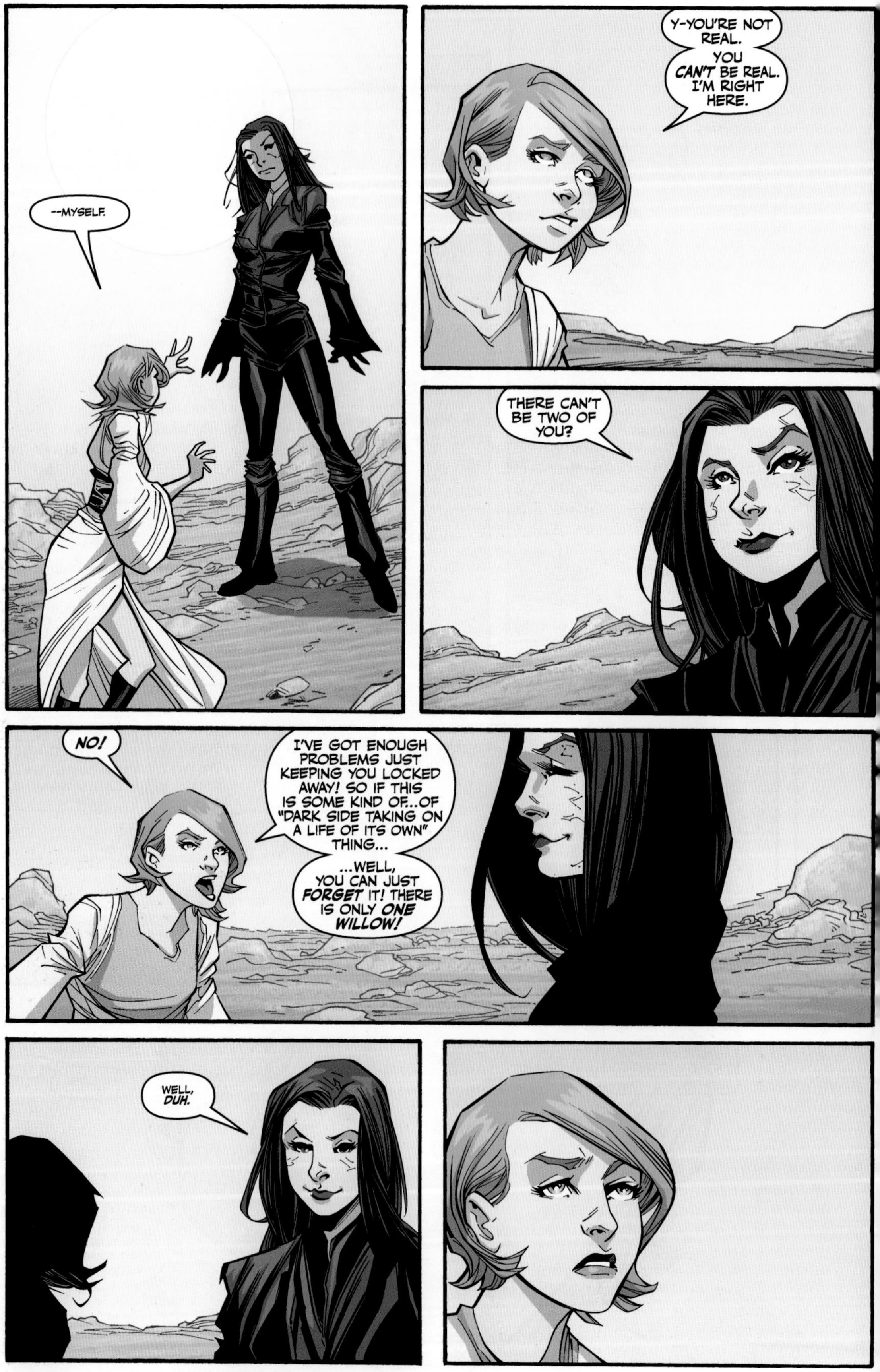

--MYSELF.
Y-YOU'RE NOT REAL.
YOU CAN'T BE REAL. I'M RIGHT HERE.
THERE CAN'T BE TWO OF YOU?
NO!
I'VE GOT ENOUGH PROBLEMS JUST KEEPING YOU LOCKED AWAY! SO IF THIS IS SOME KIND OF...OF "DARK SIDE TAKING ON A LIFE OF ITS OWN" THING...
...WELL, YOU CAN JUST FORGET IT! THERE IS ONLY ONE WILLOW!
WELL, DUH.

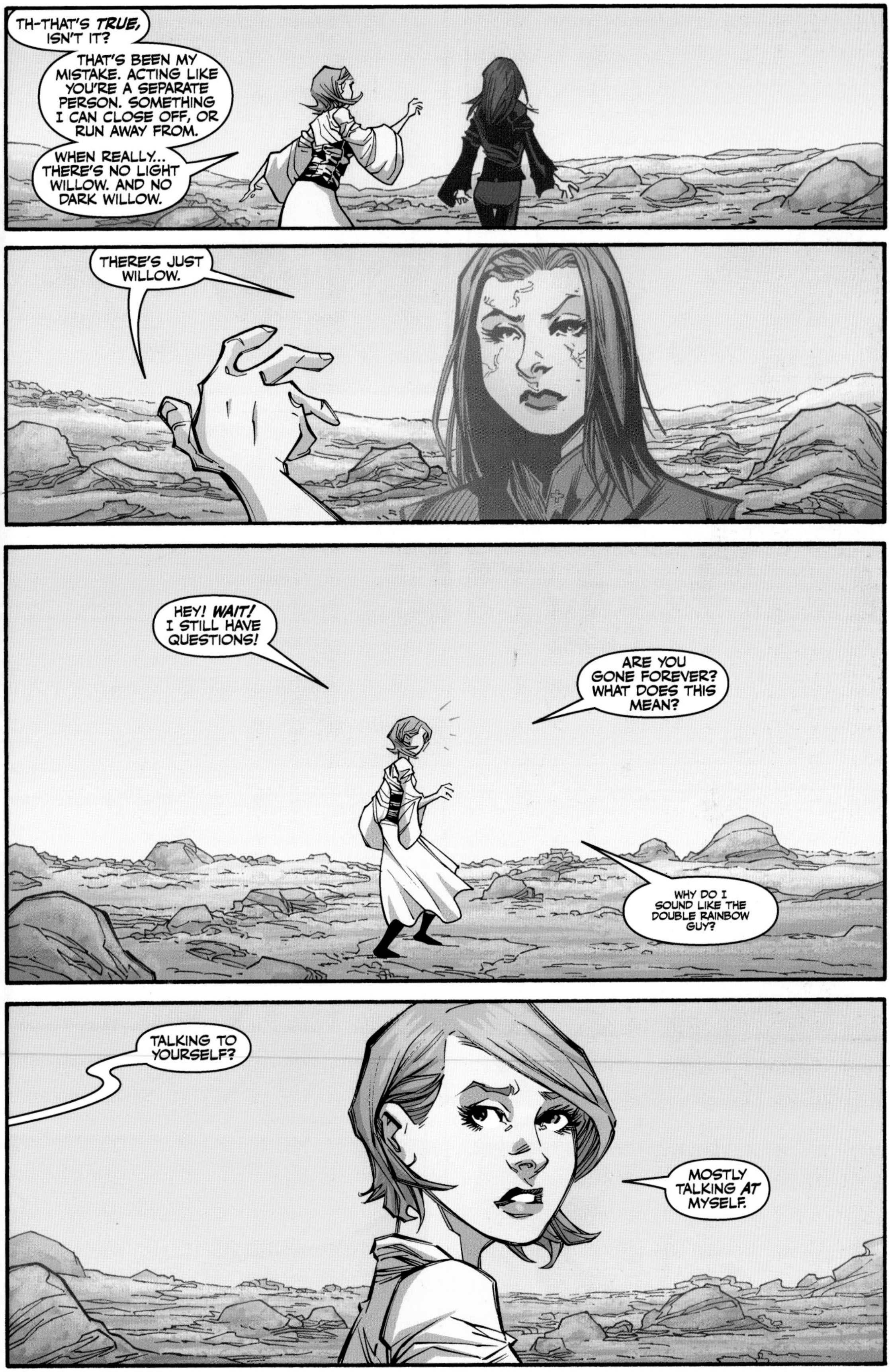
TH-THAT'S TRUE, ISN'T IT?
THAT'S BEEN MY MISTAKE. ACTING LIKE YOU'RE A SEPARATE PERSON. SOMETHING I CAN CLOSE OFF, OR RUN AWAY FROM.
WHEN REALLY... THERE'S NO LIGHT WILLOW. AND NO DARK WILLOW.
THERE'S JUST WILLOW.
HEY! WAIT! I STILL HAVE QUESTIONS!
ARE YOU GONE FOREVER? WHAT DOES THIS MEAN?
WHY DO I SOUND LIKE THE DOUBLE RAINBOW GUY?
TALKING TO YOURSELF?
MOSTLY TALKING AT MYSELF.

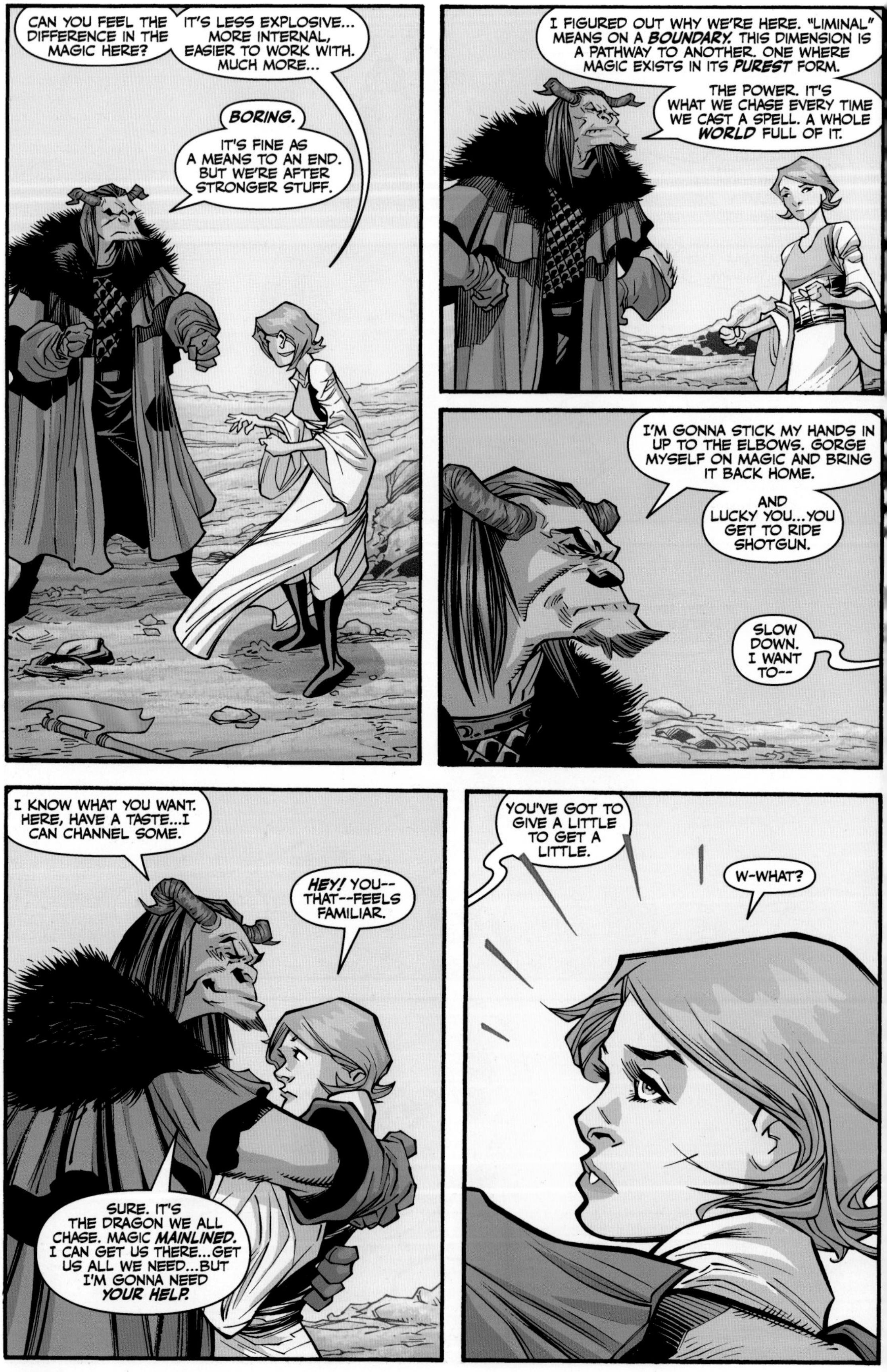

CAN YOU FEEL THE DIFFERENCE IN THE MAGIC HERE?
IT'S LESS EXPLOSIVE... MORE INTERNAL, EASIER TO WORK WITH. MUCH MORE...
BORING.
IT'S FINE AS A MEANS TO AN END. BUT WE'RE AFTER STRONGER STUFF.
I FIGURED OUT WHY WE'RE HERE. "LIMINAL" MEANS ON A BOUNDARY. THIS DIMENSION IS A PATHWAY TO ANOTHER. ONE WHERE MAGIC EXISTS IN ITS PUREST FORM.
THE POWER. IT'S WHAT WE CHASE EVERY TIME WE CAST A SPELL. A WHOLE WORLD FULL OF IT.
I'M GONNA STICK MY HANDS IN UP TO THE ELBOWS. GORGE MYSELF ON MAGIC AND BRING IT BACK HOME.
AND LUCKY YOU...YOU GET TO RIDE SHOTGUN.
SLOW DOWN. I WANT TO--
I KNOW WHAT YOU WANT. HERE, HAVE A TASTE...I CAN CHANNEL SOME.
HEY! YOU-- THAT--FEELS FAMILIAR.
SURE. IT'S THE DRAGON WE ALL CHASE. MAGIC MAINLINED. I CAN GET US THERE...GET US ALL WE NEED...BUT I'M GONNA NEED YOUR HELP.
YOU'VE GOT TO GIVE A LITTLE TO GET A LITTLE.
W-WHAT?

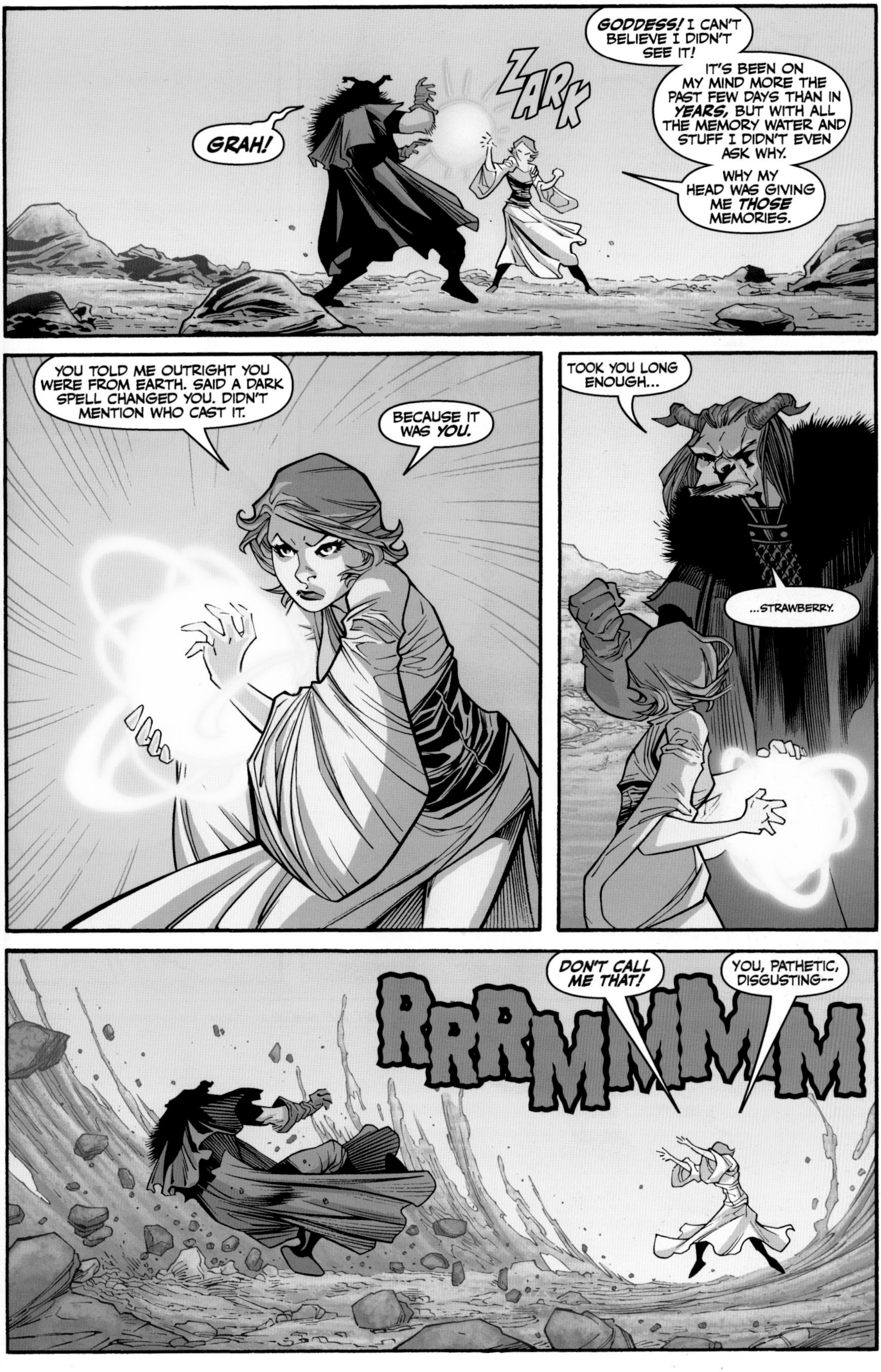
GODDESS! I CAN'T BELIEVE I DIDN'T SEE IT!
ZARK
GRAH!
IT'S BEEN ON MY MIND MORE THE PAST FEW DAYS THAN IN YEARS, BUT WITH ALL THE MEMORY WATER AND STUFF I DIDN'T EVEN ASK WHY.
WHY MY HEAD WAS GIVING ME THOSE MEMORIES.
YOU TOLD ME OUTRIGHT YOU WERE FROM EARTH. SAID A DARK SPELL CHANGED YOU. DIDN'T MENTION WHO CAST IT.
BECAUSE IT WAS YOU.
TOOK YOU LONG ENOUGH...
...STRAWBERRY.
RRRMMMMM
DON'T CALL ME THAT!
YOU, PATHETIC, DISGUSTING--

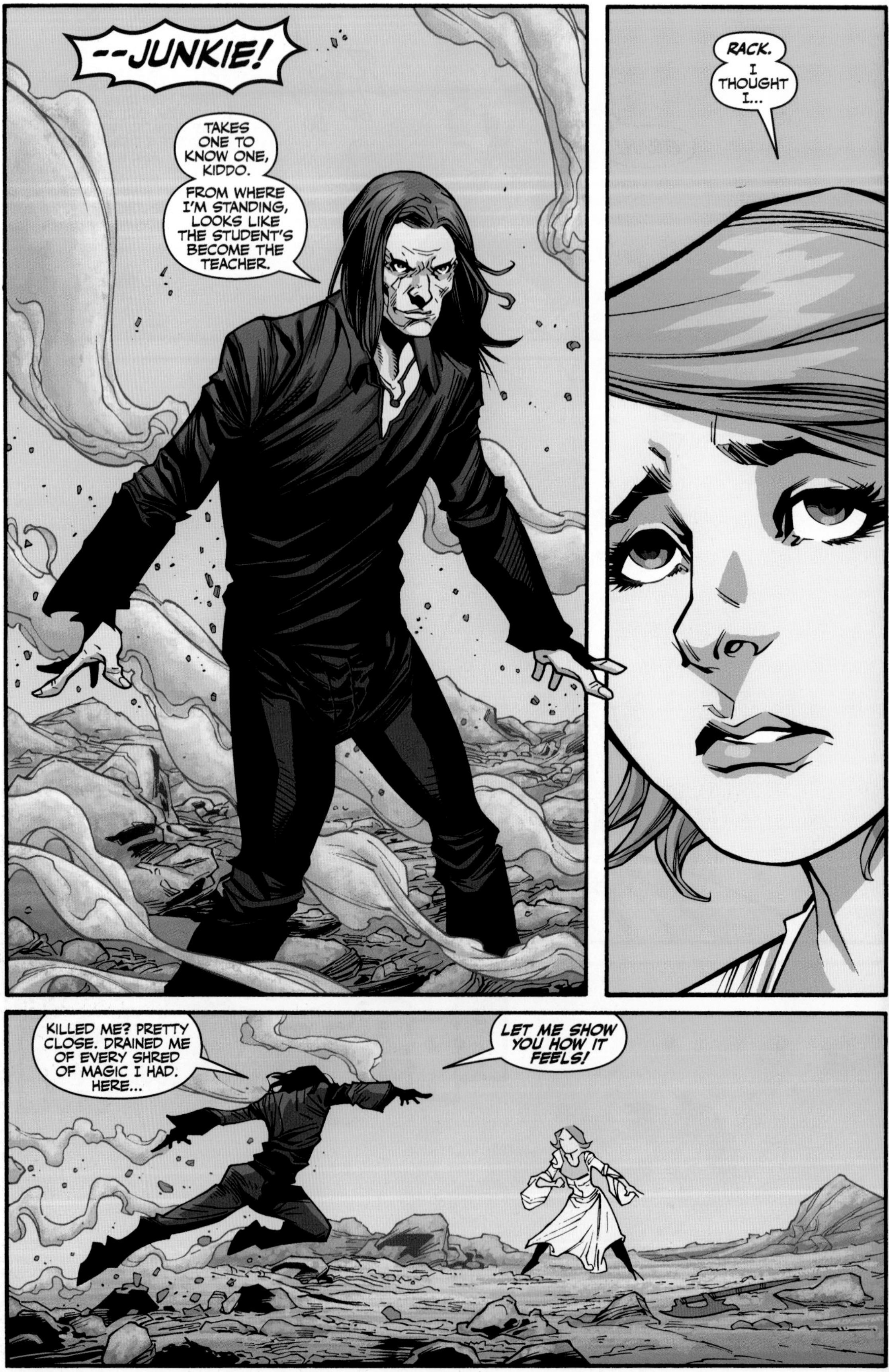
--JUNKIE!
TAKES ONE TO KNOW ONE, KIDDO.
FROM WHERE I'M STANDING, LOOKS LIKE THE STUDENT'S BECOME THE TEACHER.
RACK. I THOUGHT I...
KILLED ME? PRETTY CLOSE. DRAINED ME OF EVERY SHRED OF MAGIC I HAD. HERE...
LET ME SHOW YOU HOW IT FEELS!

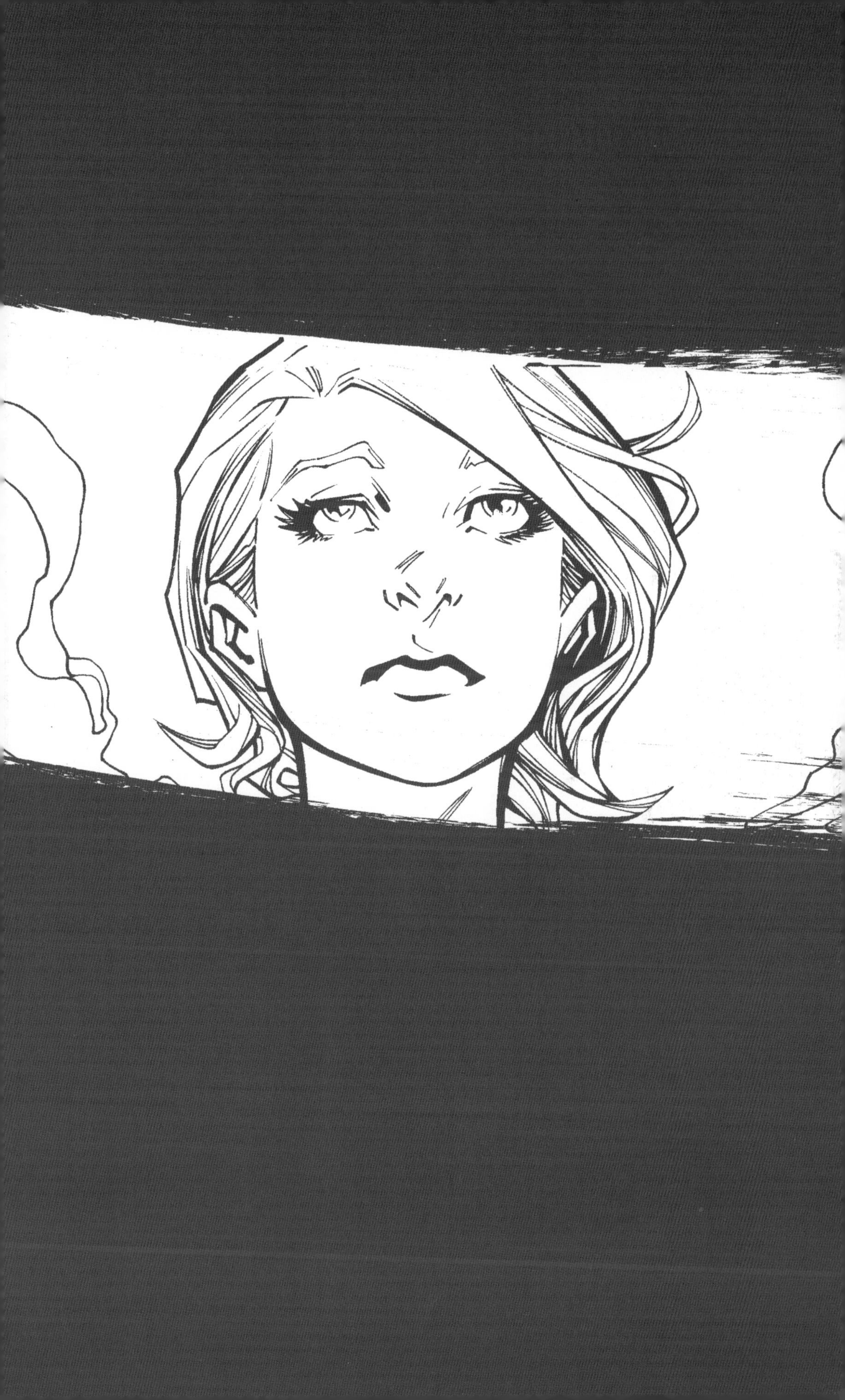

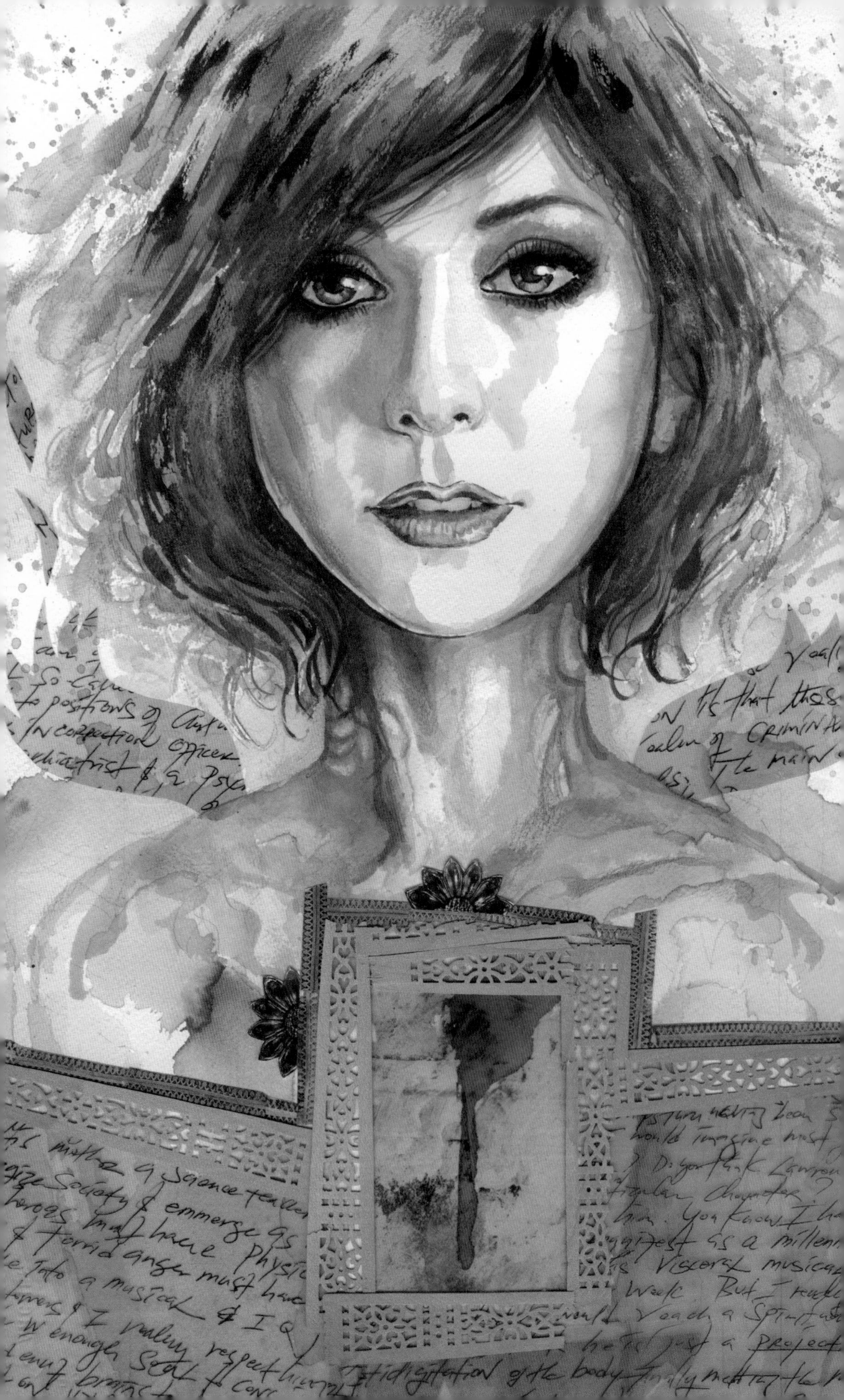

in correction officer
realm of CRIMINA
would imagine must
You know I
as a millenn
visceral musical
just a project

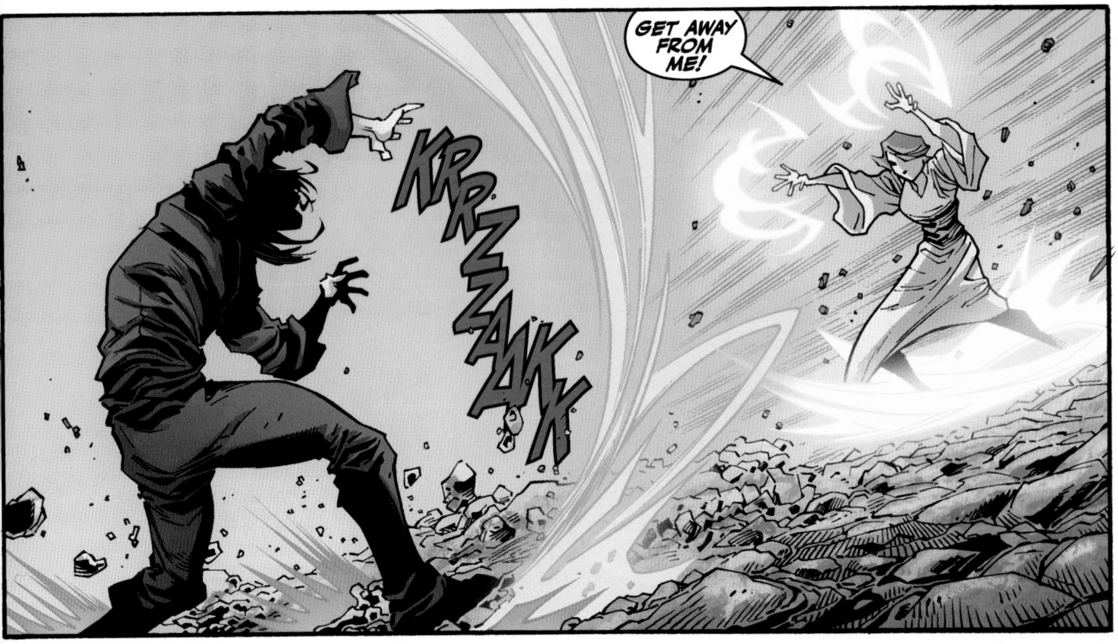
GET AWAY FROM ME!
KRRZZAKK

WONDERLAND
PART FIVE

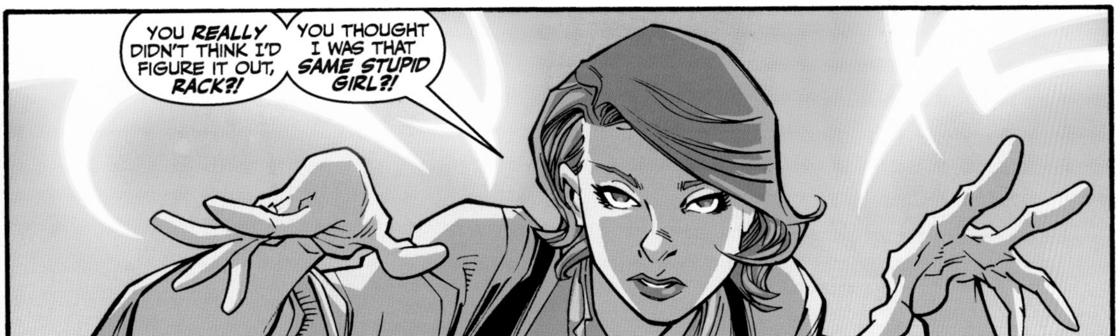
YOU REALLY DIDN'T THINK I'D FIGURE IT OUT, RACK?!
YOU THOUGHT I WAS THAT SAME STUPID GIRL?!

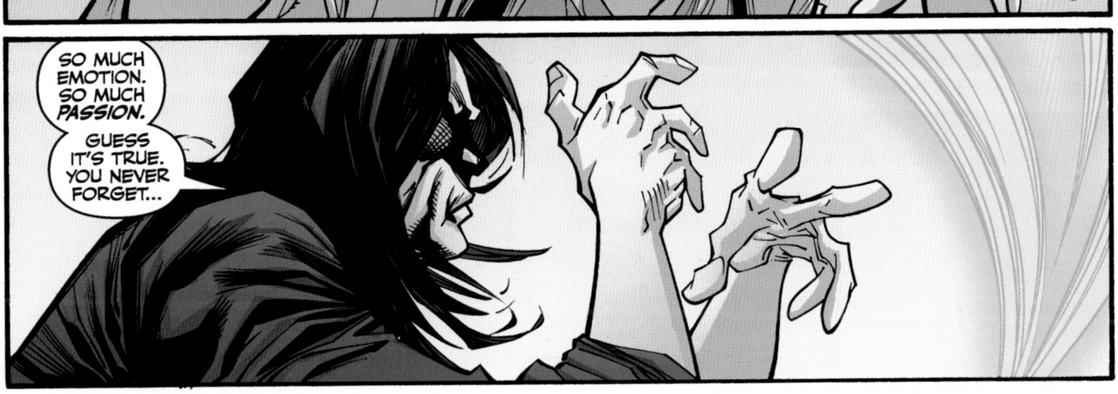
SO MUCH EMOTION. SO MUCH PASSION.
GUESS IT'S TRUE. YOU NEVER FORGET...

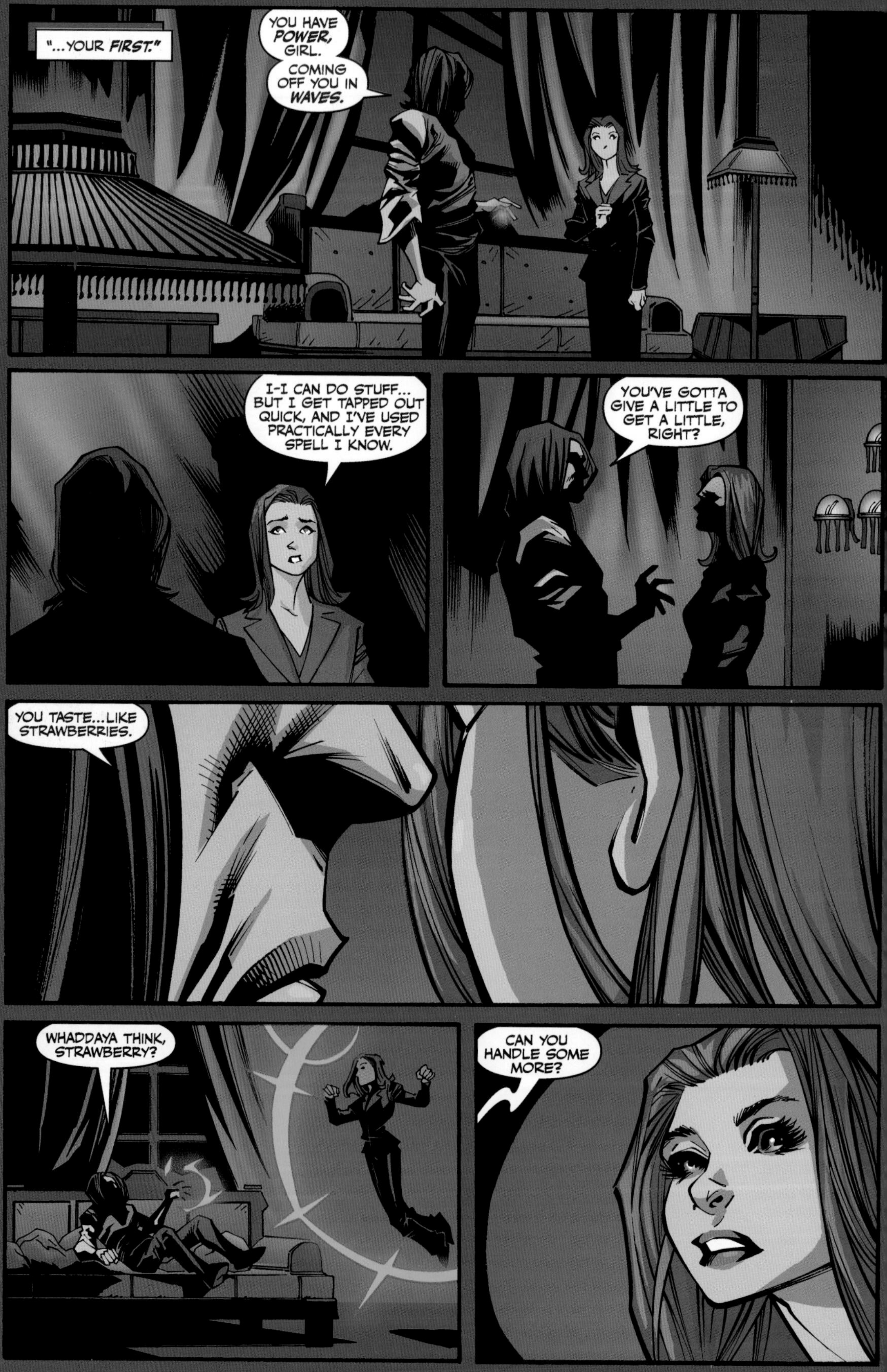
"...YOUR FIRST."
YOU HAVE POWER, GIRL.
COMING OFF YOU IN WAVES.
I-I CAN DO STUFF... BUT I GET TAPPED OUT QUICK, AND I'VE USED PRACTICALLY EVERY SPELL I KNOW.
YOU'VE GOTTA GIVE A LITTLE TO GET A LITTLE, RIGHT?
YOU TASTE...LIKE STRAWBERRIES.
WHADDAYA THINK, STRAWBERRY?
CAN YOU HANDLE SOME MORE?

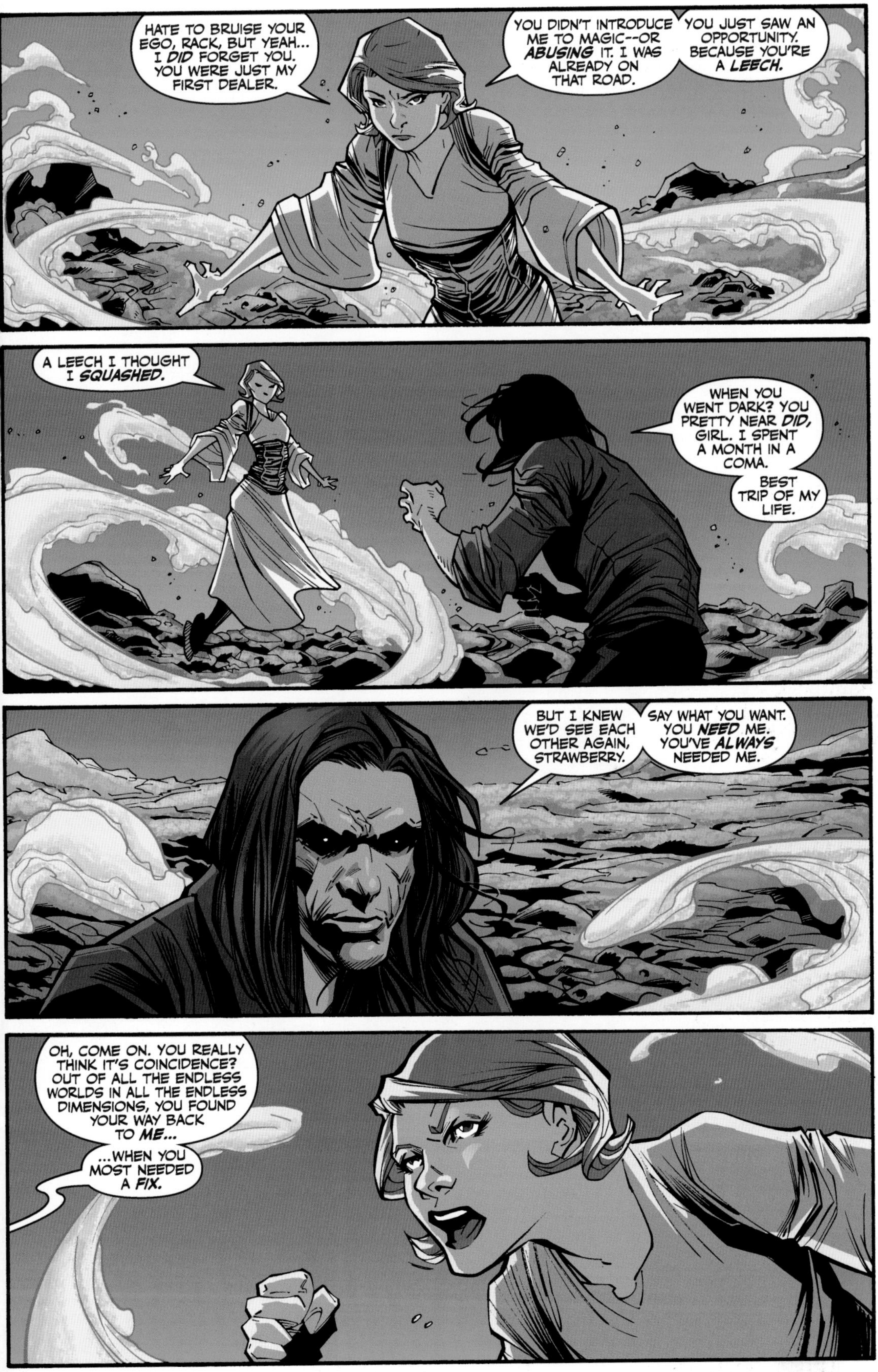
HATE TO BRUISE YOUR EGO, RACK, BUT YEAH... I DID FORGET YOU. YOU WERE JUST MY FIRST DEALER.
YOU DIDN'T INTRODUCE ME TO MAGIC--OR ABUSING IT. I WAS ALREADY ON THAT ROAD.
YOU JUST SAW AN OPPORTUNITY. BECAUSE YOU'RE A LEECH.
A LEECH I THOUGHT I SQUASHED.
WHEN YOU WENT DARK? YOU PRETTY NEAR DID, GIRL. I SPENT A MONTH IN A COMA.
BEST TRIP OF MY LIFE.
BUT I KNEW WE'D SEE EACH OTHER AGAIN, STRAWBERRY.
SAY WHAT YOU WANT. YOU NEED ME. YOU'VE ALWAYS NEEDED ME.
OH, COME ON. YOU REALLY THINK IT'S COINCIDENCE? OUT OF ALL THE ENDLESS WORLDS IN ALL THE ENDLESS DIMENSIONS, YOU FOUND YOUR WAY BACK TO ME...
...WHEN YOU MOST NEEDED A FIX.

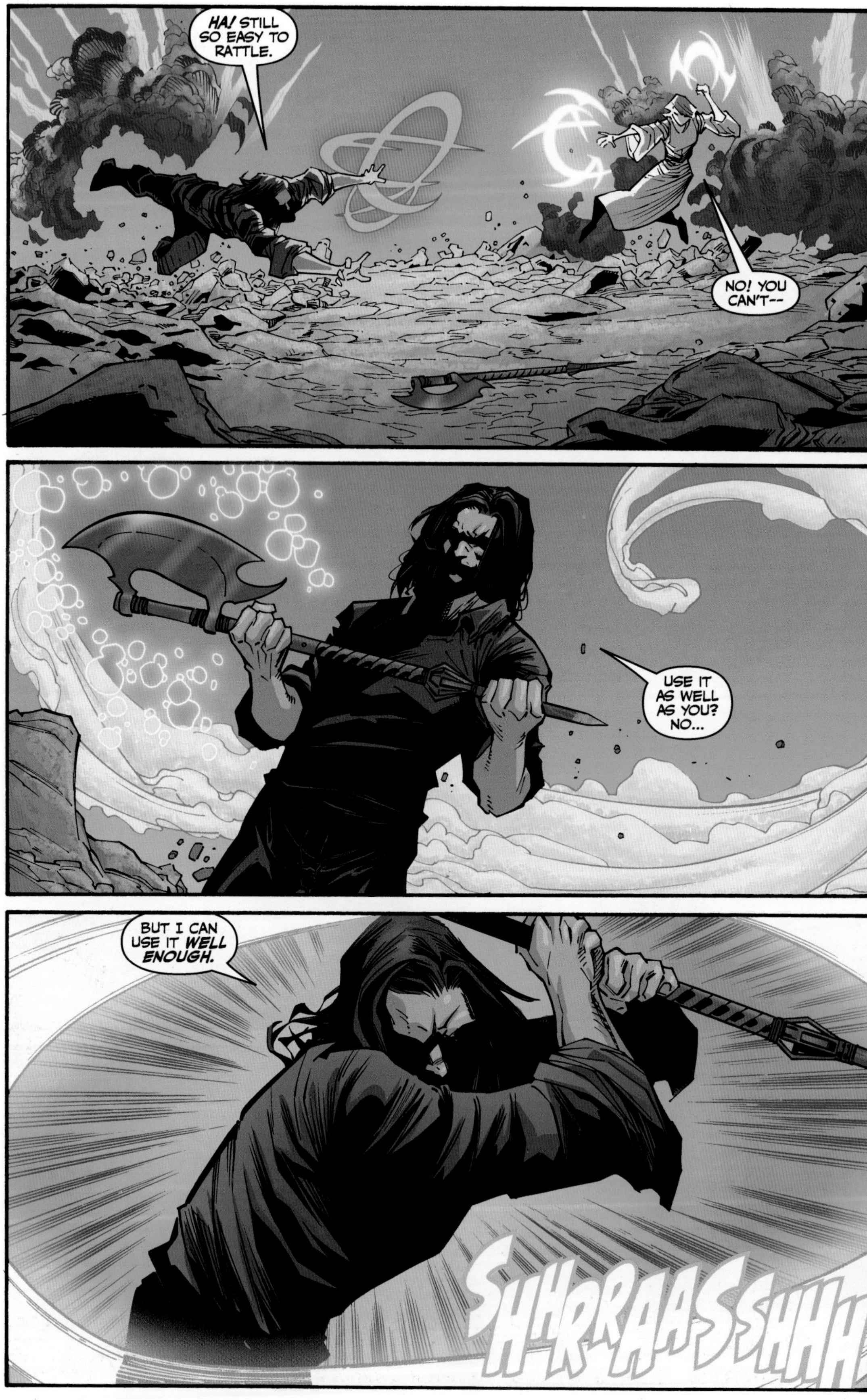

HA! STILL SO EASY TO RATTLE.
NO! YOU CAN'T--
USE IT AS WELL AS YOU? NO...
BUT I CAN USE IT WELL ENOUGH.
SHHRAASSHHH

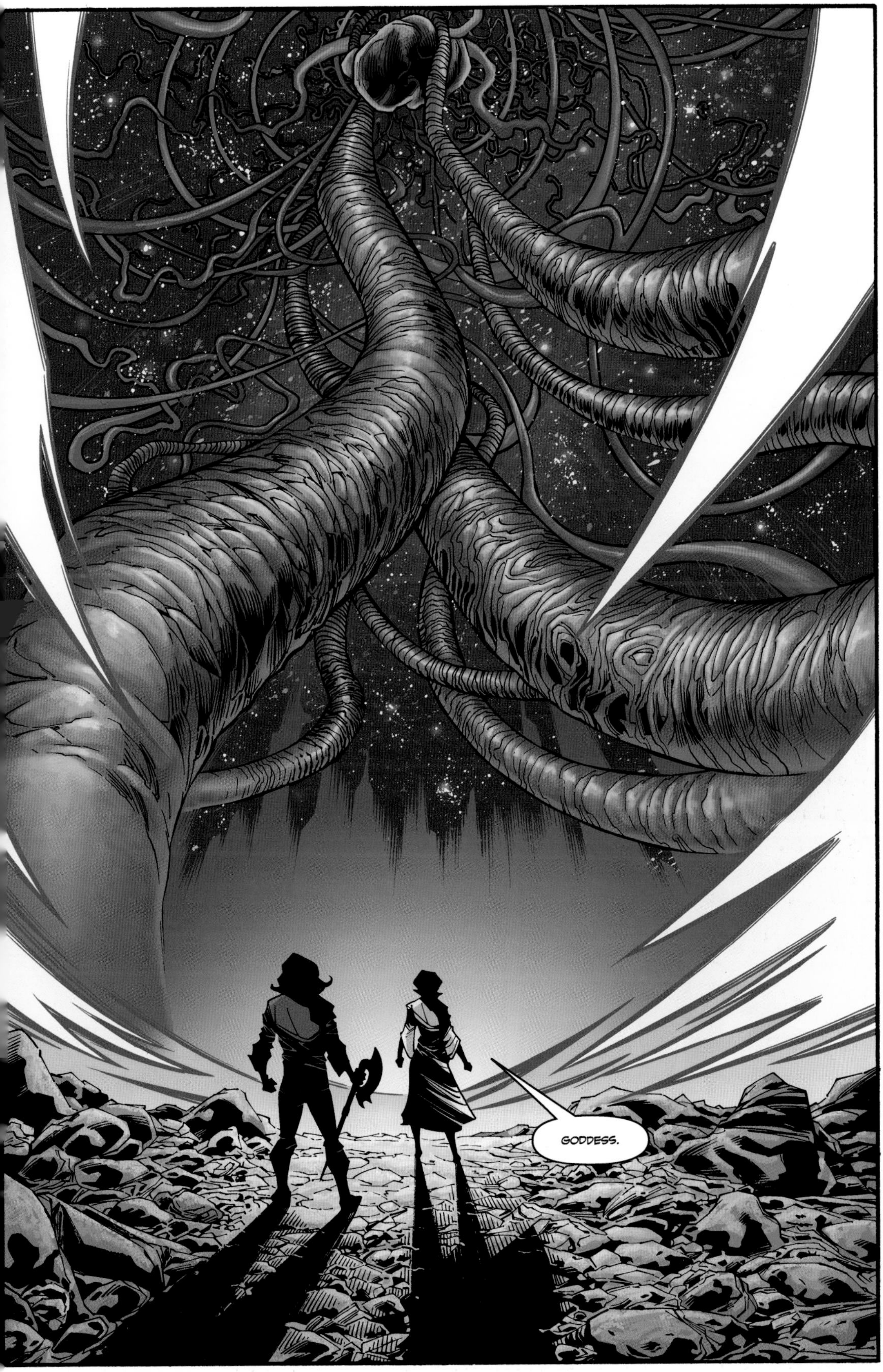
GODDESS.

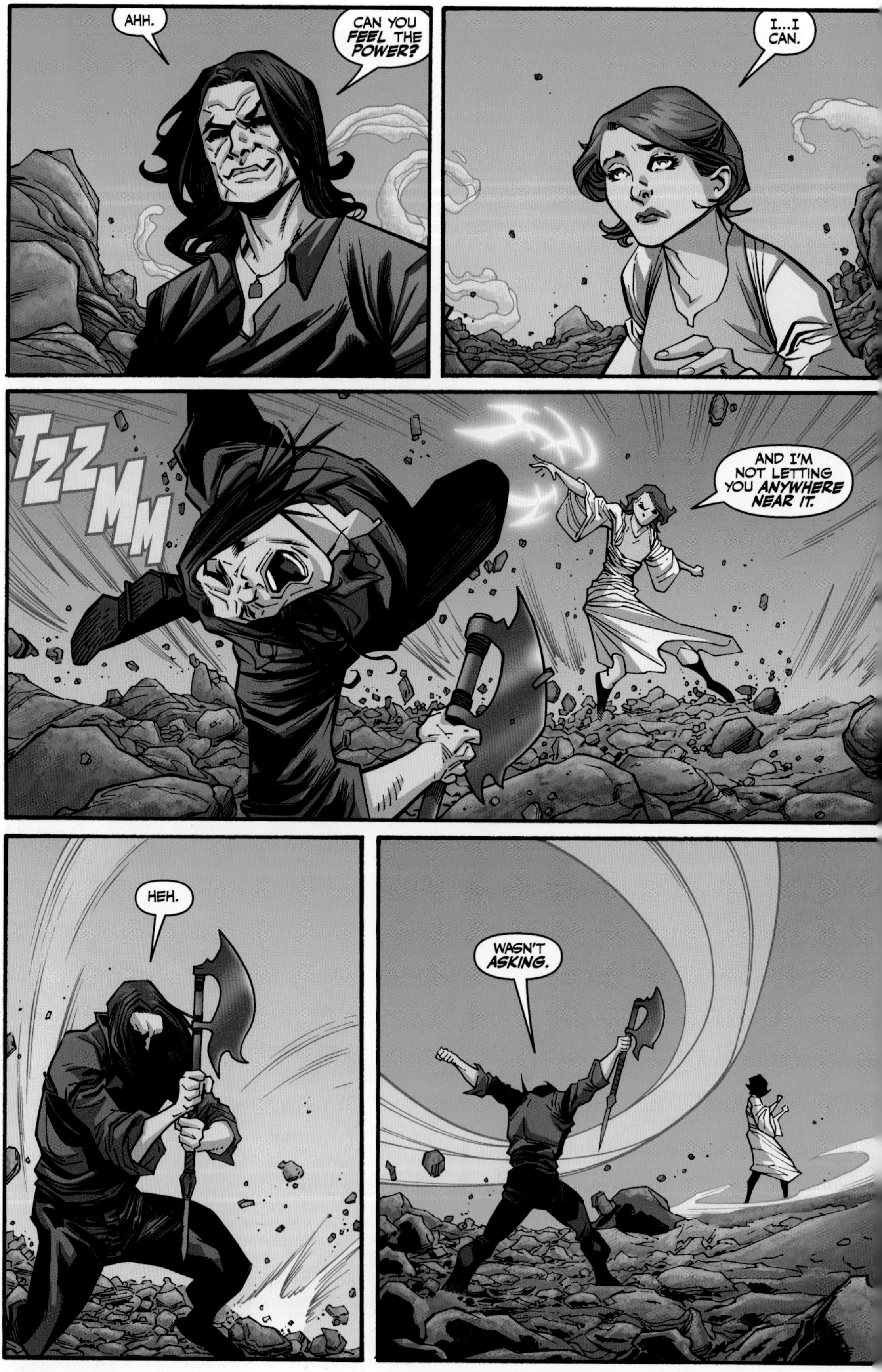
AHH.
CAN YOU FEEL THE POWER?
I...I CAN.
TZZMM
AND I'M NOT LETTING YOU ANYWHERE NEAR IT.
HEH.
WASN'T ASKING.

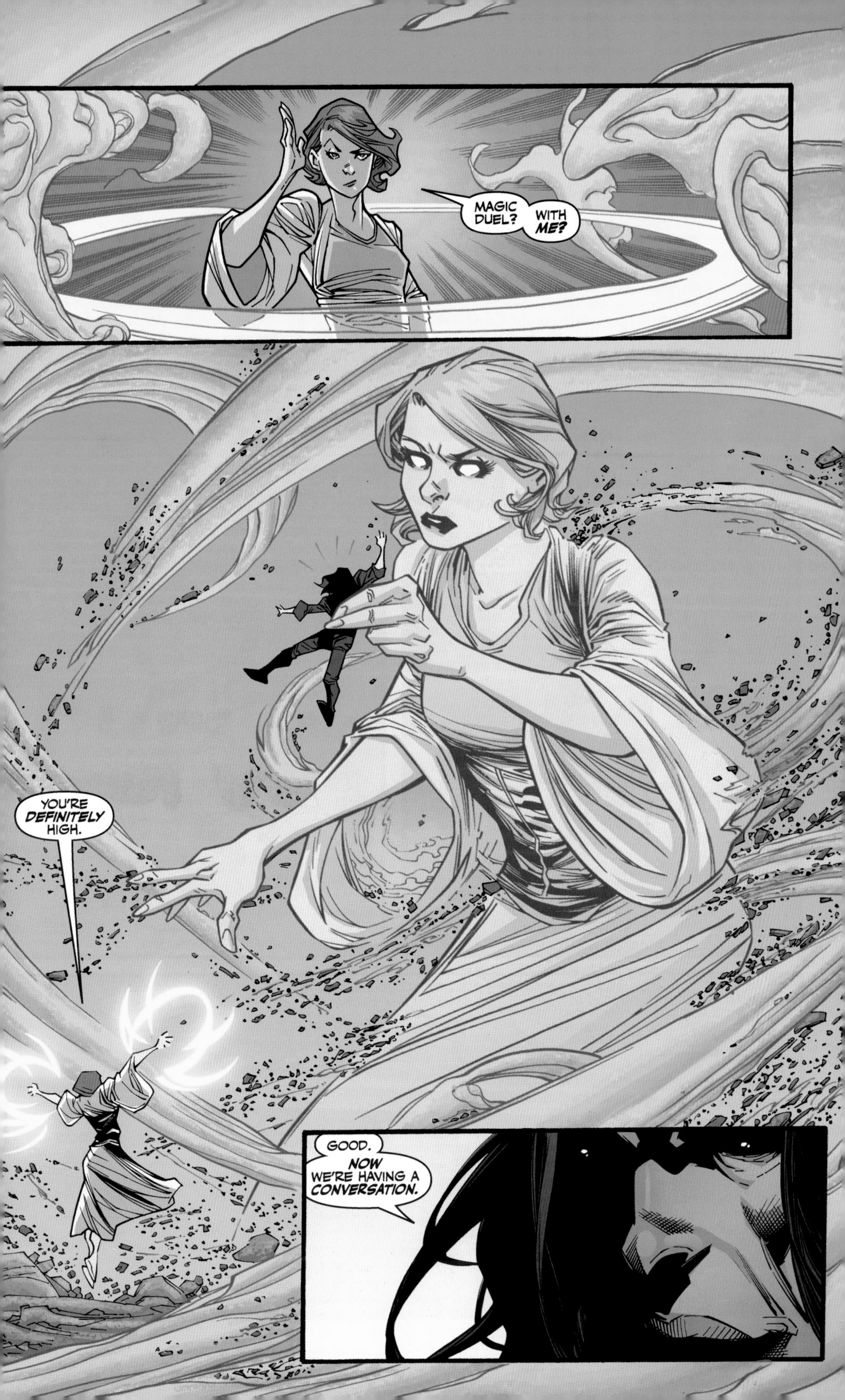
MAGIC DUEL?
WITH ME?
YOU'RE DEFINITELY HIGH.
GOOD.
NOW WE'RE HAVING A CONVERSATION.

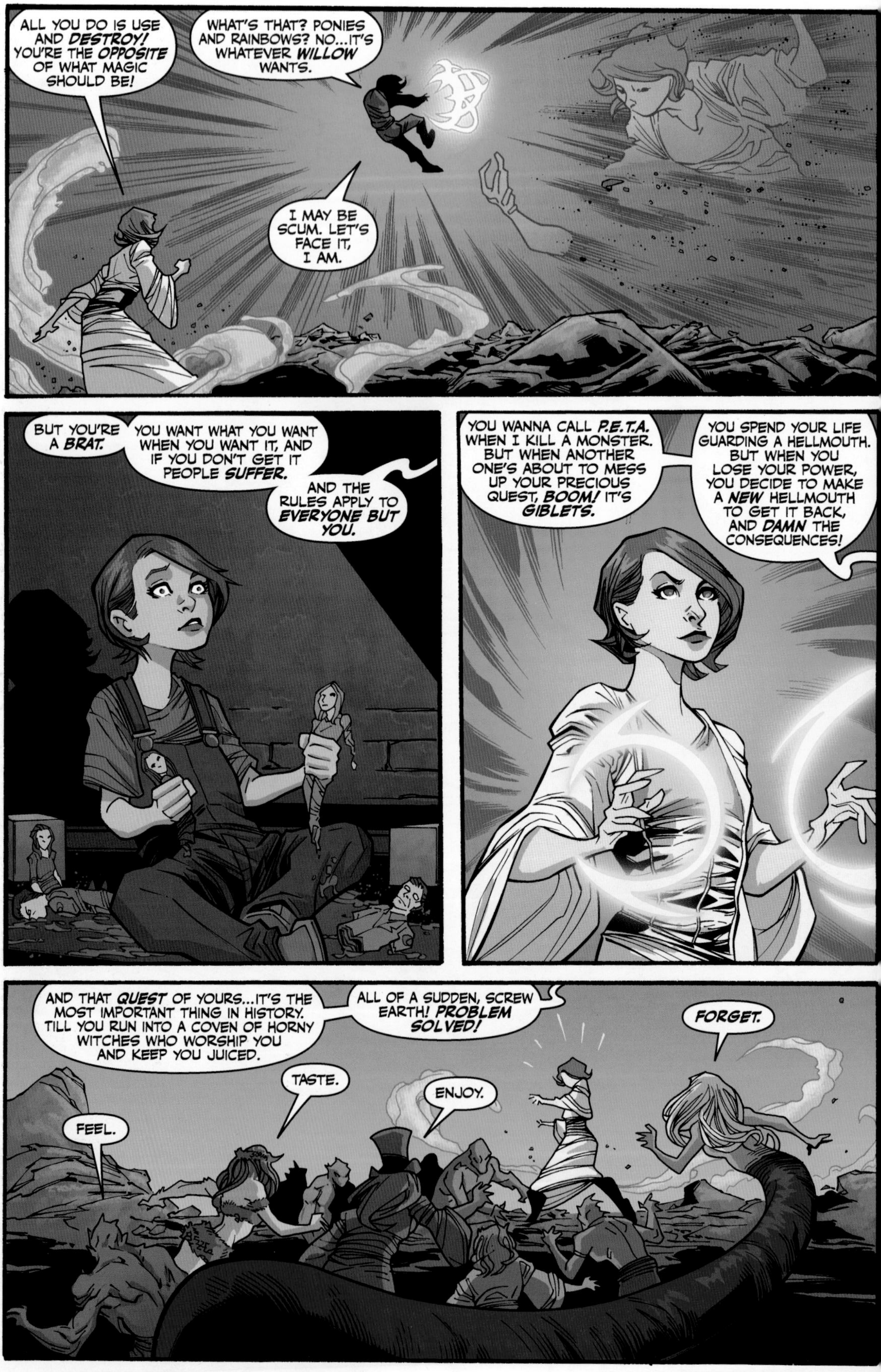
ALL YOU DO IS USE AND DESTROY! YOU'RE THE OPPOSITE OF WHAT MAGIC SHOULD BE!
WHAT'S THAT? PONIES AND RAINBOWS? NO...IT'S WHATEVER WILLOW WANTS.
I MAY BE SCUM. LET'S FACE IT, I AM.
BUT YOU'RE A BRAT.
YOU WANT WHAT YOU WANT WHEN YOU WANT IT, AND IF YOU DON'T GET IT PEOPLE SUFFER.
AND THE RULES APPLY TO EVERYONE BUT YOU.
YOU WANNA CALL P.E.T.A. WHEN I KILL A MONSTER. BUT WHEN ANOTHER ONE'S ABOUT TO MESS UP YOUR PRECIOUS QUEST, BOOM! IT'S GIBLETS.
YOU SPEND YOUR LIFE GUARDING A HELLMOUTH. BUT WHEN YOU LOSE YOUR POWER, YOU DECIDE TO MAKE A NEW HELLMOUTH TO GET IT BACK, AND DAMN THE CONSEQUENCES!
AND THAT QUEST OF YOURS...IT'S THE MOST IMPORTANT THING IN HISTORY. TILL YOU RUN INTO A COVEN OF HORNY WITCHES WHO WORSHIP YOU AND KEEP YOU JUICED.
ALL OF A SUDDEN, SCREW EARTH! PROBLEM SOLVED!
FORGET.
FEEL.
TASTE.
ENJOY.

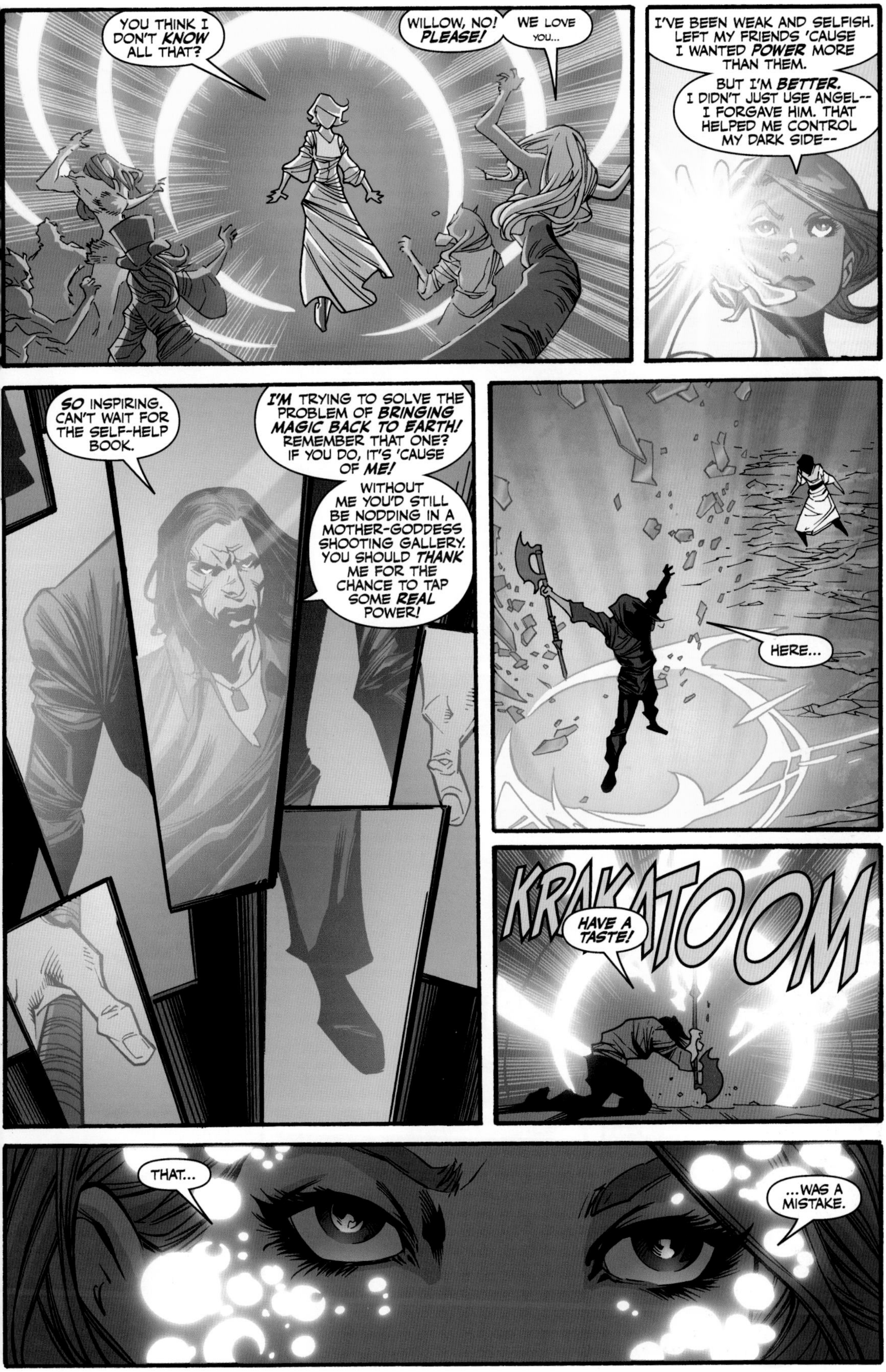

YOU THINK I DON'T KNOW ALL THAT?
WILLOW, NO! PLEASE!
WE LOVE YOU...
I'VE BEEN WEAK AND SELFISH. LEFT MY FRIENDS 'CAUSE I WANTED POWER MORE THAN THEM.
BUT I'M BETTER. I DIDN'T JUST USE ANGEL-- I FORGAVE HIM. THAT HELPED ME CONTROL MY DARK SIDE--
SO INSPIRING. CAN'T WAIT FOR THE SELF-HELP BOOK.
I'M TRYING TO SOLVE THE PROBLEM OF BRINGING MAGIC BACK TO EARTH! REMEMBER THAT ONE? IF YOU DO, IT'S 'CAUSE OF ME!
WITHOUT ME YOU'D STILL BE NODDING IN A MOTHER-GODDESS SHOOTING GALLERY. YOU SHOULD THANK ME FOR THE CHANCE TO TAP SOME REAL POWER!
HERE...
KRAKATOOM
HAVE A TASTE!
THAT...
...WAS A MISTAKE.

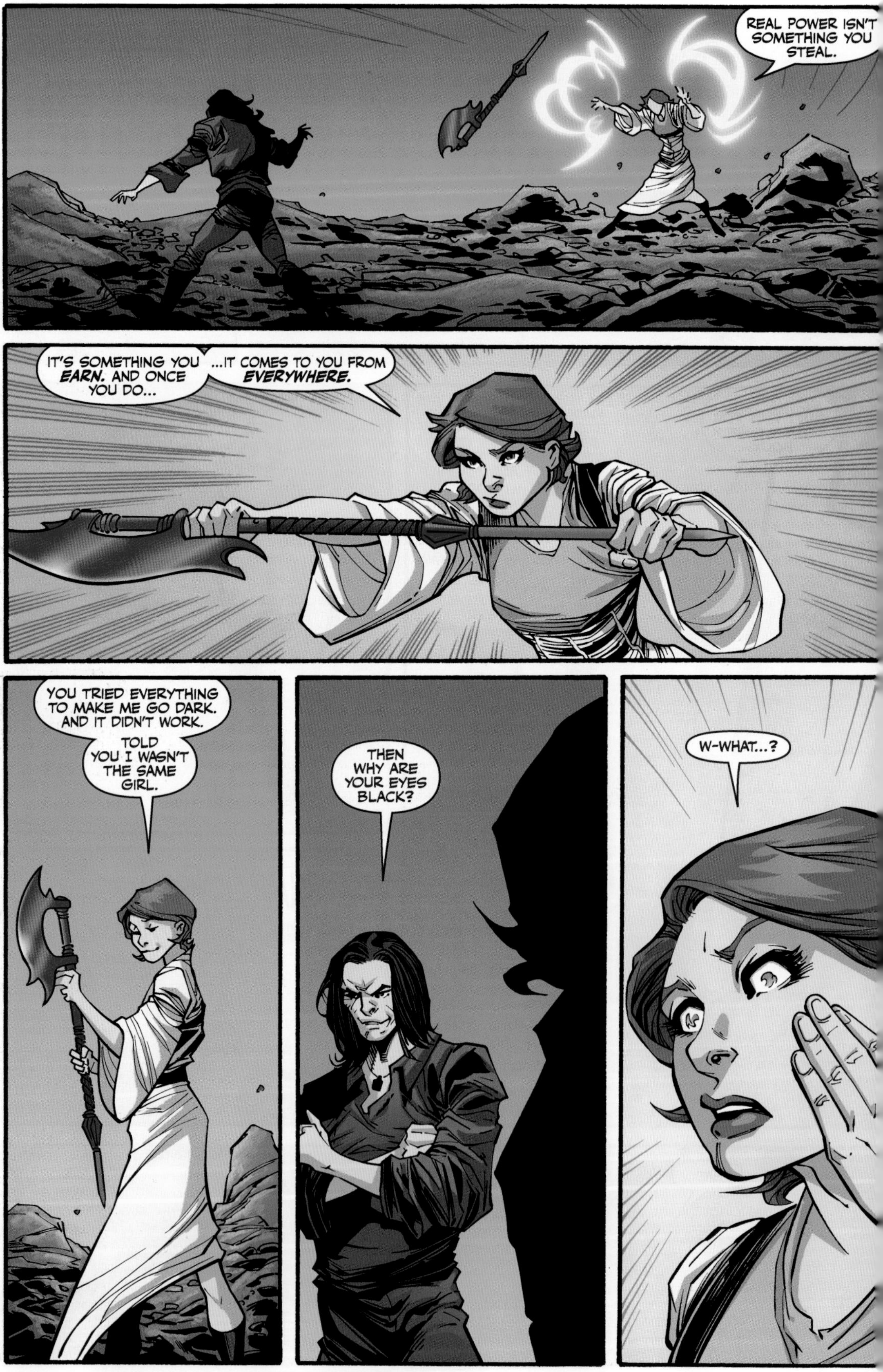
REAL POWER ISN'T SOMETHING YOU STEAL.
IT'S SOMETHING YOU **EARN.** AND ONCE YOU DO...
...IT COMES TO YOU FROM **EVERYWHERE.**
YOU TRIED EVERYTHING TO MAKE ME GO DARK. AND IT DIDN'T WORK.
TOLD YOU I WASN'T THE SAME GIRL.
THEN WHY ARE YOUR EYES BLACK?
W-WHAT...?

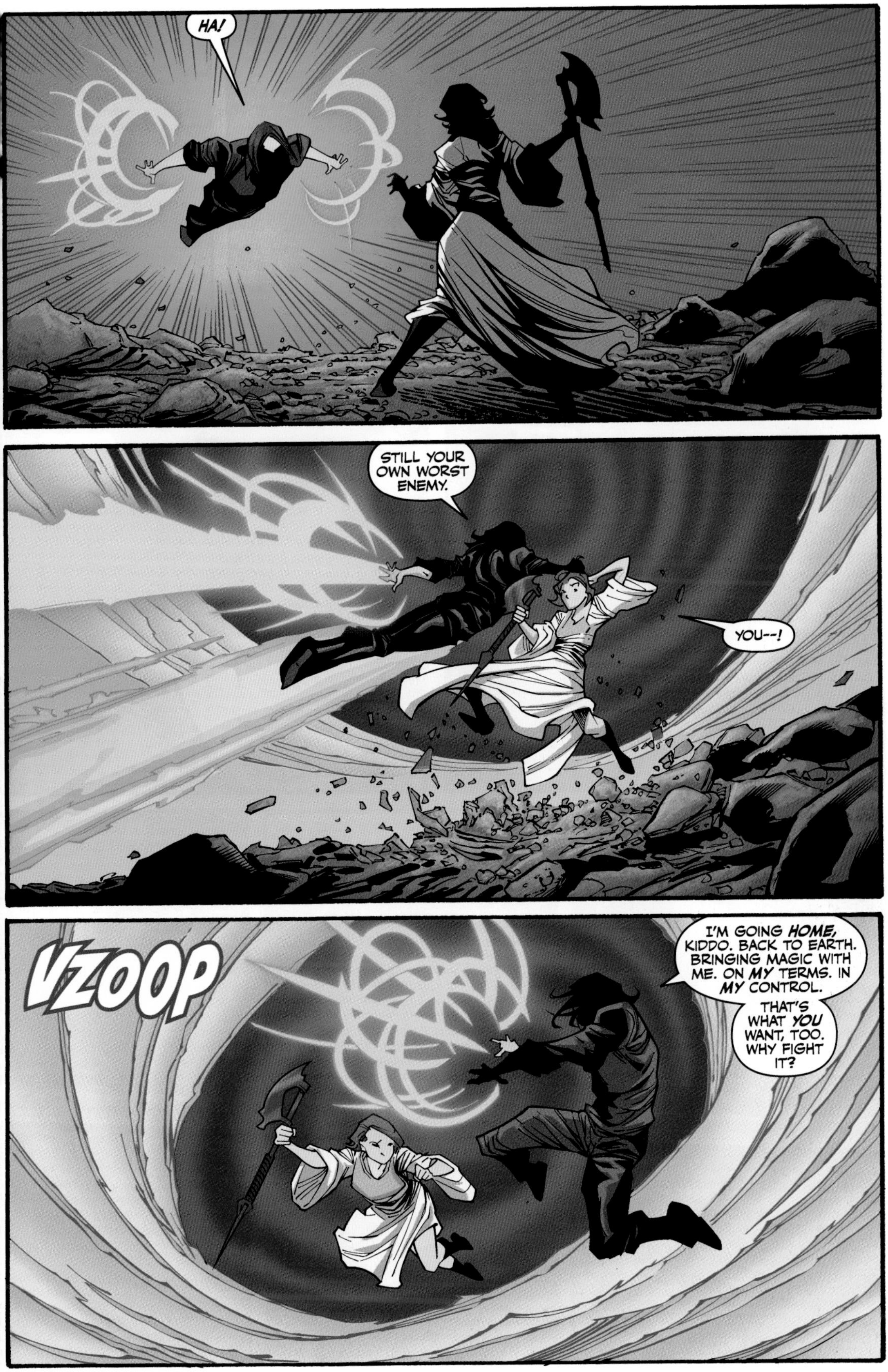
HA!
STILL YOUR OWN WORST ENEMY.
YOU--!
VZOOP
I'M GOING HOME, KIDDO. BACK TO EARTH. BRINGING MAGIC WITH ME. ON MY TERMS. IN MY CONTROL.
THAT'S WHAT YOU WANT, TOO. WHY FIGHT IT?

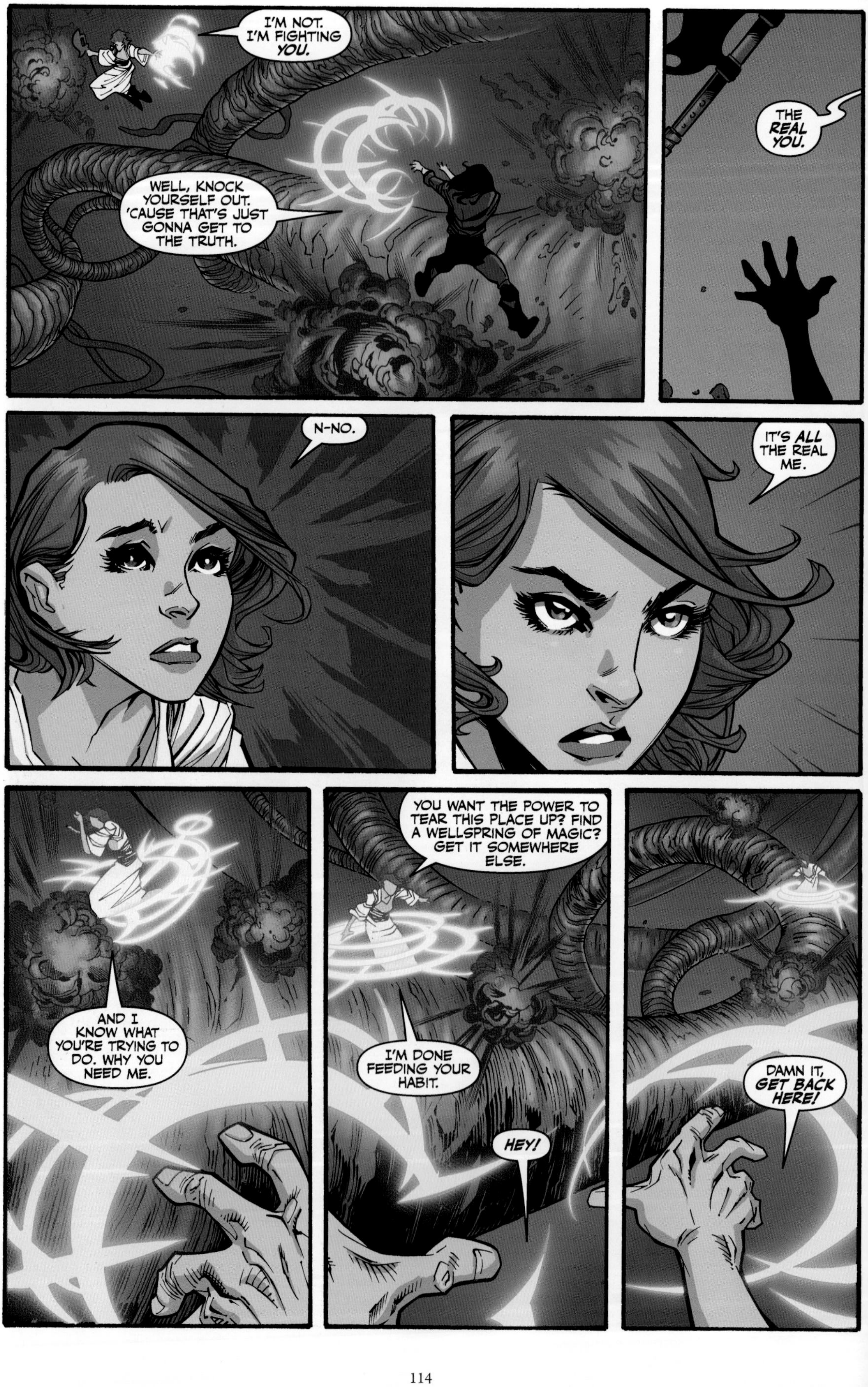
I'M NOT. I'M FIGHTING YOU.
WELL, KNOCK YOURSELF OUT. 'CAUSE THAT'S JUST GONNA GET TO THE TRUTH.
THE REAL YOU.
N-NO.
IT'S ALL THE REAL ME.
AND I KNOW WHAT YOU'RE TRYING TO DO. WHY YOU NEED ME.
YOU WANT THE POWER TO TEAR THIS PLACE UP? FIND A WELLSPRING OF MAGIC? GET IT SOMEWHERE ELSE.
I'M DONE FEEDING YOUR HABIT.
HEY!
DAMN IT, GET BACK HERE!

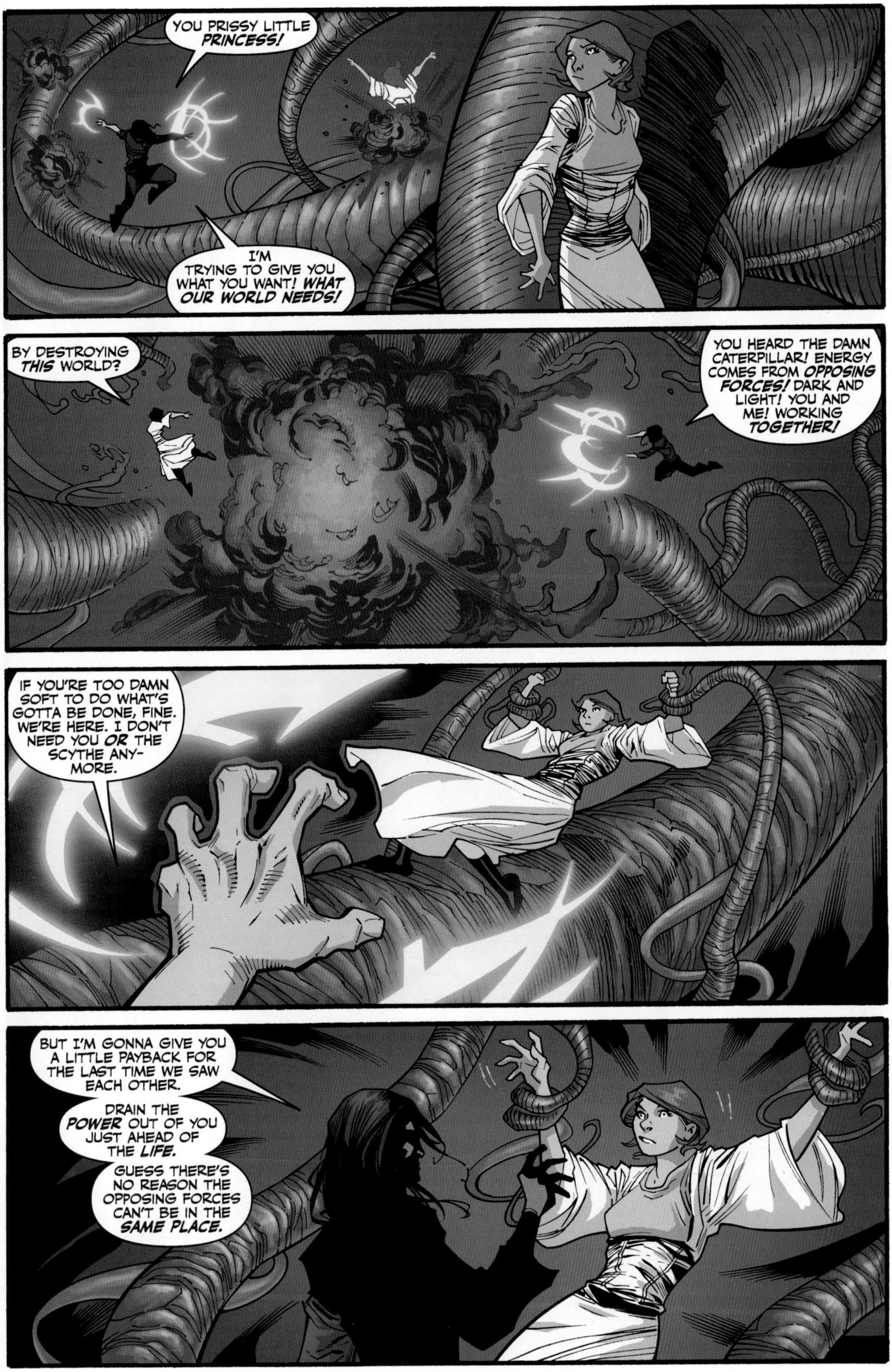

YOU PRISSY LITTLE PRINCESS!
I'M TRYING TO GIVE YOU WHAT YOU WANT! WHAT OUR WORLD NEEDS!
BY DESTROYING THIS WORLD?
YOU HEARD THE DAMN CATERPILLAR! ENERGY COMES FROM OPPOSING FORCES! DARK AND LIGHT! YOU AND ME! WORKING TOGETHER!
IF YOU'RE TOO DAMN SOFT TO DO WHAT'S GOTTA BE DONE, FINE. WE'RE HERE. I DON'T NEED YOU OR THE SCYTHE ANY-MORE.
BUT I'M GONNA GIVE YOU A LITTLE PAYBACK FOR THE LAST TIME WE SAW EACH OTHER.
DRAIN THE POWER OUT OF YOU JUST AHEAD OF THE LIFE.
GUESS THERE'S NO REASON THE OPPOSING FORCES CAN'T BE IN THE SAME PLACE.

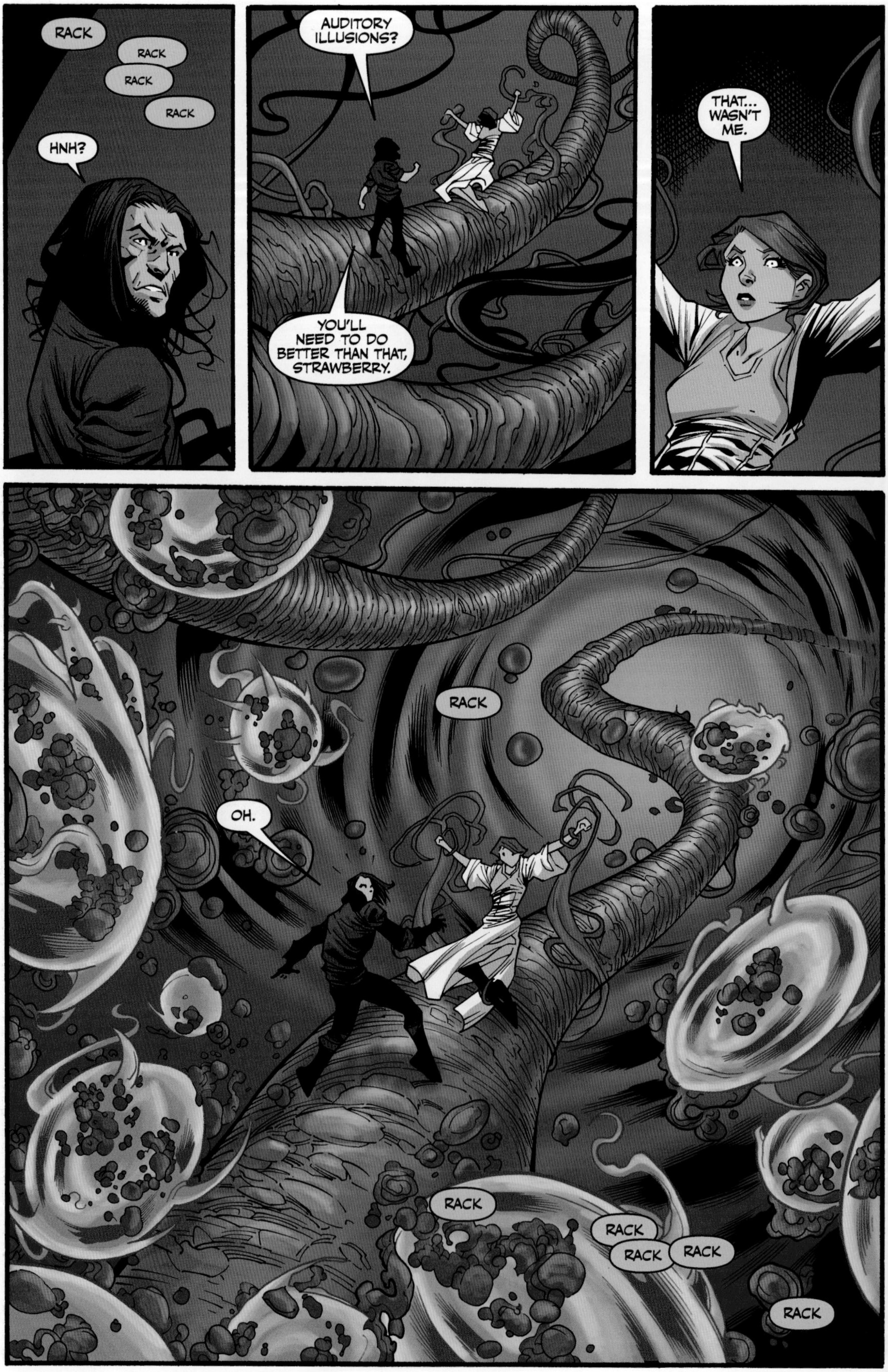
RACK
RACK
RACK
RACK
HNH?
AUDITORY ILLUSIONS?
YOU'LL NEED TO DO BETTER THAN THAT, STRAWBERRY.
THAT... WASN'T ME.
RACK
OH.
RACK
RACK
RACK
RACK
RACK

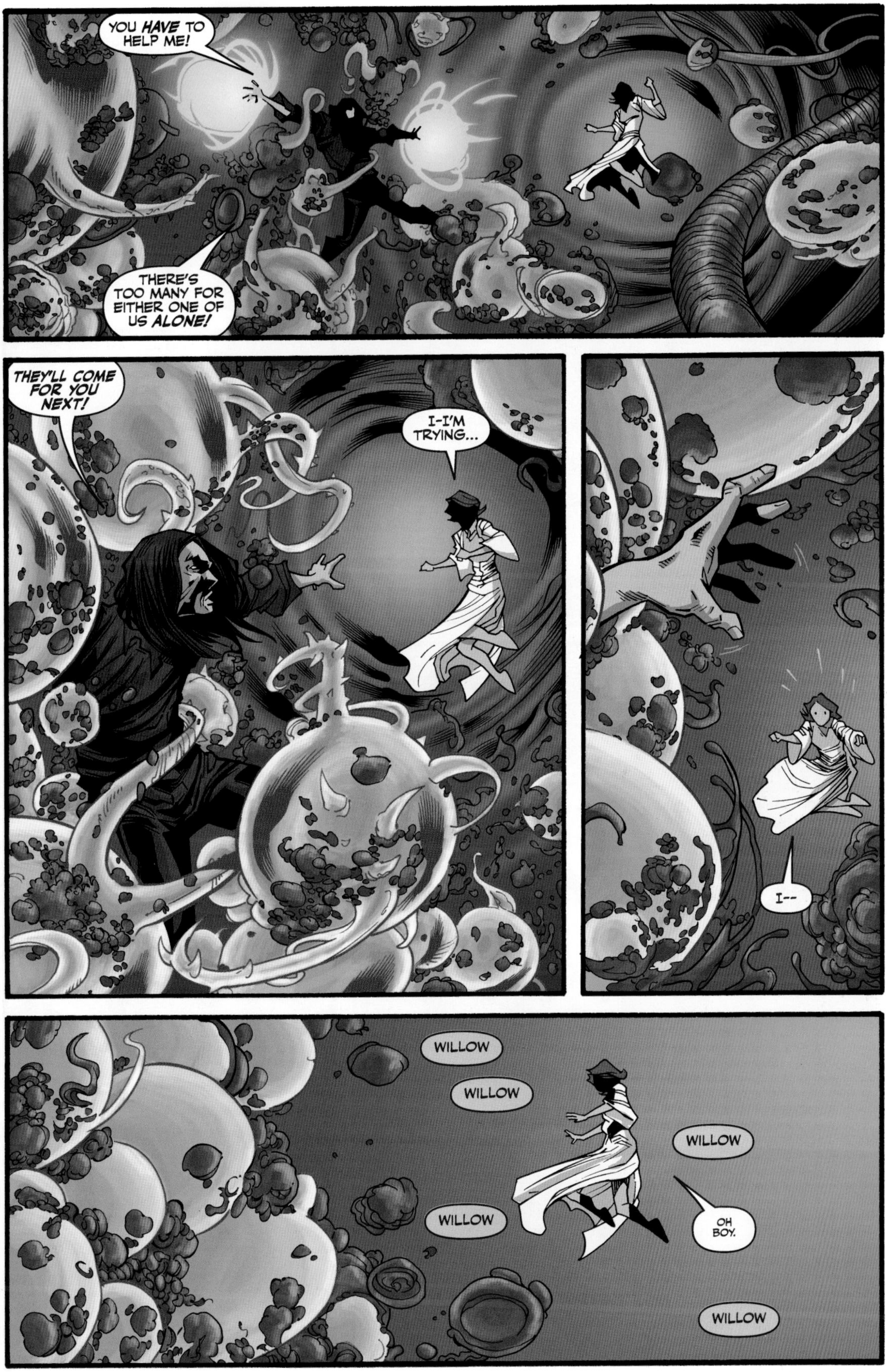
YOU HAVE TO HELP ME!
THERE'S TOO MANY FOR EITHER ONE OF US ALONE!
THEY'LL COME FOR YOU NEXT!
I-I'M TRYING...
I--
WILLOW
WILLOW
WILLOW
WILLOW
OH BOY.
WILLOW

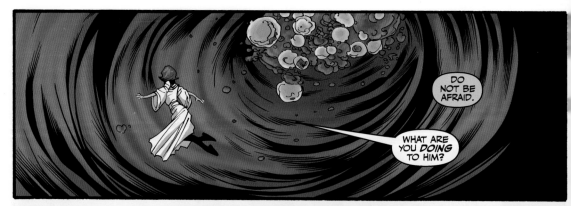

DO NOT BE AFRAID.

WHAT ARE YOU *DOING* TO HIM?

A BODY HAS DEFENSES. TO REMOVE INVADERS THAT WOULD CAUSE IT HARM.

AND... AM I--

YOU ARE AN INVADER.

BUT YOU HAVE CAUSED NO HARM.

I TRY TO BE A GOOD GUEST.

YOU SAID "A BODY." ARE YOU, LIKE, THE *EMBODIMENT* OF MAGIC?

MAGIC IS A FUNDAMENTAL FORCE. IT CANNOT BE CONTAINED IN ONE BODY. EVEN ONE THE SIZE OF A UNIVERSE.

BUT I SUPPOSE I AM AN *EMBODIMENT.*

OF WHAT?

OF MYSELF.

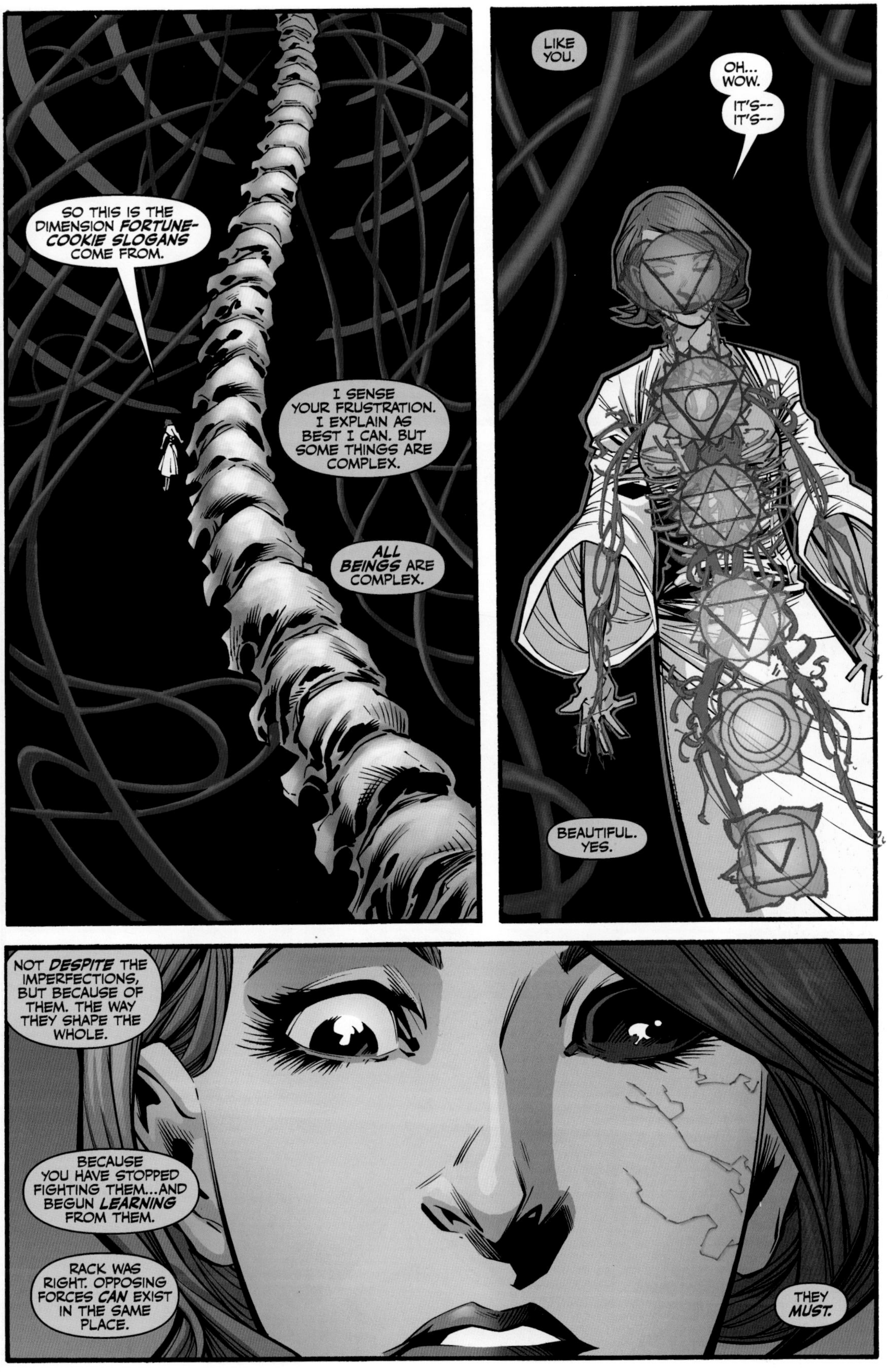
SO THIS IS THE DIMENSION FORTUNE-COOKIE SLOGANS COME FROM.
I SENSE YOUR FRUSTRATION. I EXPLAIN AS BEST I CAN. BUT SOME THINGS ARE COMPLEX.
ALL BEINGS ARE COMPLEX.
LIKE YOU.
OH... WOW. IT'S-- IT'S--
BEAUTIFUL. YES.
NOT DESPITE THE IMPERFECTIONS, BUT BECAUSE OF THEM. THE WAY THEY SHAPE THE WHOLE.
BECAUSE YOU HAVE STOPPED FIGHTING THEM...AND BEGUN LEARNING FROM THEM.
RACK WAS RIGHT. OPPOSING FORCES CAN EXIST IN THE SAME PLACE.
THEY MUST.

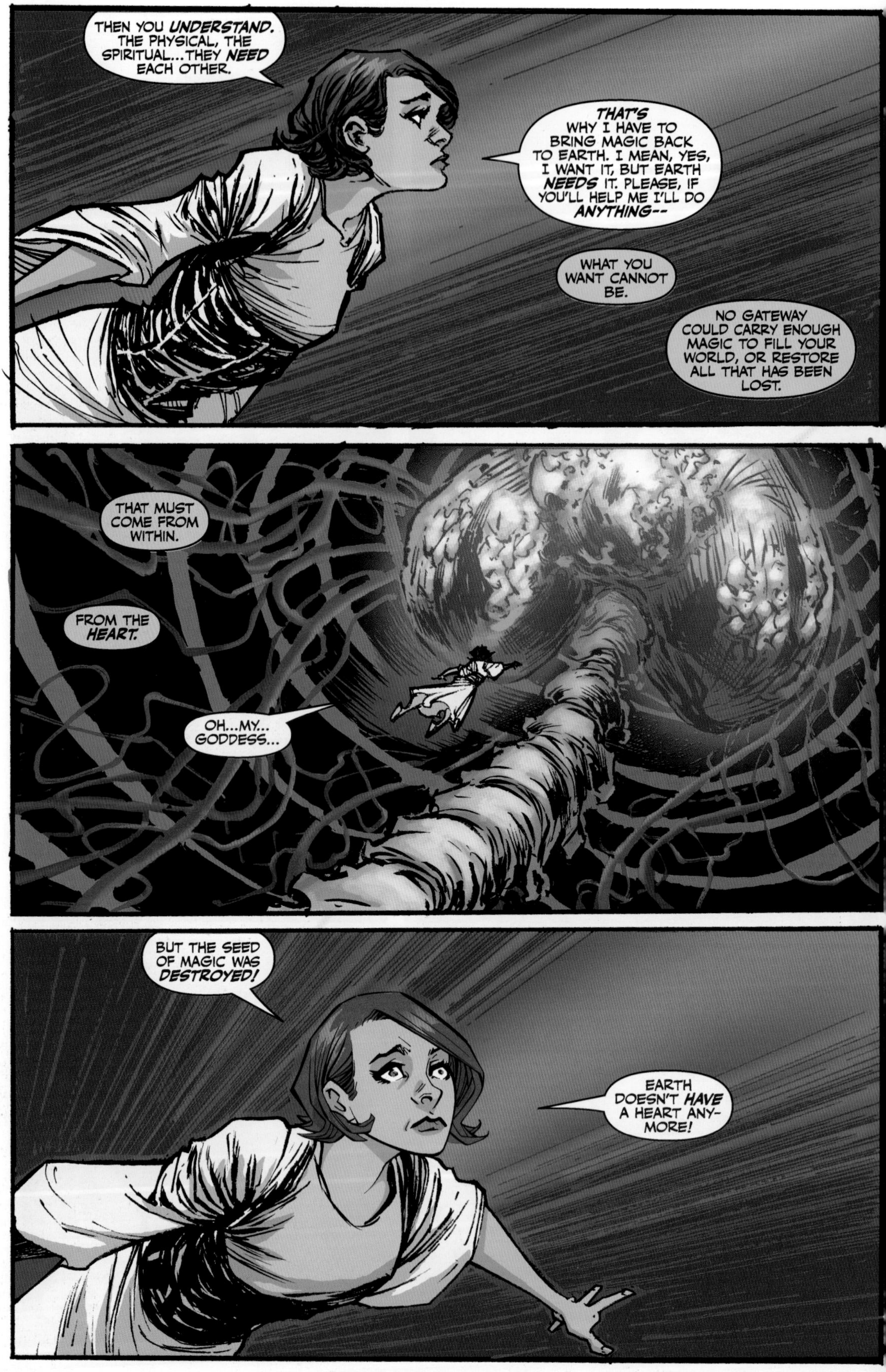
THEN YOU UNDERSTAND. THE PHYSICAL, THE SPIRITUAL...THEY NEED EACH OTHER.
THAT'S WHY I HAVE TO BRING MAGIC BACK TO EARTH. I MEAN, YES, I WANT IT, BUT EARTH NEEDS IT. PLEASE, IF YOU'LL HELP ME I'LL DO ANYTHING--
WHAT YOU WANT CANNOT BE.
NO GATEWAY COULD CARRY ENOUGH MAGIC TO FILL YOUR WORLD, OR RESTORE ALL THAT HAS BEEN LOST.
THAT MUST COME FROM WITHIN.
FROM THE HEART.
OH...MY... GODDESS...
BUT THE SEED OF MAGIC WAS DESTROYED!
EARTH DOESN'T HAVE A HEART ANY-MORE!

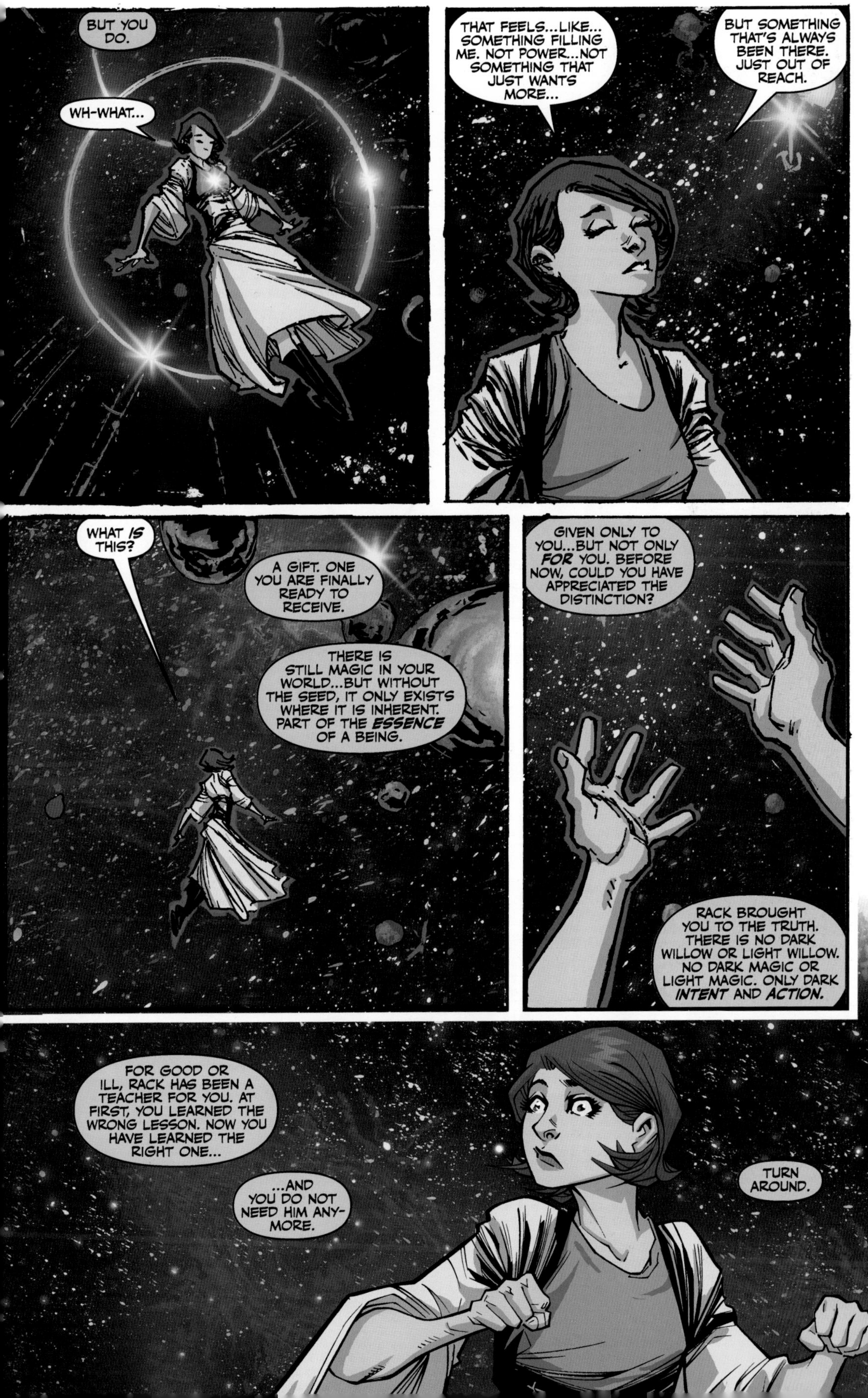
BUT YOU DO.
WH-WHAT...
THAT FEELS...LIKE... SOMETHING FILLING ME. NOT POWER...NOT SOMETHING THAT JUST WANTS MORE...
BUT SOMETHING THAT'S ALWAYS BEEN THERE. JUST OUT OF REACH.
WHAT *IS* THIS?
A GIFT. ONE YOU ARE FINALLY READY TO RECEIVE.
THERE IS STILL MAGIC IN YOUR WORLD...BUT WITHOUT THE SEED, IT ONLY EXISTS WHERE IT IS INHERENT. PART OF THE *ESSENCE* OF A BEING.
GIVEN ONLY TO YOU...BUT NOT ONLY *FOR* YOU. BEFORE NOW, COULD YOU HAVE APPRECIATED THE DISTINCTION?
RACK BROUGHT YOU TO THE TRUTH. THERE IS NO DARK WILLOW OR LIGHT WILLOW. NO DARK MAGIC OR LIGHT MAGIC. ONLY DARK *INTENT* AND *ACTION*.
FOR GOOD OR ILL, RACK HAS BEEN A TEACHER FOR YOU. AT FIRST, YOU LEARNED THE WRONG LESSON. NOW YOU HAVE LEARNED THE RIGHT ONE...
...AND YOU DO NOT NEED HIM ANYMORE.
TURN AROUND.

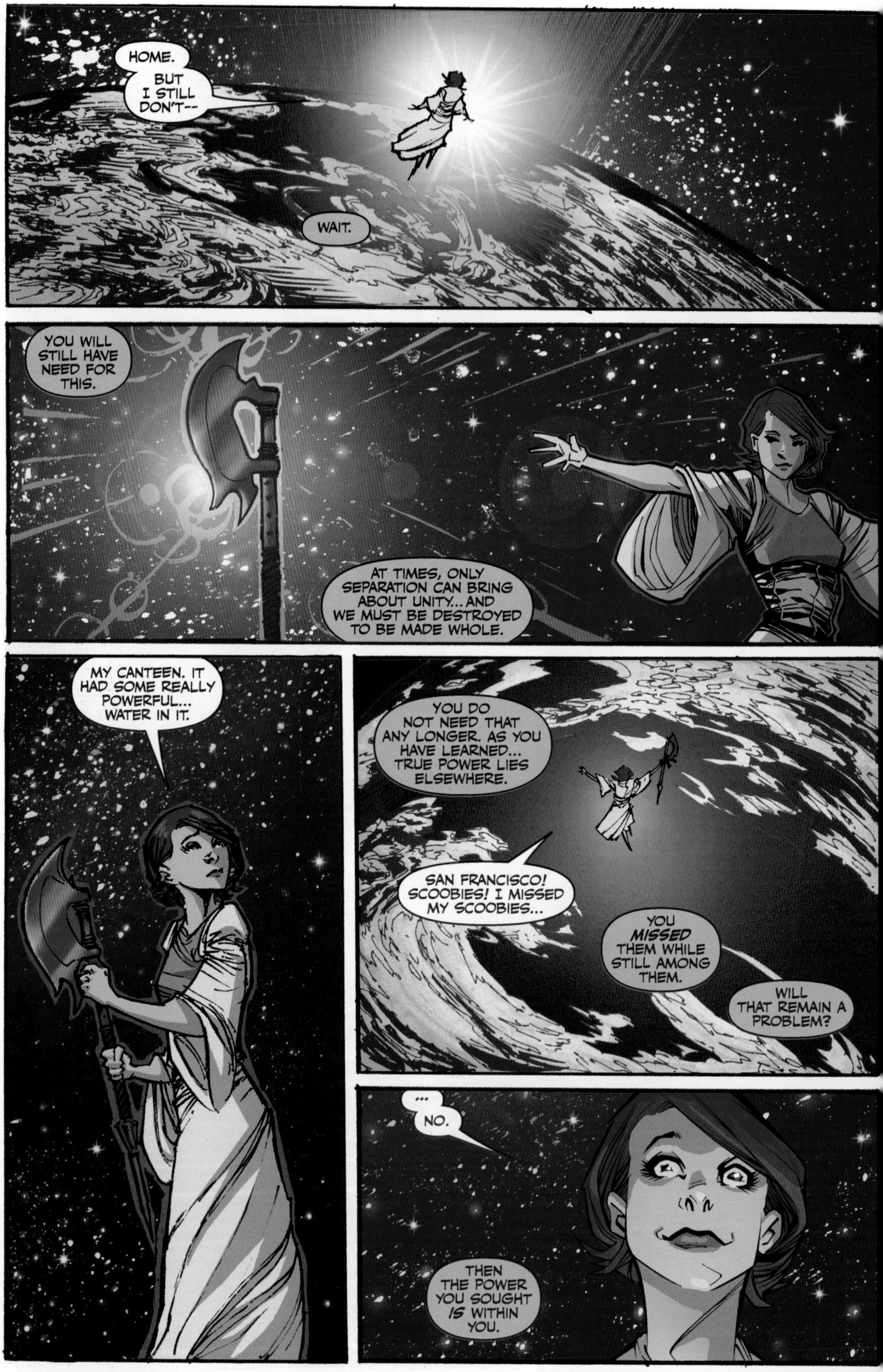
HOME.
BUT I STILL DON'T--
WAIT.
YOU WILL STILL HAVE NEED FOR THIS.
AT TIMES, ONLY SEPARATION CAN BRING ABOUT UNITY... AND WE MUST BE DESTROYED TO BE MADE WHOLE.
MY CANTEEN. IT HAD SOME REALLY POWERFUL... WATER IN IT.
YOU DO NOT NEED THAT ANY LONGER. AS YOU HAVE LEARNED... TRUE POWER LIES ELSEWHERE.
SAN FRANCISCO! SCOOBIES! I MISSED MY SCOOBIES...
YOU *MISSED* THEM WHILE STILL AMONG THEM.
WILL THAT REMAIN A PROBLEM?
... NO.
THEN THE POWER YOU SOUGHT *IS* WITHIN YOU.

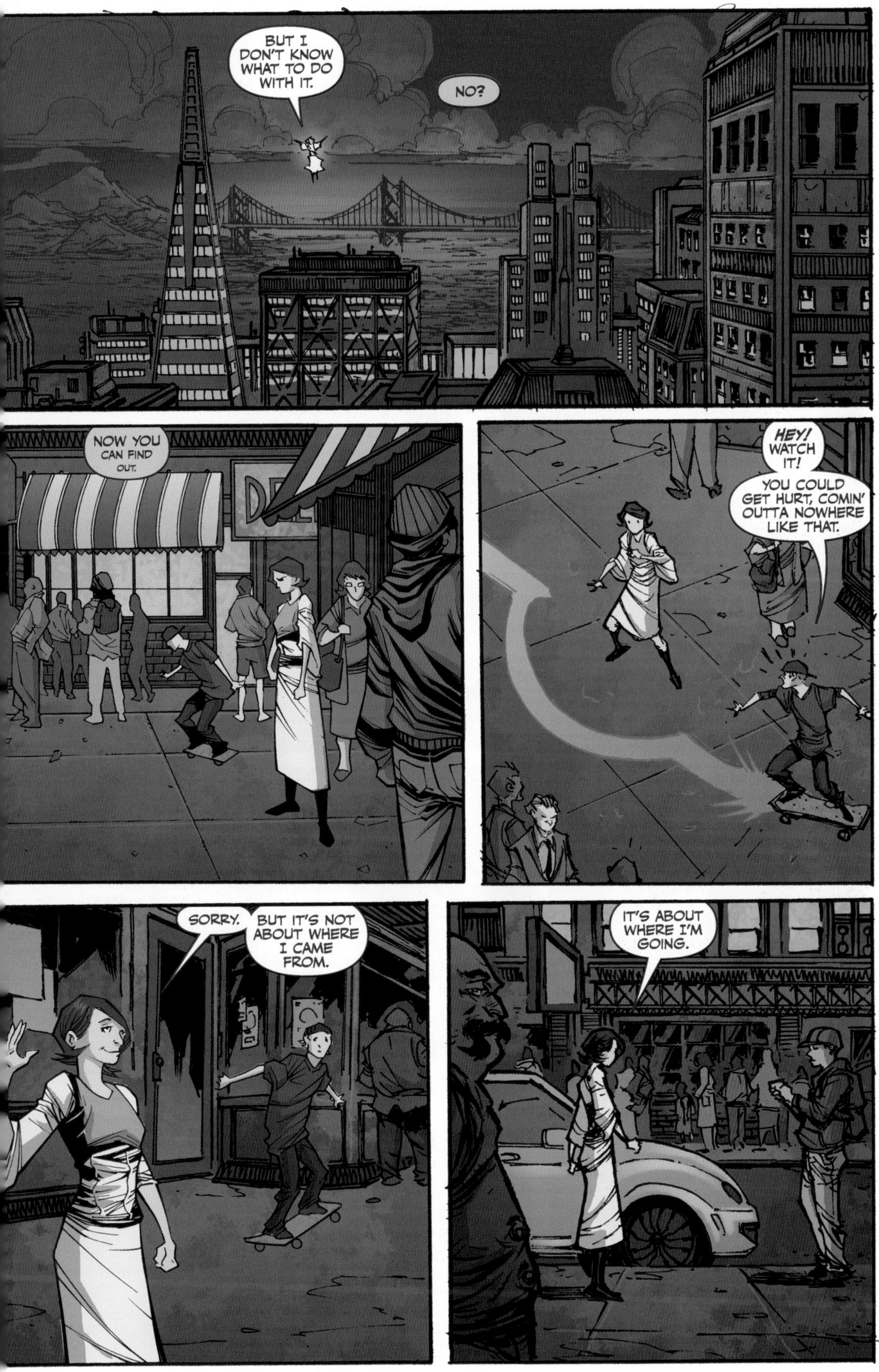
BUT I DON'T KNOW WHAT TO DO WITH IT.
NO?
NOW YOU CAN FIND OUT.
HEY! WATCH IT!
YOU COULD GET HURT, COMIN' OUTTA NOWHERE LIKE THAT.
SORRY.
BUT IT'S NOT ABOUT WHERE I CAME FROM.
IT'S ABOUT WHERE I'M GOING.

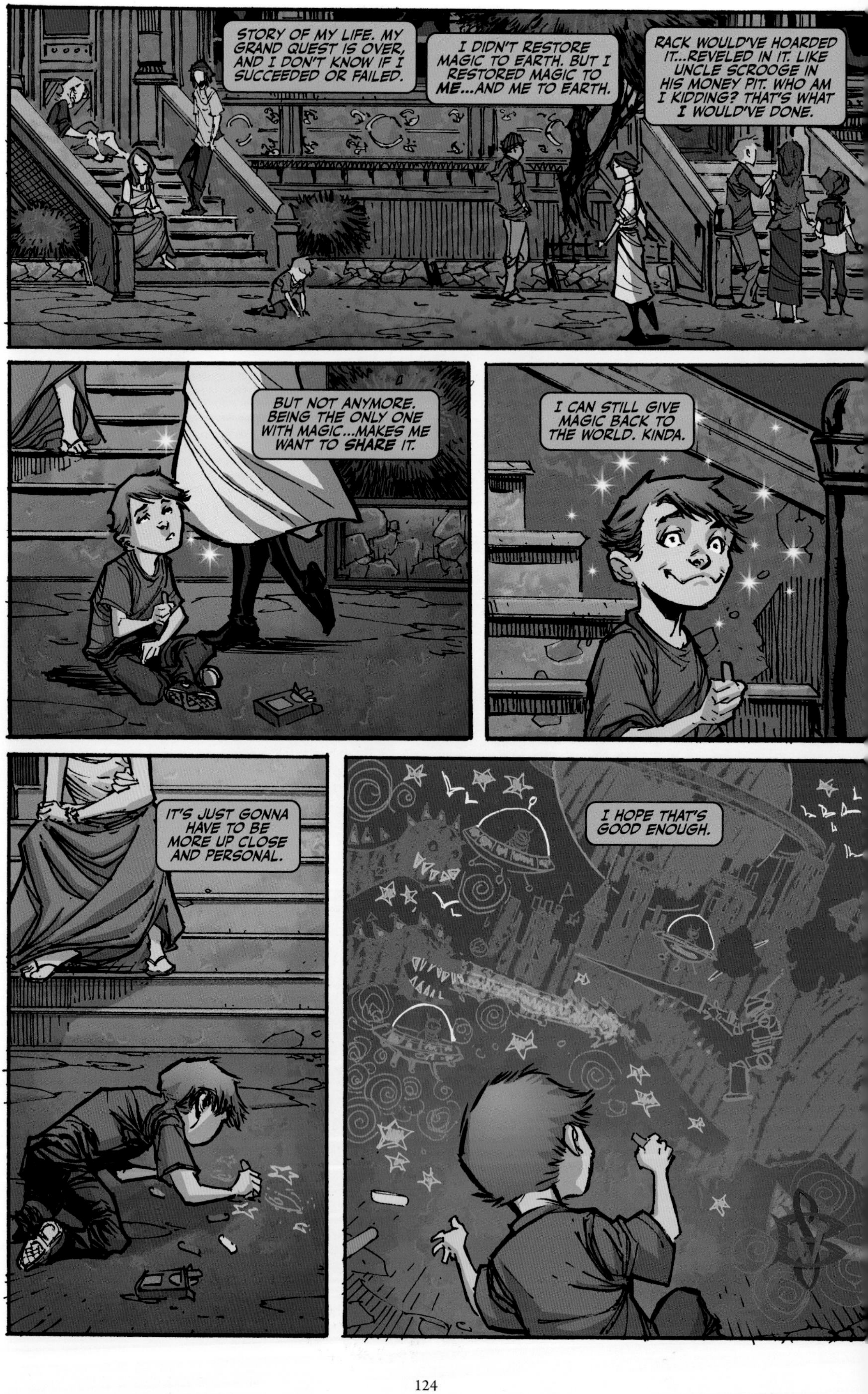
STORY OF MY LIFE. MY GRAND QUEST IS OVER, AND I DON'T KNOW IF I SUCCEEDED OR FAILED.
I DIDN'T RESTORE MAGIC TO EARTH. BUT I RESTORED MAGIC TO ME...AND ME TO EARTH.
RACK WOULD'VE HOARDED IT...REVELED IN IT. LIKE UNCLE SCROOGE IN HIS MONEY PIT. WHO AM I KIDDING? THAT'S WHAT I WOULD'VE DONE.
BUT NOT ANYMORE. BEING THE ONLY ONE WITH MAGIC...MAKES ME WANT TO SHARE IT.
I CAN STILL GIVE MAGIC BACK TO THE WORLD. KINDA.
IT'S JUST GONNA HAVE TO BE MORE UP CLOSE AND PERSONAL.
I HOPE THAT'S GOOD ENOUGH.

WILLOW: WONDERLAND COVER GALLERY *and* SKETCHBOOK

CHARACTER DESIGNS BY
BRIAN CHING

VARIANT COVER ART BY
MEGAN LARA

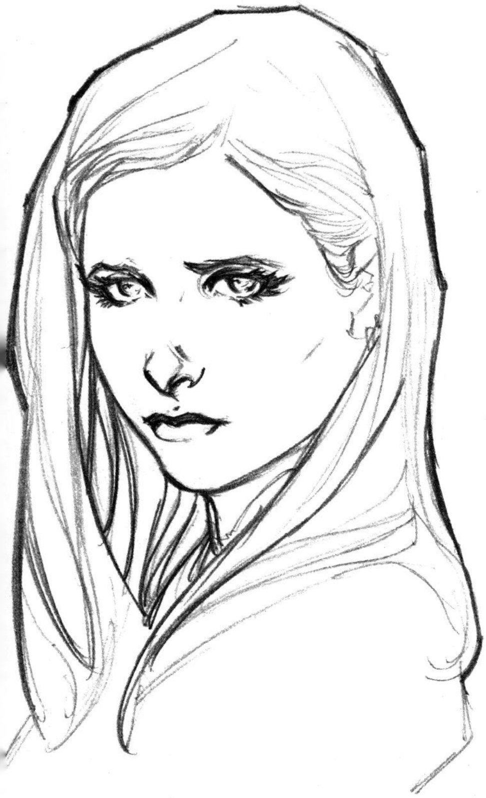

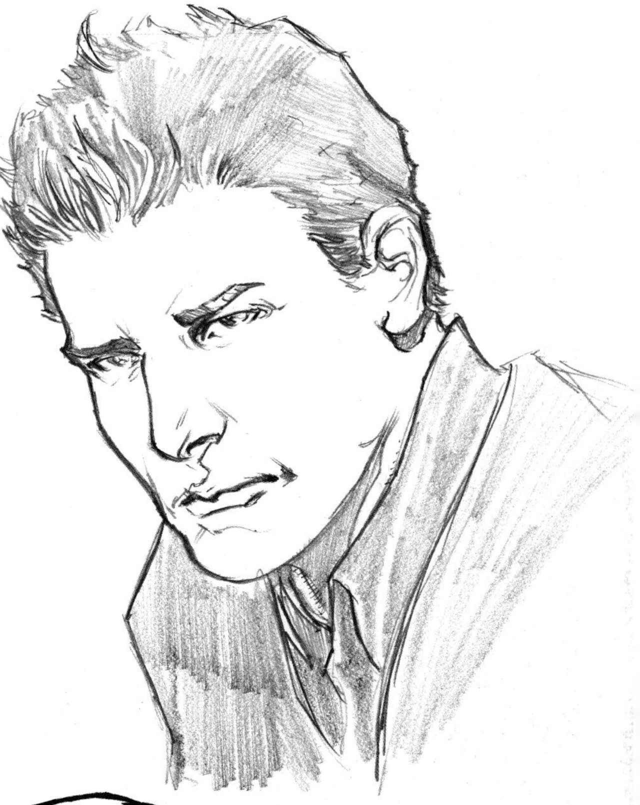

All artists that work on the Buffy *or* Angel *comics must supply likeness sketches of the actors. We send these headshots to Twentieth Century Fox, who in turn send them to the actors for approval. Once an artist is approved by a given actor, we can hire them to draw the characters in the comics. These are Brian Ching's tryouts for Buffy, Angel, and Dawn.*

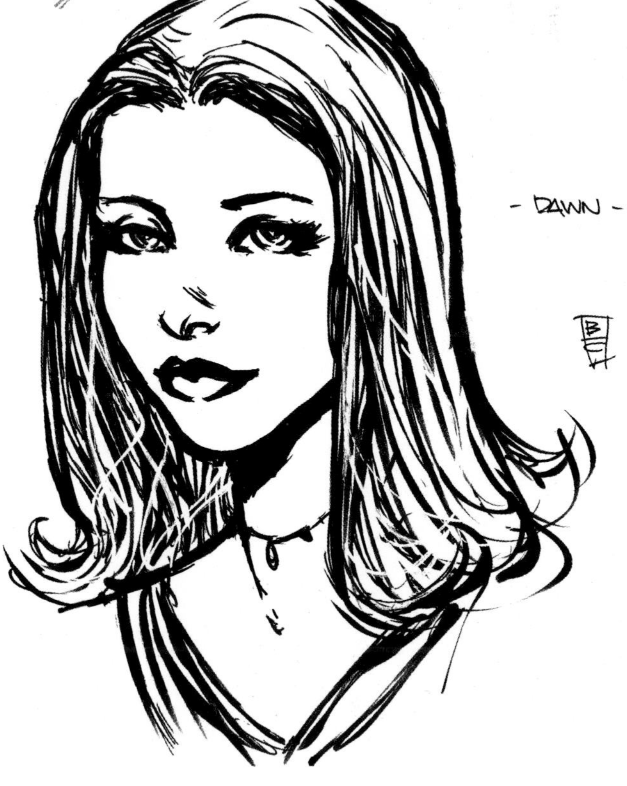
- DAWN -

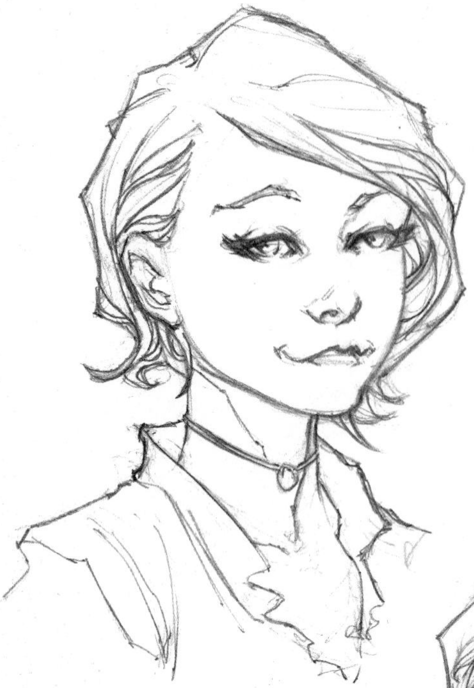

Brian's sketches of Willow balance her charming, sweet nature with her more serious and powerful side. Fashion always has a place in the Buffy *television show and in the comics, and Brian does a great job bringing Willow's evolving sense of style to this story.*

FACING: *Variant cover to* Willow #1 *by Megan Lara.*

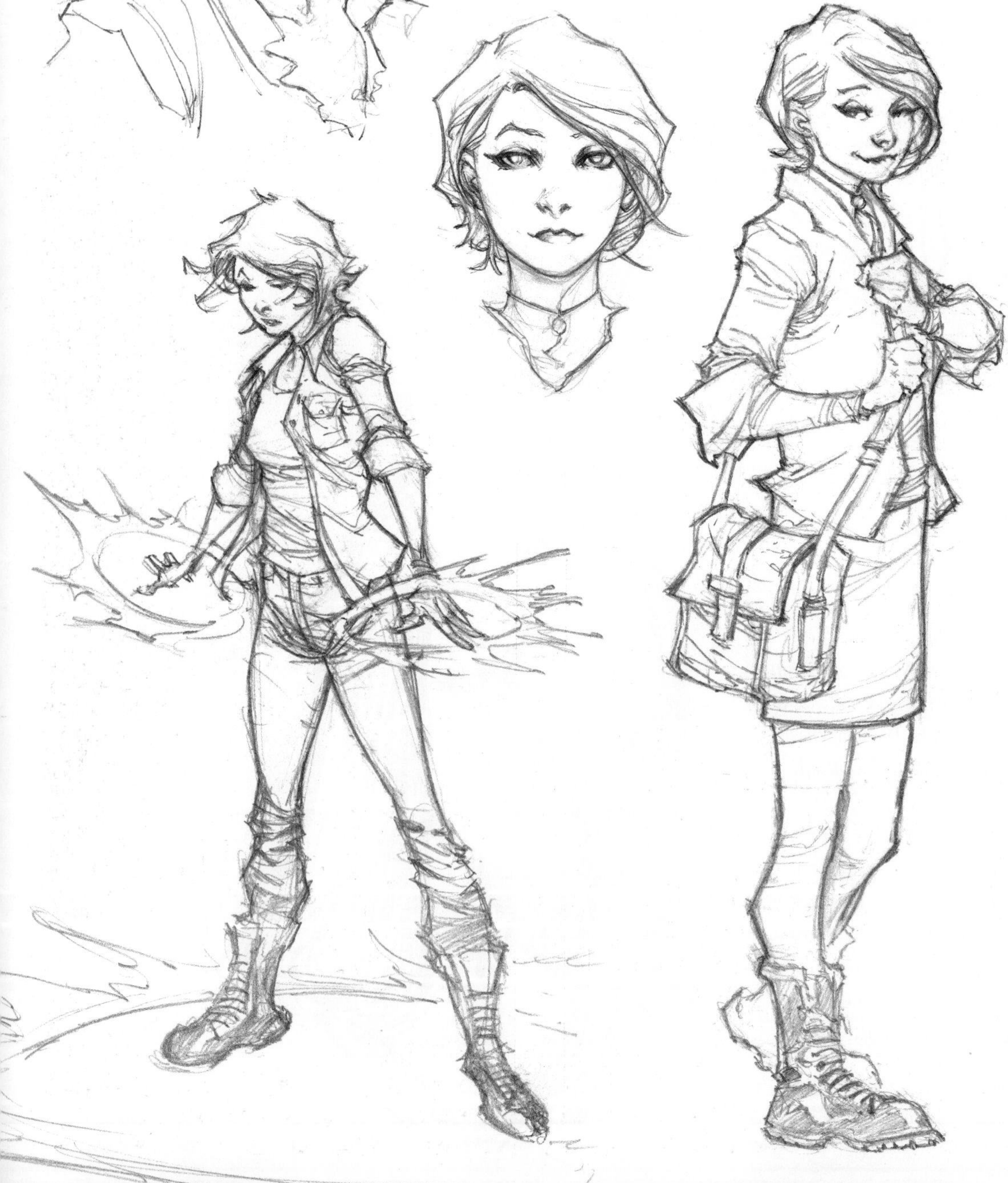

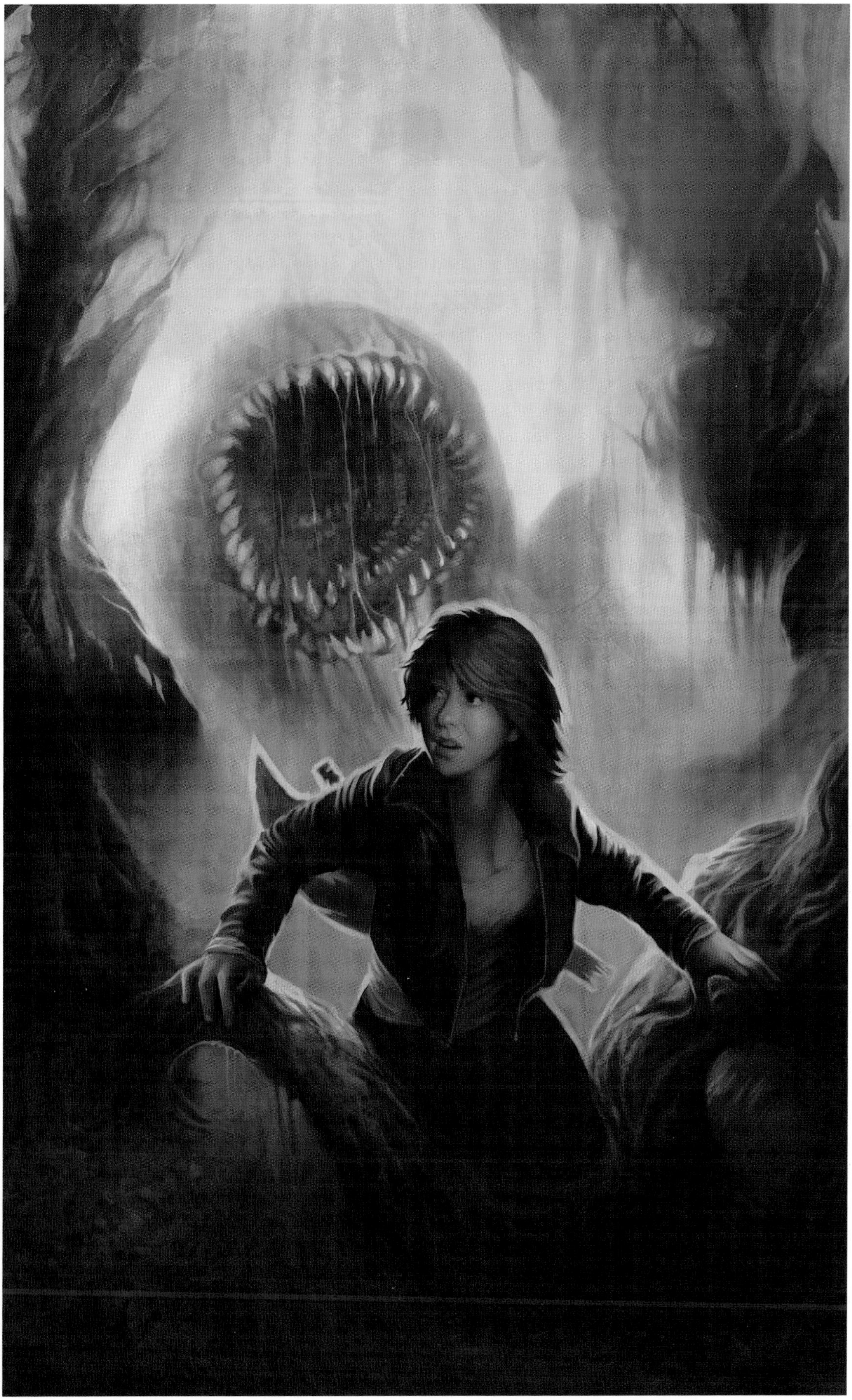

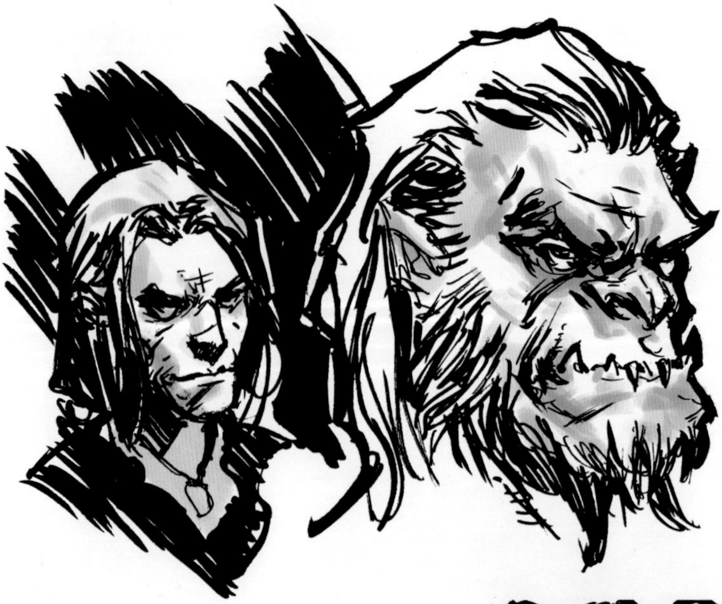

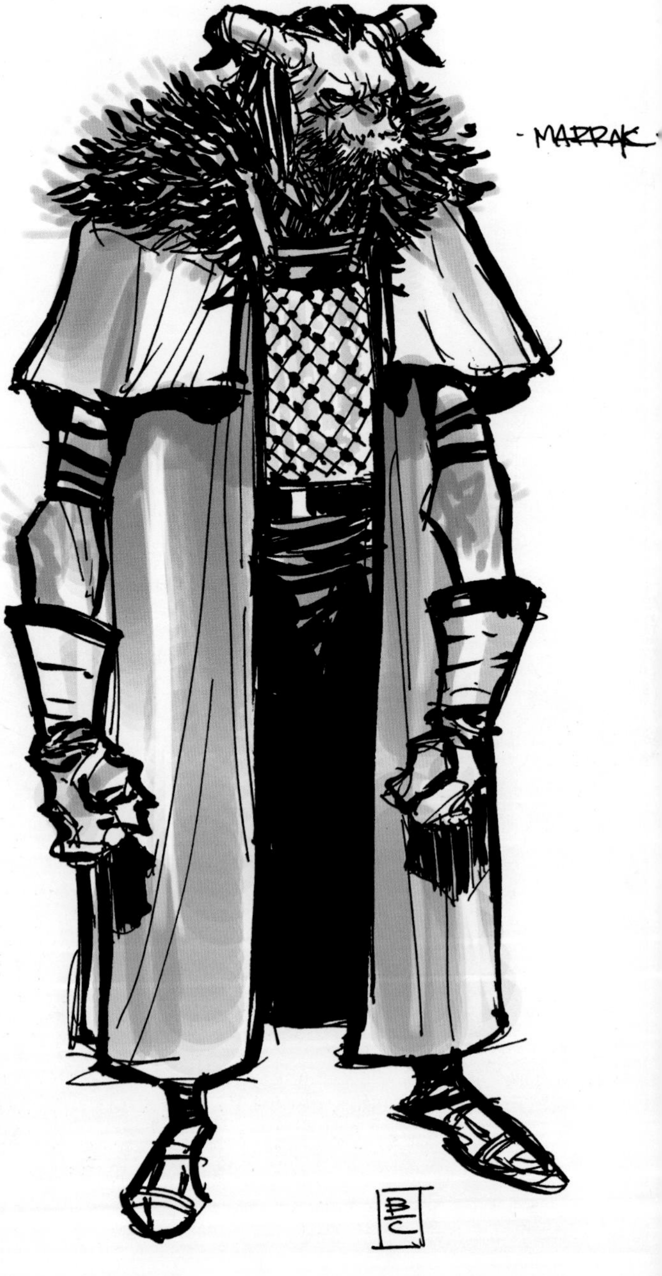
- MARRAK -

Our Big Bad, Marrak, evolved from initial sketches based on Willow's former magic-drug pusher, Rack, from Buffy *Season 6. Again, Brian perfectly balances a gentle, anthropomorphic charm with the sinister narcissism of Rack. The reader doesn't know whether or not to trust this "new" character.*

FACING: *Brian's designs for some monsters in this strange new world.*

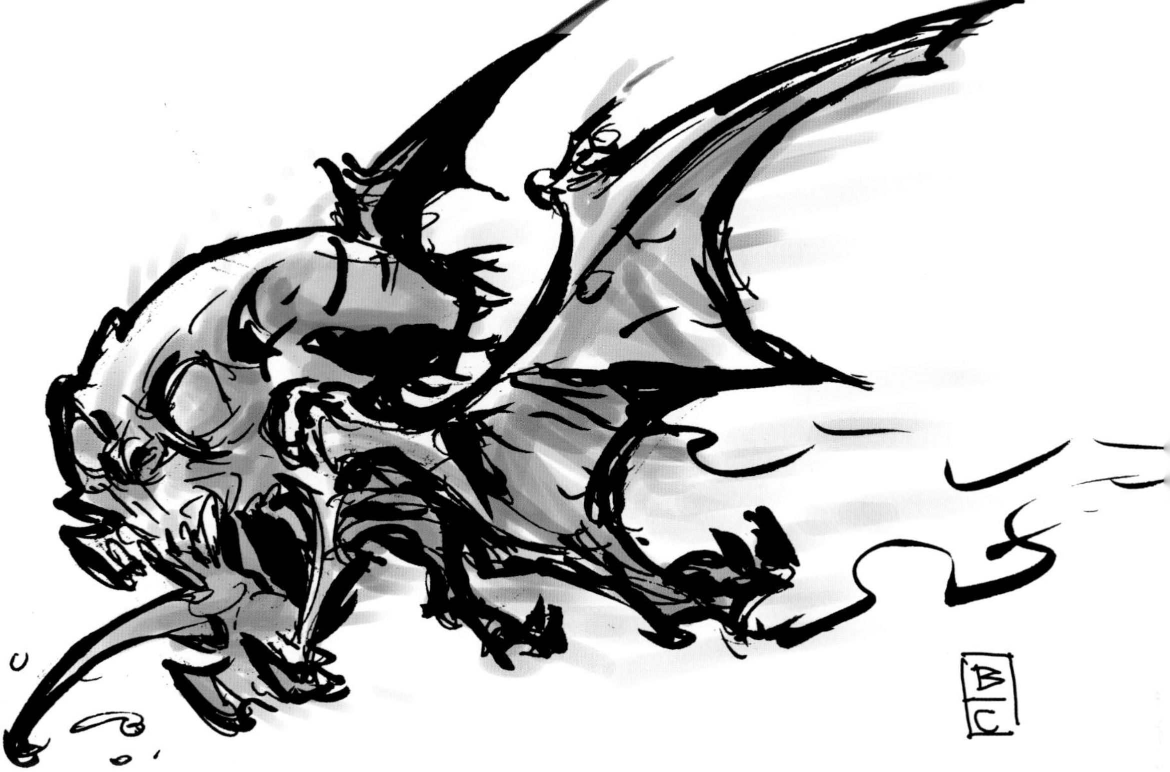

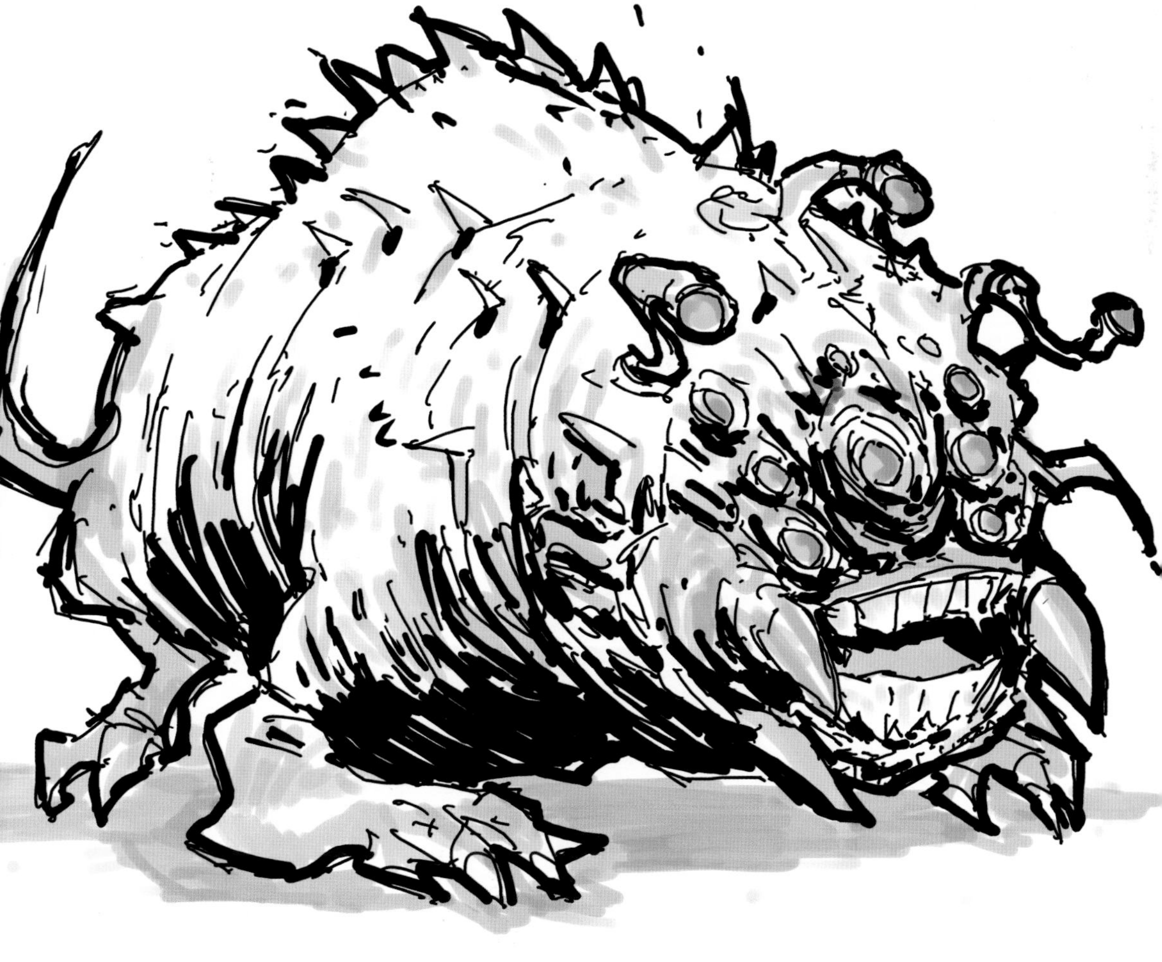

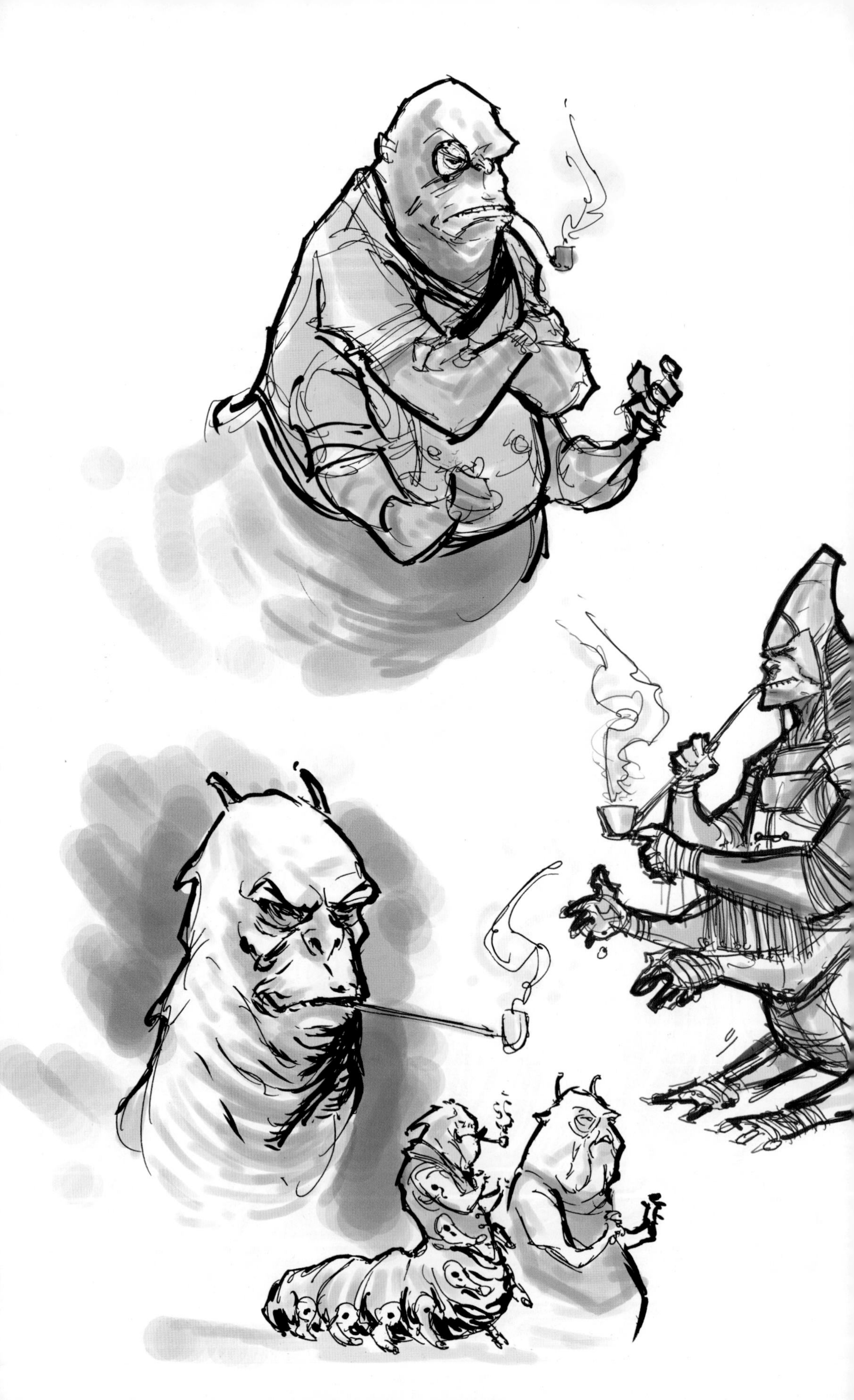

Jeff Parker was working on the outline for the series the weekend that acclaimed French cartoonist Moebius passed away. Moebius's mind-bending sci-fi and fantasy comics expanded our understanding of what comics could be, and the final design of the caterpillar character borrowed heavily from Moebius's Arzach.

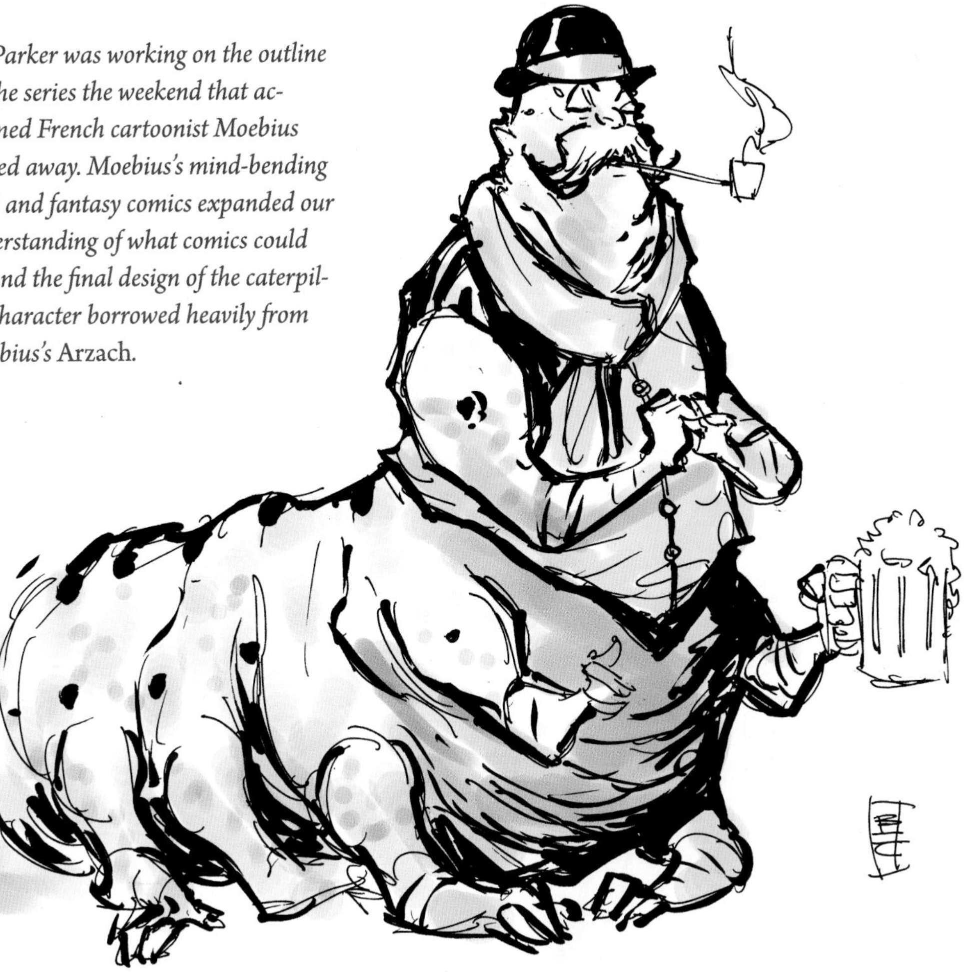

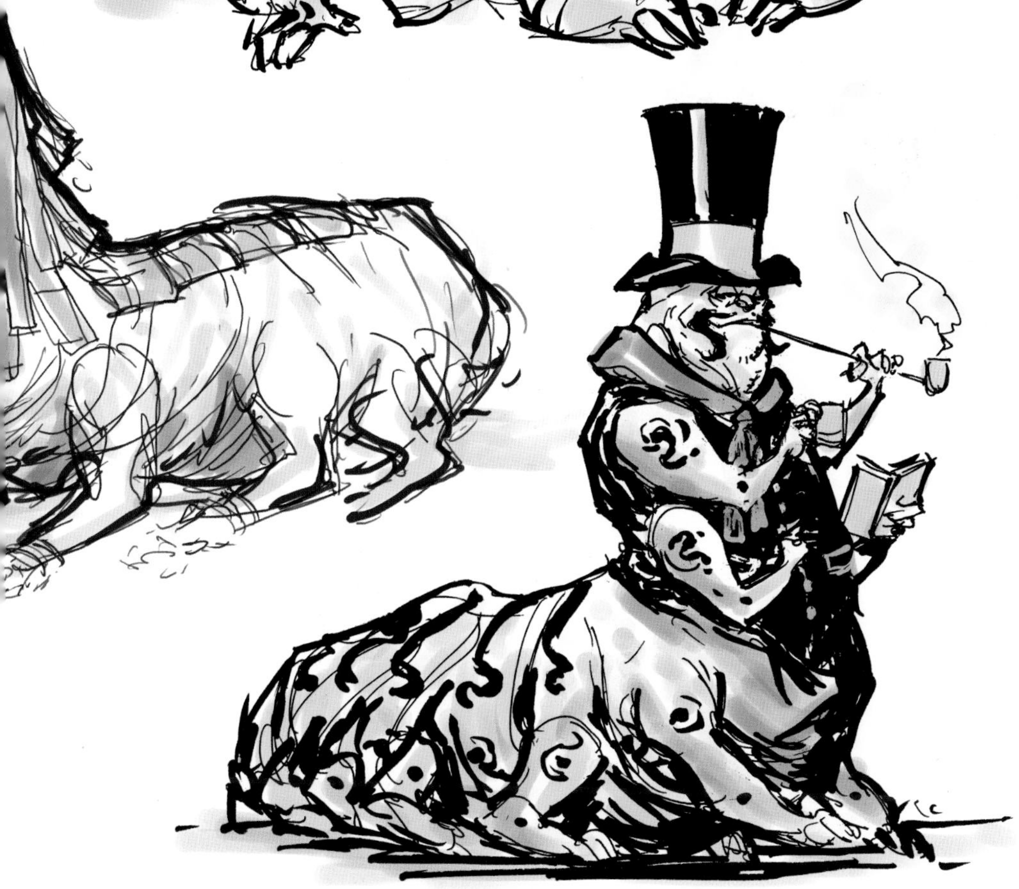

Willow had a number of costume changes throughout her adventures in Wonderland, *to address the evolving landscape and endless amount of muck that stained her clothes.*

FACING: *Variant cover to* Willow #3 *by Megan Lara.*

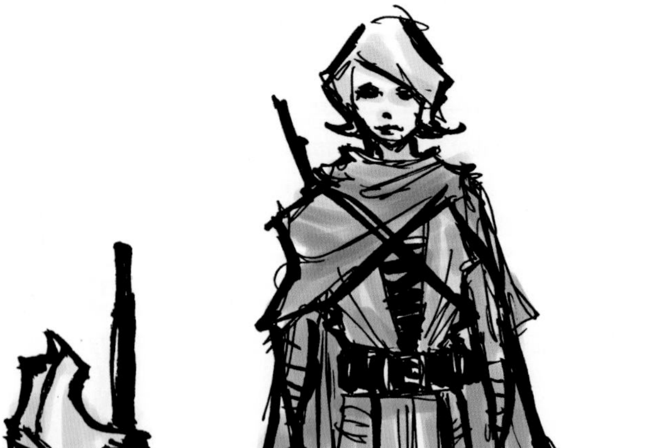

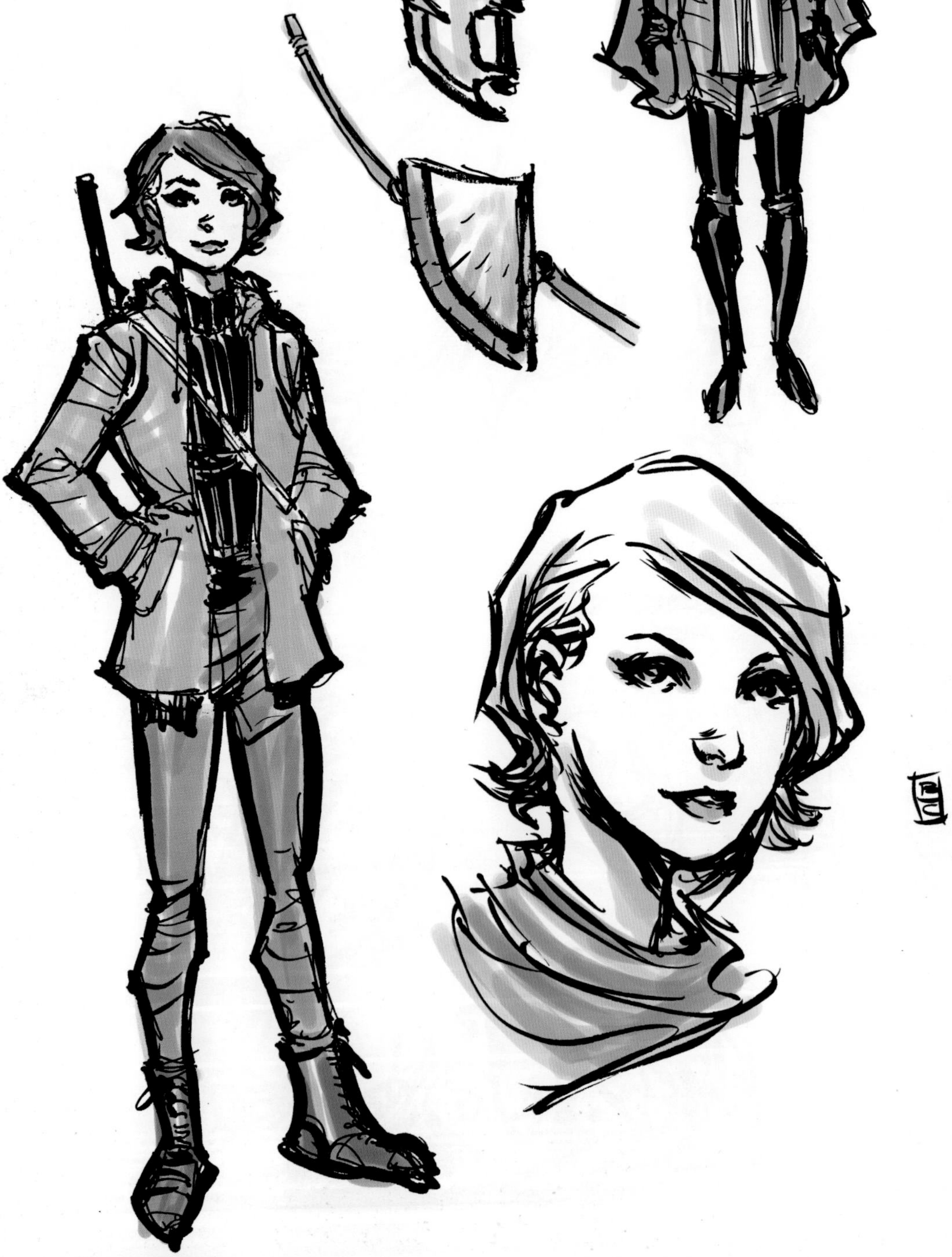

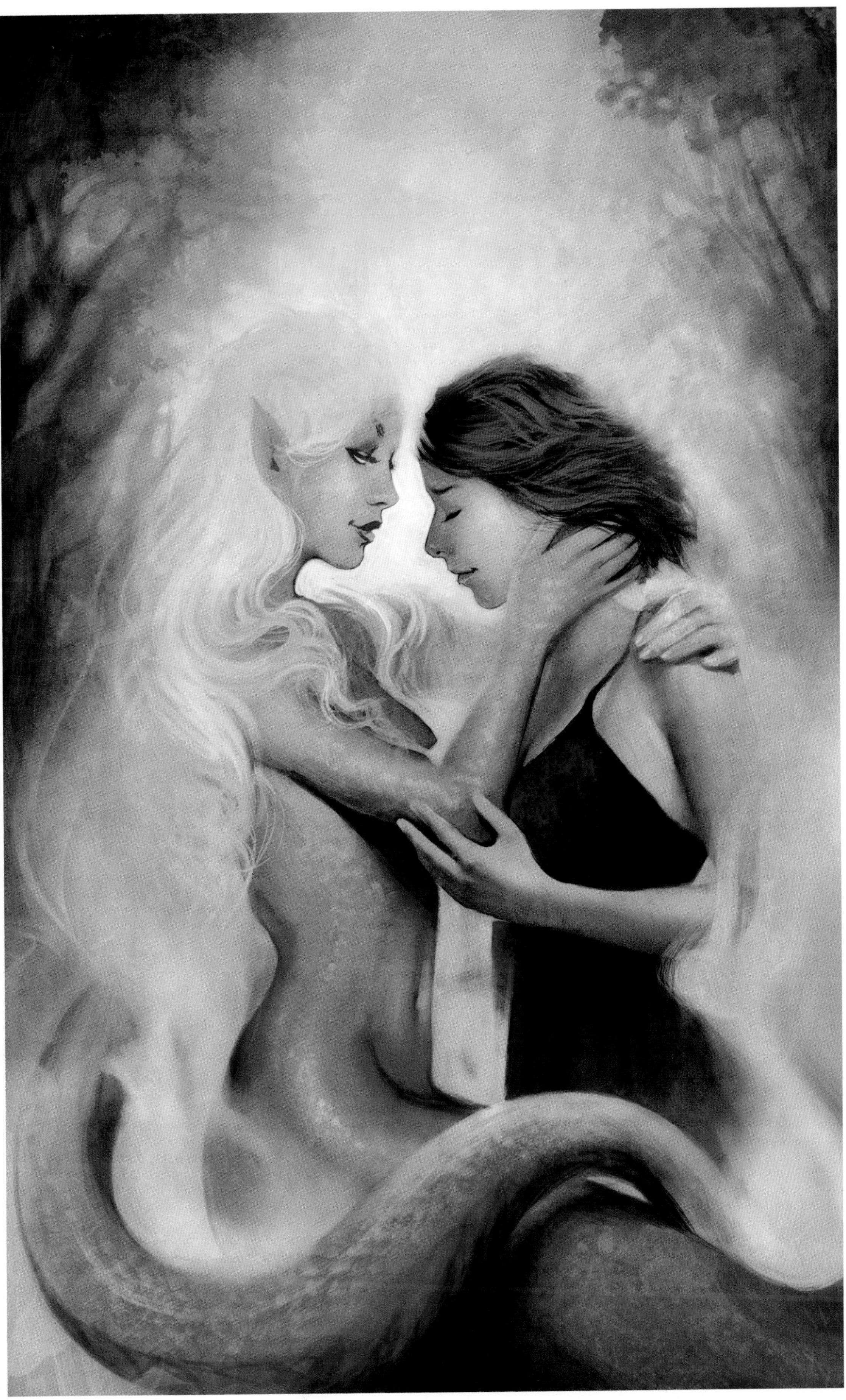

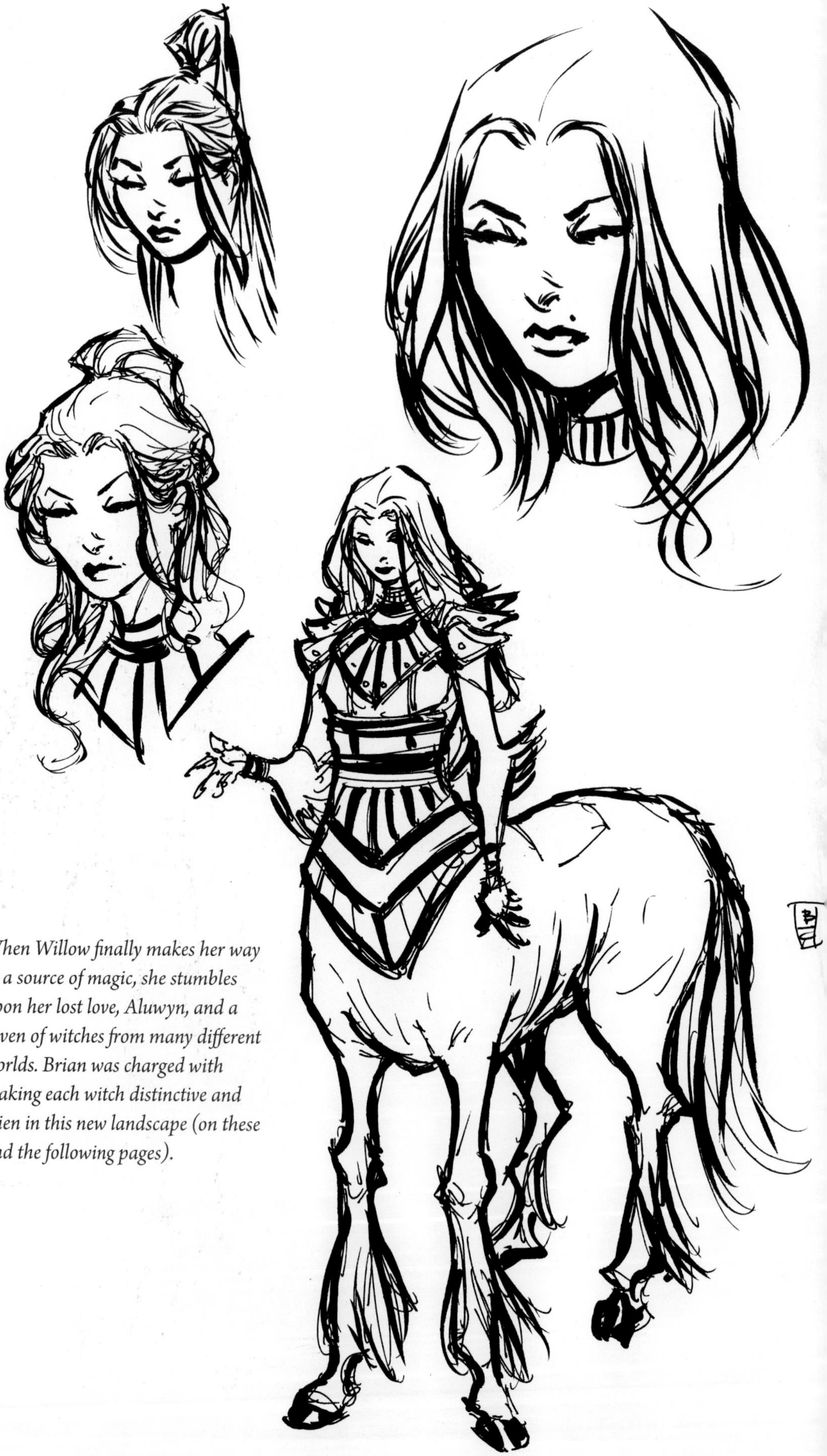

When Willow finally makes her way to a source of magic, she stumbles upon her lost love, Aluwyn, and a coven of witches from many different worlds. Brian was charged with making each witch distinctive and alien in this new landscape (on these and the following pages).

VULCANA

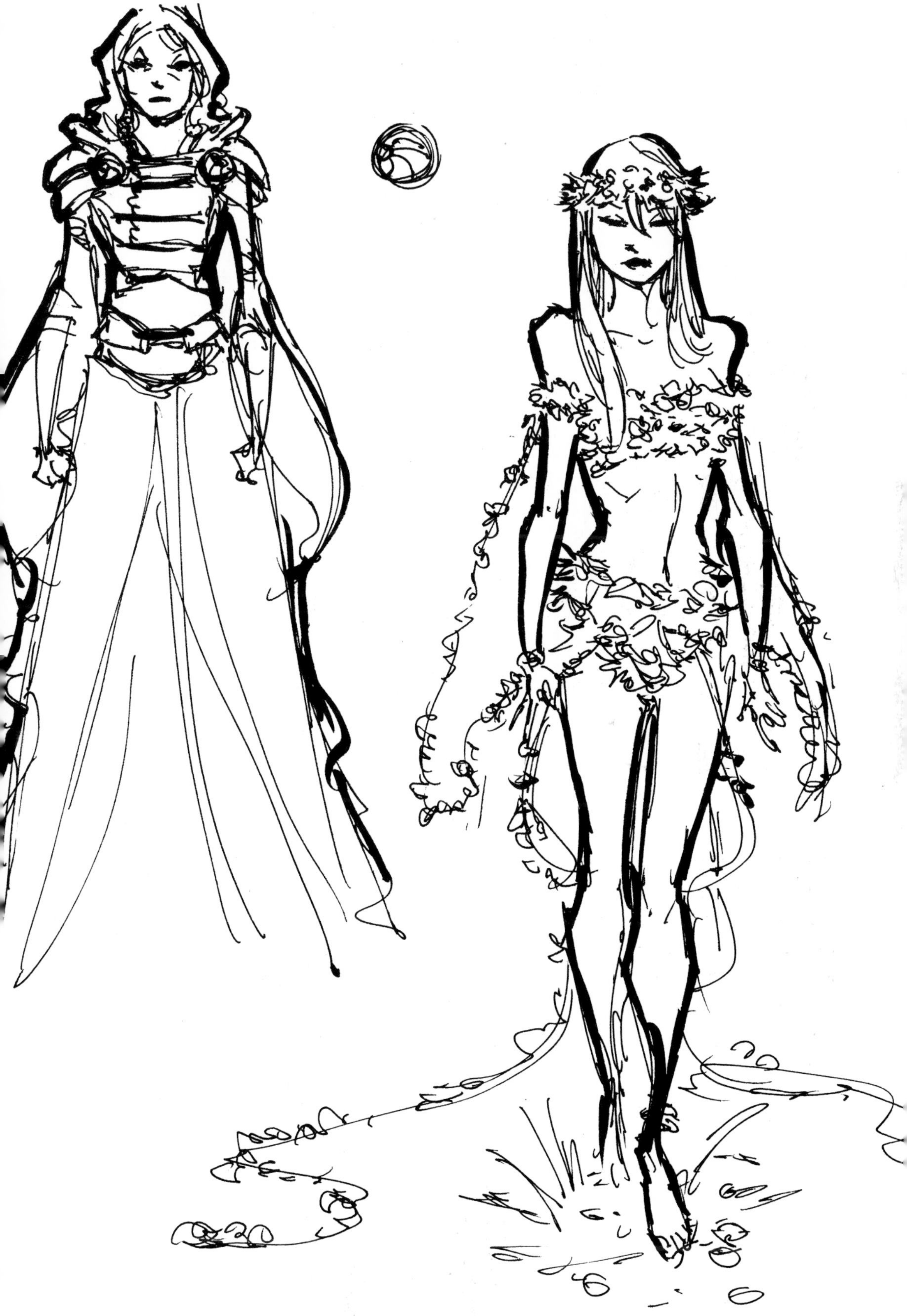

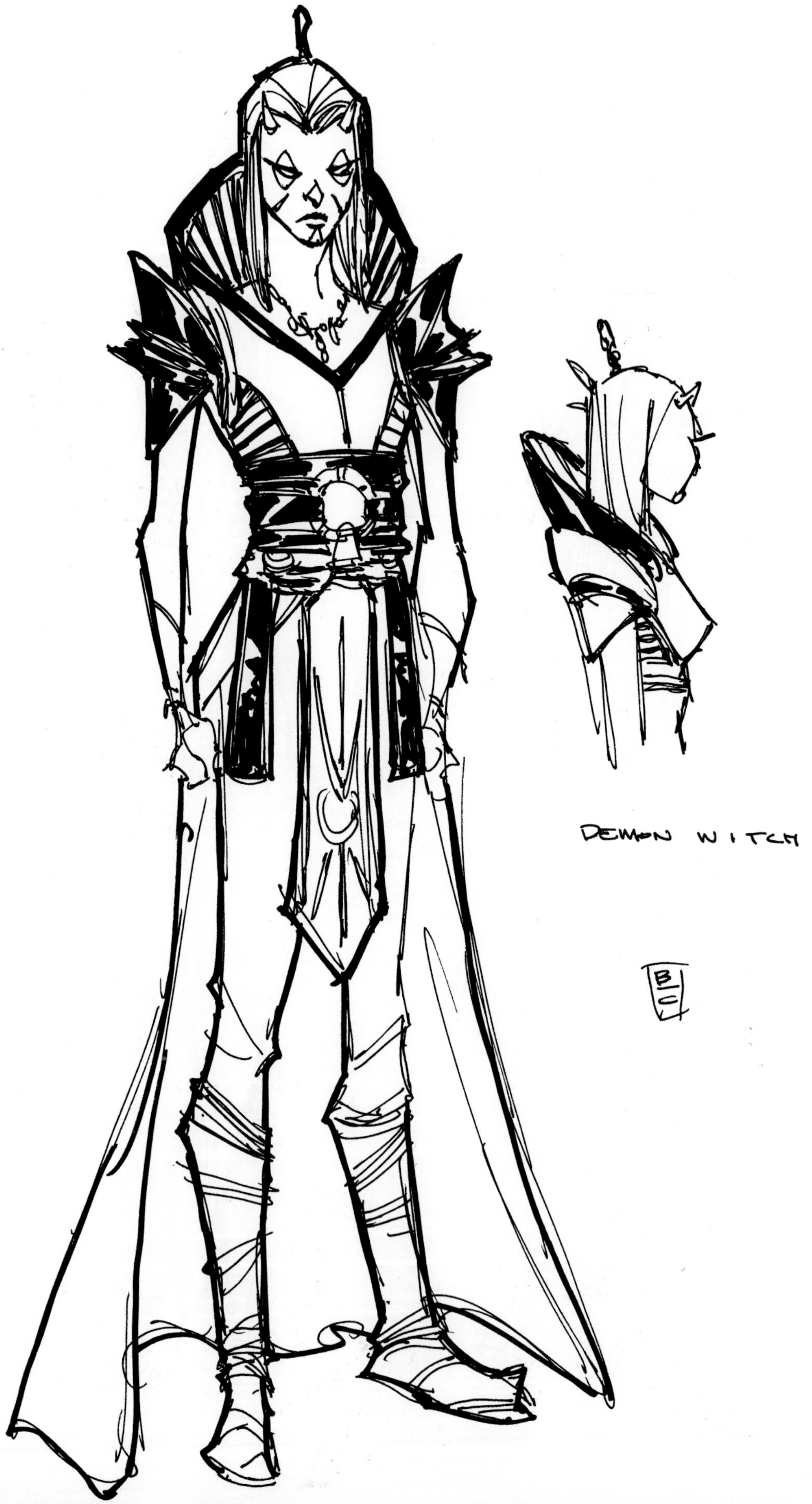
DEMON WITCH
BC

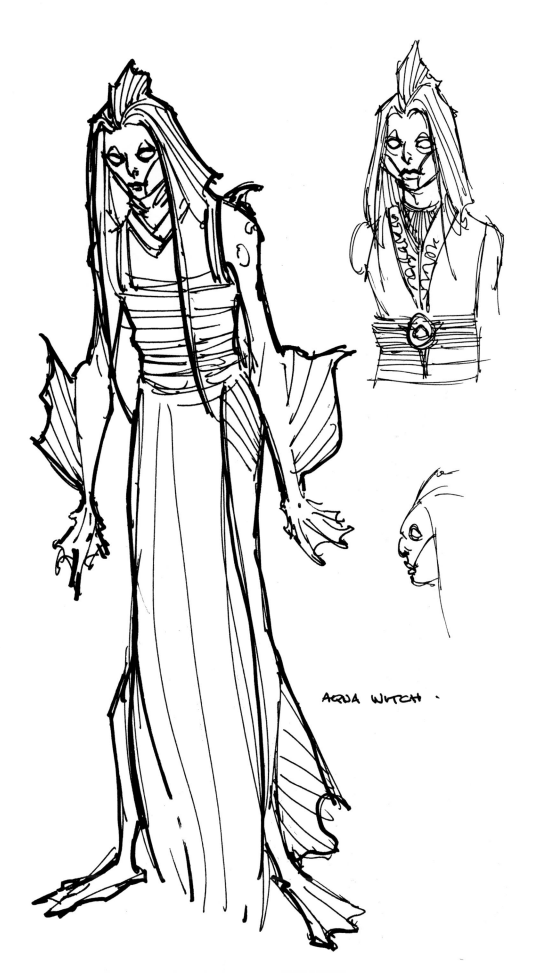

AQUA WITCH .

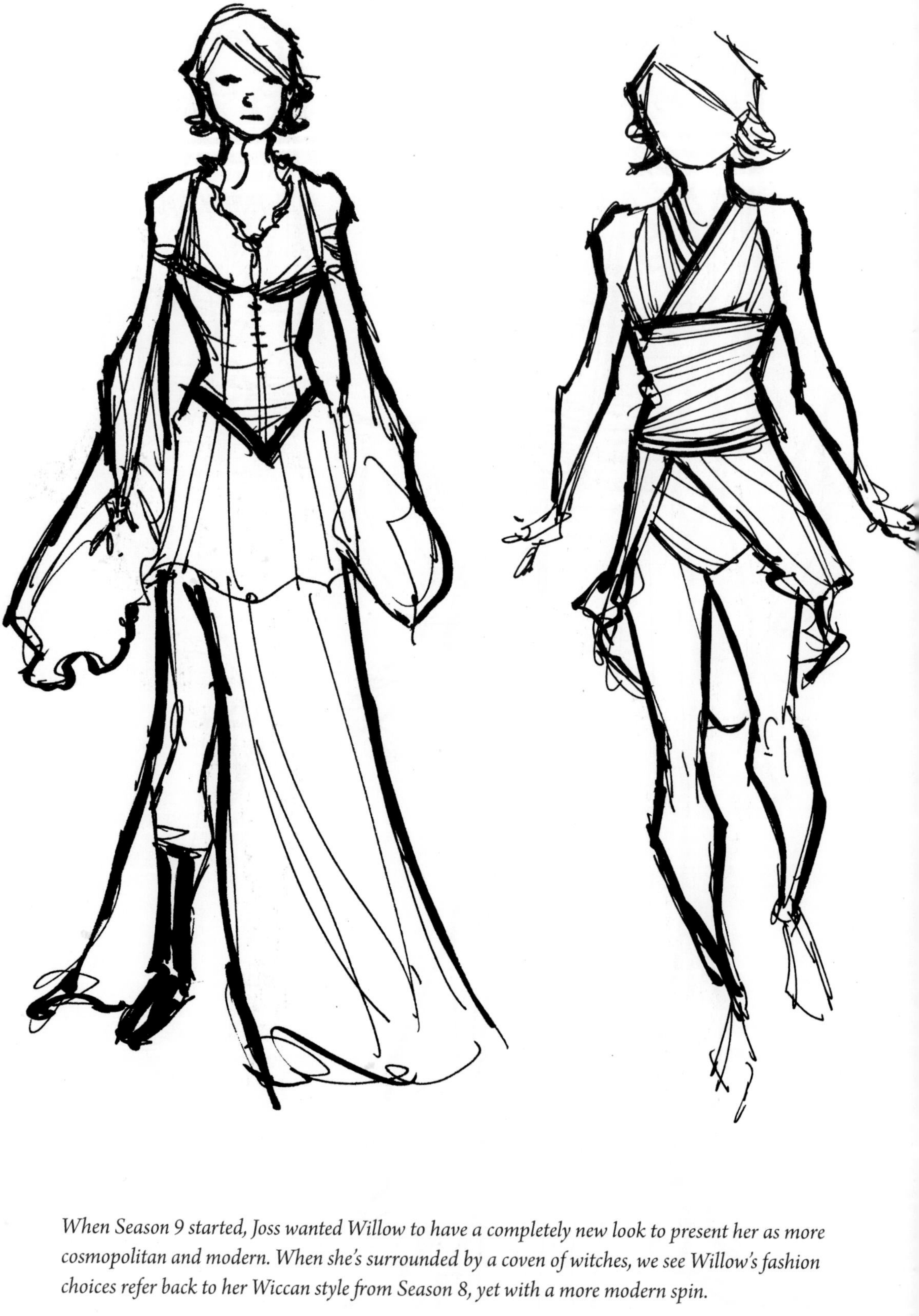

When Season 9 started, Joss wanted Willow to have a completely new look to present her as more cosmopolitan and modern. When she's surrounded by a coven of witches, we see Willow's fashion choices refer back to her Wiccan style from Season 8, yet with a more modern spin.

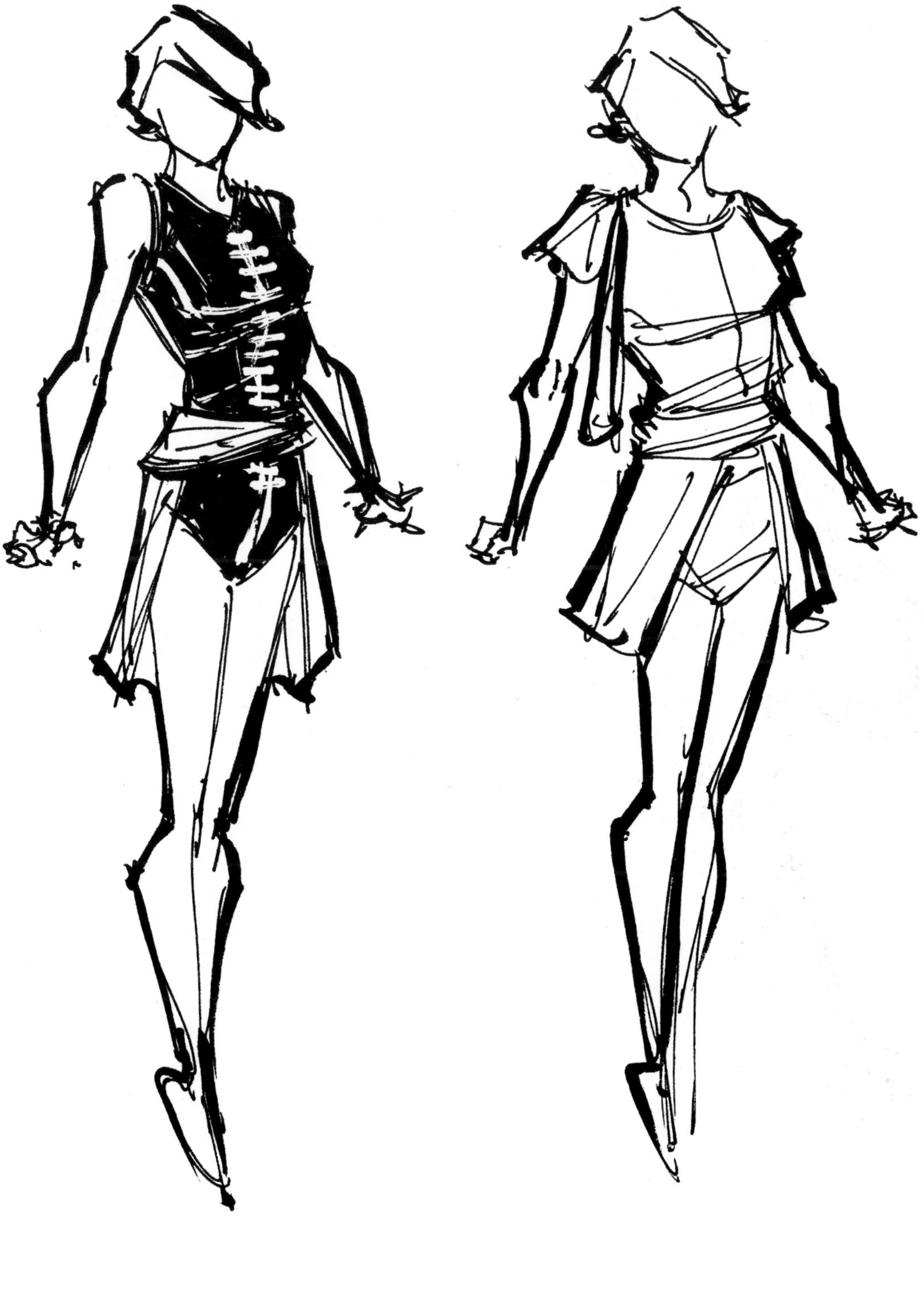

Brian's evolving sketches of Willow's swimsuit (see pages 62–64 for the final art).

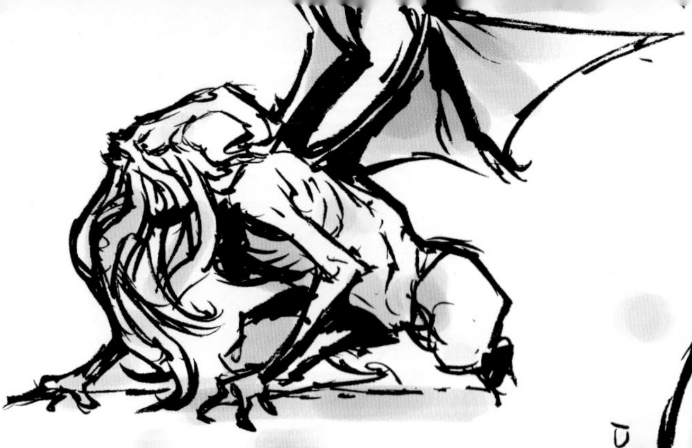

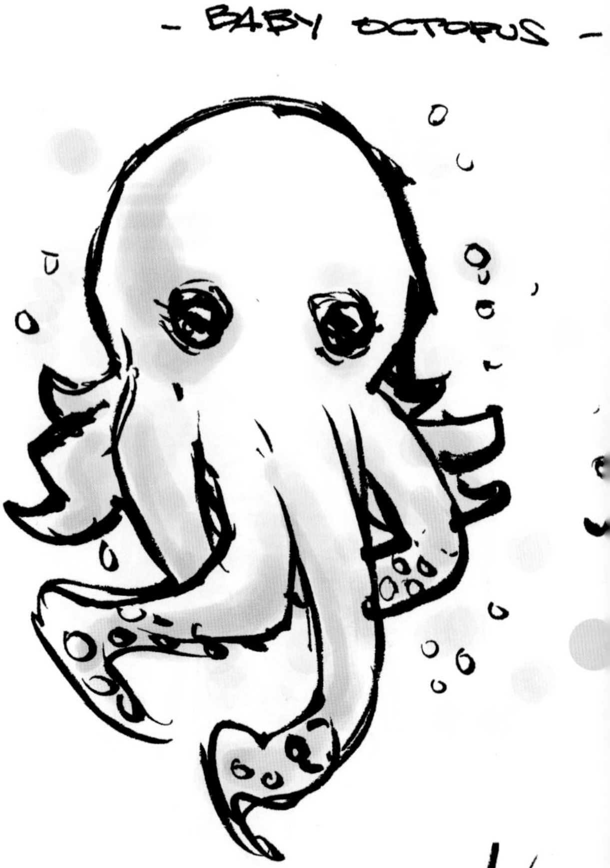
- BABY OCTOPUS -

When Willow has her confrontation with the Cthulhu creature and the adorable baby octopuses, writer Jeff Parker asked for a blend of H. P. Lovecraft and Hayao Miyazaki.

Following: Variant covers to Willow #4 *and* Willow #5 *by Megan Lara.*

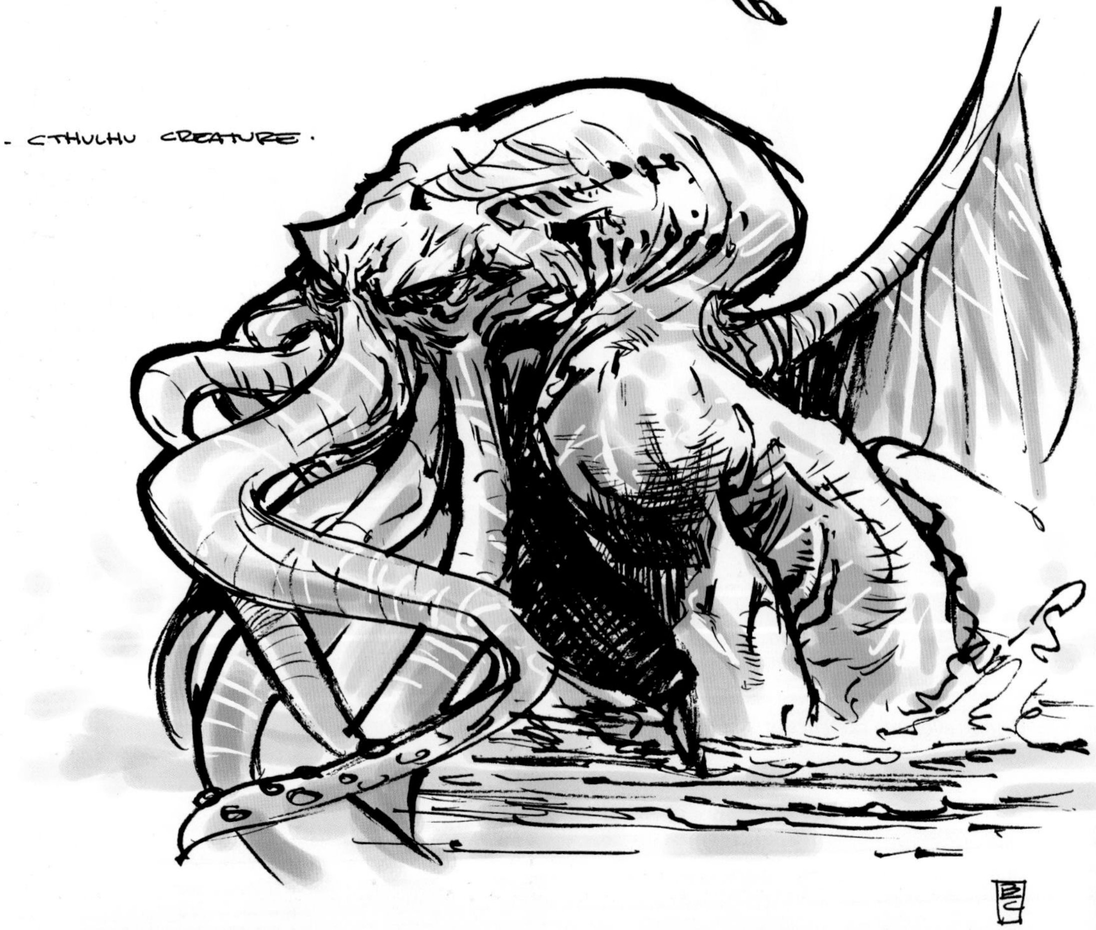
- CTHULHU CREATURE -

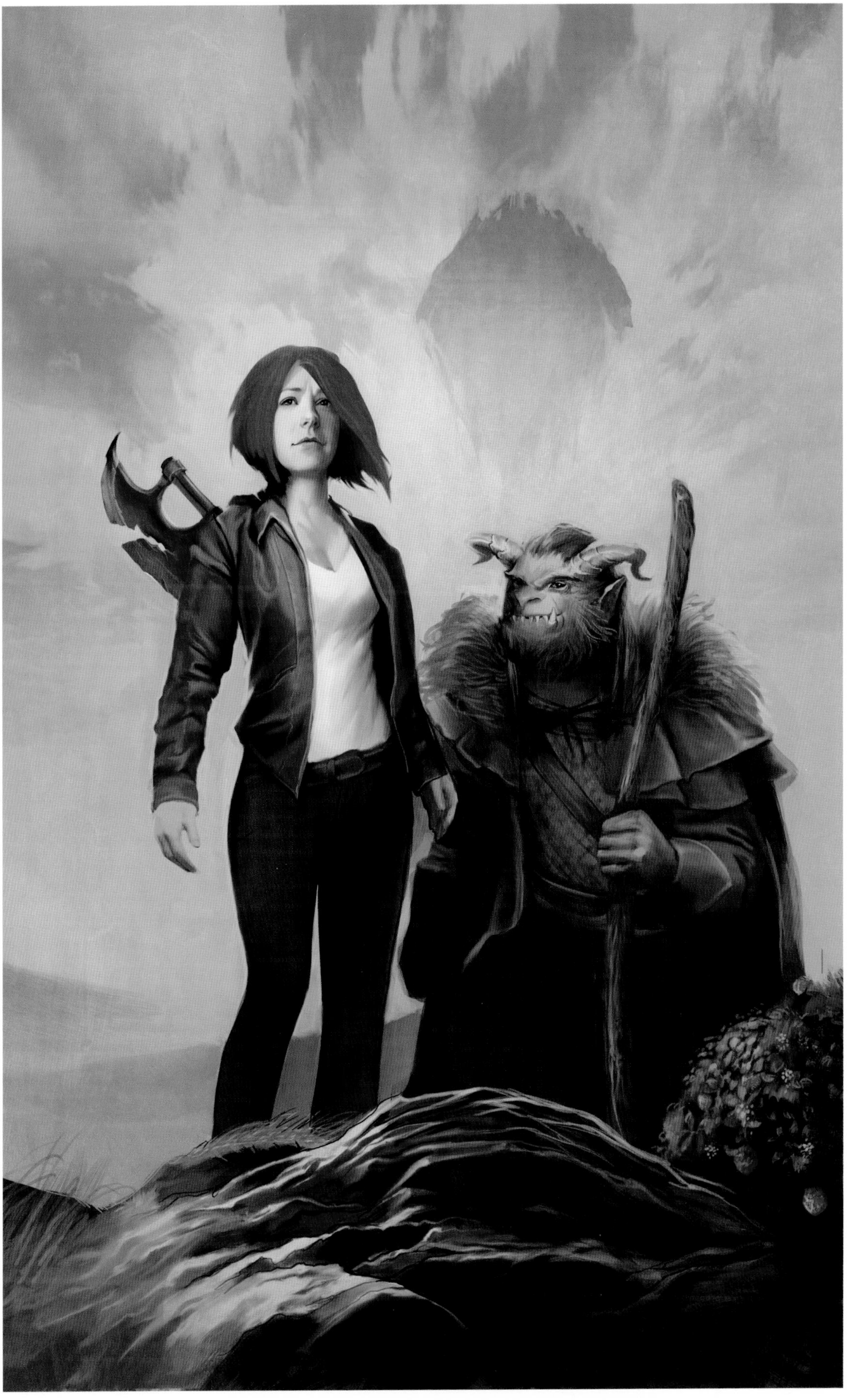

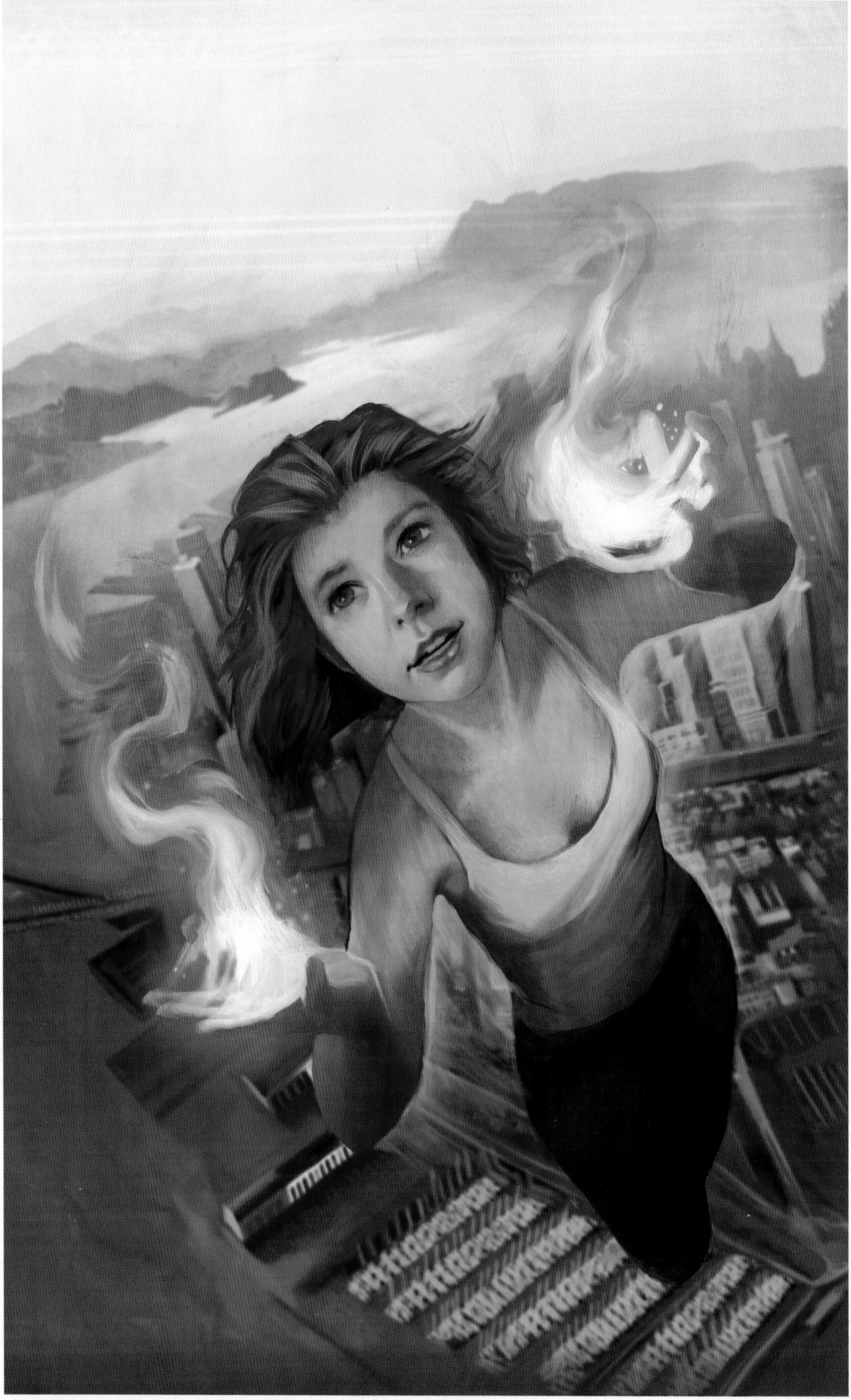

FROM JOSS WHEDON

Buffy the Vampire Slayer™

BUFFY THE VAMPIRE SLAYER SEASON 8

VOLUME 1: THE LONG WAY HOME
Joss Whedon and Georges Jeanty
ISBN 978-1-59307-822-5 | $15.99

VOLUME 2: NO FUTURE FOR YOU
Brian K. Vaughan, Georges Jeanty, and Joss Whedon
ISBN 978-1-59307-963-5 | $15.99

VOLUME 3: WOLVES AT THE GATE
Drew Goddard, Georges Jeanty, and Joss Whedon
ISBN 978-1-59582-165-2 | $15.99

VOLUME 4: TIME OF YOUR LIFE
Joss Whedon, Jeph Loeb, Georges Jeanty, and others
ISBN 978-1-59582-310-6 | $15.99

VOLUME 5: PREDATORS AND PREY
Joss Whedon, Jane Espenson, Georges Jeanty, Cliff Richards, and others
ISBN 978-1-59582-342-7 | $15.99

VOLUME 6: RETREAT
Joss Whedon, Jane Espenson, Georges Jeanty, Karl Moline, and others
ISBN 978-1-59582-415-8 | $15.99

VOLUME 7: TWILIGHT
Joss Whedon, Brad Meltzer, and Georges Jeanty
ISBN 978-1-59582-558-2 | $16.99

VOLUME 8: LAST GLEAMING
Joss Whedon, Scott Allie, and Georges Jeanty
ISBN 978-1-59582-610-7 | $16.99

BUFFY THE VAMPIRE SLAYER SEASON 8 LIBRARY EDITION

VOLUME 1
ISBN 978-1-59582-888-0 | $29.99

VOLUME 2
ISBN 978-1-59582-935-1 | $29.99

VOLUME 3
ISBN 978-1-59582-978-8 | $29.99

VOLUME 4
ISBN 978-1-61655-127-8 | $29.99

BUFFY THE VAMPIRE SLAYER SEASON 9

VOLUME 1: FREEFALL
Joss Whedon, Andrew Chambliss, Georges Jeanty, and others
ISBN 978-1-59582-922-1 | $17.99

VOLUME 2: ON YOUR OWN
Andrew Chambliss, Scott Allie, Georges Jeanty, and others
ISBN 978-1-59582-990-0 | $17.99

VOLUME 3: GUARDED
Joss Whedon, Jane Espenson, Drew Z. Greenberg, Georges Jeanty, and others
ISBN 978-1-61655-099-8 | $17.99

ANGEL & FAITH

VOLUME 1: LIVE THROUGH THIS
Christos Gage, Rebekah Isaacs, and Phil Noto
ISBN 978-1-59582-887-3 | $17.99

VOLUME 2: DADDY ISSUES
Christos Gage, Rebekah Isaacs, and Chris Samnee
ISBN 978-1-59582-960-3 | $17.99

VOLUME 3: FAMILY REUNION
Christos Gage, Rebekah Isaacs, Lee Garbett, and David Lapham
ISBN 978-1-61655-079-0 | $17.99

SPIKE

VOLUME 1: A DARK PLACE
ISBN 978-1-61655-109-4 | $17.99

WILLOW

VOLUME 1: WONDERLAND
ISBN 978-1-61655-145-2 | $17.99

AVAILABLE AT YOUR LOCAL COMICS SHOP OR BOOKSTORE!
To find a comics shop in your area, call 1-888-266-4226. For more information or to order direct:
On the web: DarkHorse.com • E-mail: mailorder@darkhorse.com • Phone: 1-800-862-0052 Mon.–Fri. 9 AM to 5 PM Pacific Time

ALSO FROM JOSS WHEDON

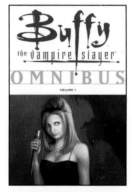

BUFFY THE VAMPIRE SLAYER OMNIBUS
VOLUME 1
ISBN 978-1-59307-784-6 | $24.99
VOLUME 2
ISBN 978-1-59307-826-3 | $24.99
VOLUME 3
ISBN 978-1-59307-885-0 | $24.99
VOLUME 4
ISBN 978-1-59307-968-0 | $24.99
VOLUME 5
ISBN 978-1-59582-225-3 | $24.99
VOLUME 6
ISBN 978-1-59582-242-0 | $24.99
VOLUME 7
ISBN 978-1-59582-331-1 | $24.99

BUFFY THE VAMPIRE SLAYER: PANEL TO PANEL
ISBN 978-1-59307-836-2 | $19.99

ANGEL OMNIBUS
Christopher Golden, Eric Powell, and others
ISBN 978-1-59582-706-7 | $24.99

TALES OF THE SLAYERS
*Joss Whedon, Amber Benson, Gene Colan, P. Craig
Russell, Tim Sale, and others*
ISBN 978-1-56971-605-2 | $14.99

TALES OF THE VAMPIRES
Joss Whedon, Brett Matthews, Cameron Stewart, and others
ISBN 978-1-56971-749-3 | $15.99

BUFFY THE VAMPIRE SLAYER: TALES HARDCOVER
ISBN 978-1-59582-644-2 | $29.99

FRAY: FUTURE SLAYER
Joss Whedon and Karl Moline
ISBN 978-1-56971-751-6 | $19.99

**SERENITY VOLUME 1: THOSE LEFT BEHIND
SECOND EDITION HARDCOVER**
Joss Whedon, Brett Matthews, and Will Conrad
ISBN 978-1-59582-914-6 | $17.99

**SERENITY VOLUME 2: BETTER DAYS AND
OTHER STORIES HARDCOVER**
*Joss Whedon, Patton Oswalt, Zack Whedon, Patric
Reynolds, and others*
ISBN 978-1-59582-739-5 | $19.99

**SERENITY VOLUME 3: THE SHEPHERD'S
TALE HARDCOVER**
Joss Whedon, Zack Whedon, and Chris Samnee
ISBN 978-1-59582-561-2 | $14.99

DR. HORRIBLE AND OTHER HORRIBLE STORIES
Joss Whedon, Zack Whedon, Joëlle Jones, and others
ISBN 978-1-59582-577-3 | $9.99

DOLLHOUSE VOLUME 1: EPITAPHS
*Andrew Chambliss, Jed Whedon, Maurissa Tancharoen,
and Cliff Richards*
ISBN 978-1-59582-863-7 | $18.99